INSIDE
THE BELLY OF AN
ELEPHANT

INSIDE
THE BELLY OF AN
ELEPHANT

A MOTORCYCLE JOURNEY OF LOSS, LEGACY AND ULTIMATE FREEDOM

TODD LAWSON

Foreword by Bruce Kirkby

RMB

For information on purchasing bulk quantities of this book, or to obtain media
excerpts or invite the author to speak at an event, please visit rmbooks.com and
select the "Contact" tab.

RMB | Rocky Mountain Books Ltd.
rmbooks.com
@rmbooks
facebook.com/rmbooks

Cataloguing data available from Library and Archives Canada
ISBN 9781771605755 (softcover)
ISBN 9781771605762 (electronic)

All photographs are by Todd Lawson unless otherwise noted.

Design: Lara Minja, Lime Design

Printed and bound in Canada

We would like to also take this opportunity to acknowledge the traditional
territories upon which we live and work. In Calgary, Alberta, we acknowledge
the Niitsítapi (Blackfoot) and the people of the Treaty 7 region in Southern Alberta,
which includes the Siksika, the Piikuni, the Kainai, the Tsuut'ina, and the Stoney
Nakoda First Nations, including Chiniki, Bearpaw, and Wesley First Nations.
The City of Calgary is also home to Métis Nation of Alberta, Region III. In Victoria,
British Columbia, we acknowledge the traditional territories of the Lkwungen
(Esquimalt and Songhees), Malahat, Pacheedaht, Scia'new, T'Sou-ke, and
W̱SÁNEĆ (Pauquachin, Tsartlip, Tsawout, Tseycum) peoples.

We acknowledge the financial support of the Government of Canada through
the Canada Book Fund and the Canada Council for the Arts, and of the province
of British Columbia through the British Columbia Arts Council and the Book
Publishing Tax Credit.

CONTENTS

"In the beginning of time the skies were filled with flying elephants. Every night they lay down in the same place in the sky, and dreamt with one eye open. When you gaze up at the stars at night, you are looking into the unblinking eyes of elephants, who sleep with one eye open to best keep watch over us."

GREGORY COLBERT, *Ashes and Snow: A Novel in Letters*

MOTORCYCLE
JOURNEY

2004

Latin America tour
October 2004 – May 2006
23 countries, 44,000 km

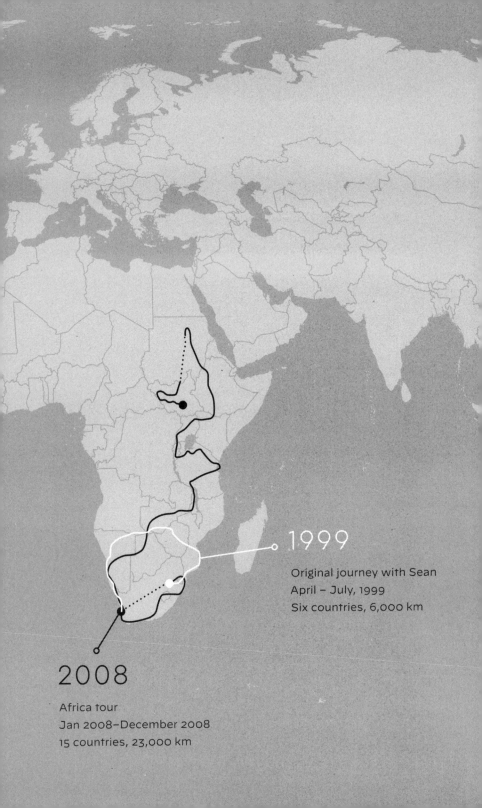

1999

Original journey with Sean
April – July, 1999
Six countries, 6,000 km

2008

Africa tour
Jan 2008–December 2008
15 countries, 23,000 km

BRUCE KIRKBY

I first met Todd in Whistler, at the Multiplicity storytelling festival. As one of the organizers, he had invited me to town to present, and I was dropping bags in my hotel room when the phone rang. It was Todd, suggesting we take a few ski runs together before the evening gala. We found each other outside the upper gondola station, and after shaking hands and slapping backs, Todd took off at a breakneck pace, weaving to and fro across the slopes, making sure no mogul went unjumped. In fairness, I had failed to mention I wasn't much of an alpine skier. Amid flailing attempts to keep his orange jacket in sight, I suddenly crossed skis with an Australian woman who zigged when I zagged, spinning us both around like tops. Her furious boyfriend chased me down the mountain like a bellowing moose, even as I chased Todd. That evening, I walked onto the stage with a noticeable limp.

Months later I was back in Whistler again. Aware that I was a keen paddleboarder, Todd suggested we make a run down the Cheakamus River. I'd never paddled whitewater aboard an SUP before, but I was game and Todd assured me I'd be fine. What could go wrong? The afternoon ended in the Squamish clinic, where a nurse patiently wove seven stitches into the thin skin of my shin.

So my earliest vision of Todd was that of a sort of crazy man. He possessed baffling skills, enviable exuberance and unshakable confidence. And he seemed untethered from cares in a way I didn't recognize. Despite three decades experience in the outdoor industry myself—working as a guide, author and photographer—Todd seemed to exist on a plane I had never encountered. And one that I was curious about.

I suspect that is precisely how Todd's older brother Sean—whom this deeply moving book is posthumously centred on—must have appeared to many of those who crossed his path during Sean's short, blazing time on this planet. It was certainly how Sean appeared to Todd in his formative years: someone he looked up to enormously, who burned bright but also felt illusory or fleeting, occupying an orbit that Todd dreamed of sharing but could never quite find.

The sprawling story opens as the two brothers' trajectories begin to move closer and they embark together on a motorcycle odyssey through raw Africa. Tragically, it was a journey only Todd would return from.

Driven by love and survivor's guilt, Todd soon sets out again by motorcycle, this time on a journey that will span continents and years, accompanied by his (admirably resolute) partner Christina. Ostensibly, their goal is to spread Sean's ashes to the four winds—a wonderfully fitting tribute to one who could never be contained. But ultimately the journey demands that Todd wrestle with those most primal of human angsts: mortality, meaning and connection.

Todd's writing, like his journey, is remarkably unapologetic. F@#$ it, he says, this is what went down, warts and all. His ruthless honesty reminds me at times of Anthony Bourdain on two wheels. But that would diminish what he has accomplished in these pages, for Todd writes with what all writers seek but not all will find: a voice that is unmistakably his own.

The book itself is staggeringly ambitious in scope. We are taken to exotic landscapes, meet absorbing characters, experience unimaginable twists and turns, but most importantly we watch a young man come of age in a complex world. On his journey of healing, Todd not only bridges the gap with his enigmatic older brother but also discovers his own unique orbit.

And in these pages, for a brief time, we share that orbit. We travel alongside a man who is heartfelt, sincere, audacious, brutally honest, and most definitely not crazy. (Well, not too crazy anyways!) And through his eyes, we are given a chance to reflect on the things that matter in life: family, friendships, forgiveness, strength, the kindness of strangers, and the wonders that still exist out there, on the road.

Savour the ride!

BRUCE KIRKBY
Author of *Blue Sky Kingdom, A Family Journey into the Heart of the Himalaya*
April 2023

– PROLOGUE –

It's four o'clock in the morning when the harsh ring of a landline wakes me from a deep sleep. On the other end, the trembling voice of Dr. Debbie casts a grim shadow over my groggy state. I throw on some clothes and charge out the door, trying hard to hold back the fear that's making every hair in my body stand on end. The night guard at the front gate asks me a question, but I can't hear him through my helmet. I'm drowning in panic, and yell at him to open the fucking gate. Speeding onto the highway, the morning chill rips through my clothes as Dr. Debbie's worried voice keeps replaying over and over in my head. *Todd, you've got to make it here as soon as you possibly can.*

I soon see the exit for Soweto Township and realize where I am, and what I'm doing – trying to find my way in the dark through one of the most dangerous slums in all of Africa. Apartheid is only a few years removed, and this is no white man's land, not for a foreigner alone on a motorcycle in the darkest hours of night. The mood feels murky and surreal, like I'm riding at slow motion through a dimly lit movie set. Clusters of street urchins huddle together smoking cigarettes around fires in rusted barrels. They all look at me, slowly turning their heads one by one as I ride past, but I try to avoid eye contact, realizing that I don't really know where I am and have no recollection of how to get to the hospital.

I have spent the last three days clutching my brother's hand in the intensive care unit at the Chris Hani Baragwanath Hospital, watching his condition deteriorate rapidly since he was diagnosed. But the doctors had hope. Sean was in top physical shape and fighting hard against the rapid onset of *Plasmodium falciparum* – the most severe strain of the malaria parasite species, also known as cerebral malaria. If not treated within 24 hours from the sign of the first symptoms, it can progress to severe illness, often death. Every year in Africa almost a million people lose their lives to the disease.

Stuffed full of tubes in that hospital bed, Sean couldn't respond verbally when I spoke to him, but he would blink his eyes ever so slightly – a minuscule sign that helped me realize *he* knew I was beside him. And I knew he was still with us, fighting in silence.

When Sean fell into a drug-induced sleep, I walked silently to the pay phone at the top of the stairwell and called everyone I could think of, everyone except our own mother; I didn't have the guts to deliver such alarming news to her. I had even downplayed the urgency when we called just 72 hours previous.

"Please pray for Sean," I begged those who answered my collect calls. "He's been diagnosed with malaria and is in very serious condition. I'm with him now at his bedside but I need you to spread the word to everyone you know. Please send positive healing prayers. He is fighting hard and the doctors are doing everything they can."

I imagined summoning up the presence of every person that we'd met throughout southern Africa for the past eight months to join me in manifesting Sean's immediate recovery.

It feels like I'm in survival mode, speeding through the township, straight through every intersection, stop sign and "robot," as South Africans call traffic lights. Cresting the top of a hill, I see the shining lights of a massive building in the distance. *That must be the hospital. This has to be it.* I see a bold green-and-white H sign high on a light pole and breathe a sigh of relief. Turning sharply left, I nearly hit a ragged dog hobbling on three feet. He skitters away. My heart is thumping. Pulling up to the hospital gate, my face is a mess of tears and grief. An armed guard walks out of his little night shack and asks me where I'm headed.

"My brother is in the ICU. Where is the entrance?"

He looks at me blankly. "You must first sign in please."

"He doesn't have long to live! Where is the ICU?!" I yell.

My bike is still running, my hands freezing cold. *Fuck this, I'm not waiting.* The guard still has the boom down, and I see just enough room to squeeze past the cement pole on the right. I gun it, suddenly remembering the back entrance to the intensive care building from my first visit three days ago. I make an impulsive sharp turn to the right along a row of narrow wards and park in the last stall between a white van and a chain link fence. The guard is coming after me, but I don't care. I hastily rip off my helmet and pull open the door, running up three flights of concrete stairs with my heart pounding out of my chest.

The first person I see is Dr. Debbie Ibbotson. Her nervous, sympathetic eyes shoot a hole right through me.

"He was doing fine until about an hour ago, Todd. He stopped breathing and we had to pump him with adrenaline to get his heart going again. I'm so sorry. We've been doing everything we can. He's breathing again but very faintly. I don't know how much longer we can keep him alive."

I slump into a quivering mess on the floor.

"Todd, listen to me. I've called your parents, they're on the way."

Oh my god, is this really happening right now? Sean needs me. Now. Gather some strength, for fuck's sake. Dr. Debbie pulls me up, gives me a deep, caring hug and peels away the curtain. Sean is lying peacefully on his back, hoses and wires and beeping machines plugged into his body. *This can't be happening. Why? Why? Why? Not my brother. Not like this.* Sobbing uncontrollably, I grab my hair with both hands and pull as hard as I can. Intense emotion rages through my body. *Poor Mom. This is going to ruin her.* She's already lost two husbands in her life, and now to lose her first-born son... it's ripping me to pieces.

A hunger pang fires inside my belly. I can't remember the last time I ate. I walk outside of the hospital and squint into the sky, feeling the energy of the sun warm my body. Guilt takes over and unleashes everything it's got. I break down beside my motorcycle and punch the seat again and again and again until my hands hurt. Looking into the sky, I scream at the full capacity of my being: "Jesus fucking Christ, Todd, why didn't you take him to the hospital sooner?! Why didn't we listen to Kenny? You're such a fucking idiot! Please, God, help us, please let my brother live!"

The volume of my voice startles a Black woman nearby.

"What is wrong, my child?" she asks, walking quickly towards me with her palms to the sky. "Please, calm down, my boy. God is with us. He is all around."

She holds me tightly in a motherly embrace, and I clutch her plump body, crying in sporadic shrieking outbursts like a boy who has fallen off his bicycle for the first time.

"God is watching, my child, God is watching," she says calmly, holding my head against her bosom.

In that moment, she's all I have. I don't want to let her go.

PART ONE

HOME ON THE PLAIN

STONY PLAIN, ALBERTA • December 1977

On a crisp fall morning in September 1975, Sean had raked a huge pile of crunchy yellow leaves in the front yard of our home in Edmonton, Alberta. Sean was 5, two years older than me, and it was his plan to bury ourselves inside the mound and wait for our dad, Michael, to open the front door, at which point we'd spring up from the pile and scare him. The plan worked like a charm, although Dad was undoubtedly faking it. Little did I know that this was the last and only memory I'd ever possess of our father.

Less than two weeks later, Dad and his friend William took off to hunt moose in the coniferous forests and willow muskegs of west-central Alberta. They carried with them a pair of high-powered rifles, lots of ammunition, and plenty of booze. The day after they arrived at camp, Dad called my mom from a gas station pay phone and said, somewhat uncharacteristically, "Everything is okay here, we're all set up. Kiss my boys goodbye for me."

The next evening, he and a First Nations guide were paddling the canoe back to camp after a hunt, the rhythmic dip of their paddles the only sound breaking the calm in the fading light of dusk. William had stayed ashore, hanging back at camp and swigging a bottle of whiskey by the fire. After an hour alone, William spotted the two paddlers a quarter mile from shore and thought that firing a "warning shot" somewhere near the canoe would be a funny way to scare them; a prank that somehow made sense in his drunken mind. That blast from William's bolt-action .30-06 rifle missed its imaginary mark and instead hit a real one, blowing the back of my father's head off in an instant. The bullet entered near the left temple, shattered his skull and buried itself in the chest of the guide paddling at the canoe's stern. The guide survived, but my dad was gone.

Mom was on the family farm in Flat Lake, Alberta, at the time with her three young boys: Sean, me and Bradley, our 8-month-old baby brother, when the heart-shattering call came from the police through the wires of a crackly rural party-line.

The farm belonged to our immigrant homesteader grandparents John and Helen Marchuk, who, together with their respective parents and siblings, had escaped the grasp of poverty on the heels of the Bolshevik Revolution (1917–23) that affected many parts of Poland. In 1925, my great-grandfather Jacob Marczuk (the name changed to Marchuk in Canada) had made the long voyage from his homeland to Argentina in an attempt to secure land and a better life for his family. Somehow, he ended up choosing Canada instead, having heard talk of free, available land in the western prairies. Many Polish families took heed, fleeing their troubled homeland to find new opportunities in the Great White North.

On July 18, 1929, together with their children and several other townspeople from the village of Ortel Królewski Pierwszy, my great-grandparents Jacob and Paulina Marchuk boarded the 524-foot-long Scandinavian American steamship *Frederik VIII*, in Gdańsk, Poland, and made the life-changing journey across the Atlantic, arriving at Pier 21 in Halifax, Nova Scotia, on August 3 – exactly one month before the Great Depression.

Like many immigrants who arrived on those rocky shores, their eyes were dazzled by broadside posters with exaggerated typography on every street corner, touting *Free Farms of 160 Acres in the West. Climate the Healthiest in the World. Great Fertile Plains.* The Marchuks, including 19-year-old Jan (John) and his sister Sabina, rode the Canadian Pacific Railway more than 4000 kilometres across the country, and both ended up in the small community of St. Paul, Alberta, where they holed up at the Lavoie Hotel, spending their life savings while waiting for their land to become available. Near penniless after a few months, the immigrants had to learn English and figure out life in Canada during the hardscrabble times of the Great Depression. But at least they had their own pieces of land – claimed under the Dominion Lands Act, an 1872 law aimed to encourage the settlement of the Canadian Prairies. The act offered ownership of 160 acres of land (for a ten-dollar registration fee) to any man over the age of 18 or any woman heading a household. Some 1.25 million homesteads were made available over an expanse of 80 million hectares, the largest survey grid in the world. From 1870 to 1930, roughly 625,000 land patents were issued to homesteaders, and hundreds of thousands of settlers poured into the region.

However, instead of "Great Fertile Plains as far as the eye could see" – like the posters had promised – the land that Jacob and Paulina had purchased was surrounded by difficult terrain covered in trees and rocks. But they were the lucky ones; there was a small two-bedroom log house tucked away at the edge of the forest that would become their new home. Here, their long, arduous homesteading life began in earnest.

My grandmother Helen (née Zarzyski) and her family had made the exact same voyage a year prior, but hard luck had befallen them almost immediately, when a fire lit to keep hordes of hungry mosquitoes at bay engulfed a nearby granary that contained all their family possessions. Desperate, they went from farmhouse to farmhouse begging the neighbours for some eggs or a loaf of bread to get through the week. They offered to work the fields in exchange for some money, but the other farmers couldn't afford to pay. My great-grandmother Katherine became so distraught that she succumbed to a nervous breakdown, forcing my grandmother and her two sisters to look after themselves while still in their youth. Katherine struggled with bouts of depression for two continuous years.

Through sheer determination, the Marchuks and Zarzyskis survived their first hard winters, chipping away at the harsh life of homesteading one day at a time. All the firewood to heat their small wooden
homes came from falling, sawing and splitting trees by hand. A single
winter's woodpile measured 60 feet long, 16 feet wide, and 8 feet high.
In the spring, they planted gardens that provided peas and carrots and
beets and potatoes. The Marchuks managed to buy a cow so they could
drink milk and make cheese and butter, then a chicken so they could
eat eggs. More cows were bought, and they sold the calves for income.
Hardworking and devoutly religious, both my grandparents' families
toiled from dusk to dawn in the fields, picking wild berries and mush-
rooms to supplement their meagre diet, when they weren't picking
rocks. They often wondered why they had even left Poland. And the
Marchuks and Zarzyskis were just two of the hundreds of thousands
of immigrant families building a nation in this same fashion.

As fate would have it, the Marchuks (Jacob, Paulina, John and Sabina) and Zarzyskis (Kathrine, Nicholas, Stella, Mary and Helen) lived
across the road from one another in Vilna, Alberta. Helen eventually
met John, 10 years her senior, and they fell in love and married on
February 13, 1941 at the Sacred Heart Church. Eight months later, on
September 19, 1941, they welcomed their first daughter, Wanda, into
the world.

In the summer of 1945, John and Helen purchased a 320-acre parcel
of land in an area known as Flat Lake, loaded up their worldly belongings into a horse and buggy and forged out into the wild to build their
future together on their very own farm. With rocks to pick and fences
to build and animals to look after, they knew they'd need more hands
to help and began adding to their family. My mother, Rita, was born
on October 1, 1945, and her brother, Edmund, on March 3, 1953.

At nine months old, Mom was diagnosed with celiac disease. Every
week she and her parents would take a horse and buggy – sometimes
equipped with a wood stove for the coldest winter days – to the nearby
town of Elk Point to see Dr. Miller, leaving in the dark and returning
in the dark – no matter rain, sleet, snow, hail, thunder or lightning.

Grandpa John would also administer needles to my mom while they both cried; he didn't want to give her the needle any more than she wanted to get pricked, but it was to save her.

Other than the rare trip into town for staples like flour and sugar, they carved out an entirely self-sufficient existence, canning everything from fruits and vegetables to pickled chicken feet, head cheese and pork hocks, all kept in glass jars and stored in the underground cellar to get them through the cold months ahead. Nothing ever went to waste, not even blood or intestines, which were used to make sausage after a pig had been slaughtered.

As time marched on and the children grew into teenagers, eventually things on the farm got better. The Marchuk family began to harvest crops with regularity and they started to slowly accumulate a few trappings of modern society: a workhorse Massey-Harris farm tractor one year, a baby-blue Fargo truck the next; and a few years after that, Christmas holidays were changed forever when Santa Claus delivered a 1976 Ski-Doo snowmobile, complete with a cushy-seated sleigh to pull behind. With our speed-loving Uncle Ed and his wife, Auntie Cathy, behind the handlebars, we three boys would spend hours riding around the farm, taking turns with our older cousins Russell and Lucille. In spite of round-the-clock hard work, the whole family relished the open spaces and community connections with other farmers in the area. Here, they were truly free, and the pride of owning land made it all worthwhile. Their love of the outdoors deepened. When it came time to harvest crops, community work parties would go from one farm to the next until all the work was done. No farm was left alone.

Throughout the 1960s the three Marchuk siblings – Wanda, Ed and Rita – all left the farm to pursue education and opportunity in Edmonton, returning often to continue to help their parents with livestock, harvesting crops and baling hay. Carving out her own life in the "big city" of Edmonton, Mom soon met a charming young professional (his family operated Chicago Vocational School) named Michael Lawson. They had met in 1967 at an apartment building in Edmonton, when

Michael Lawson had knocked on the door of mom's apartment a few times in a row, always to borrow a cup of sugar or flour, or anything that was "missing" from a recipe he wanted to make. They quickly fell in love and soon bought a modest new house near Storyland Valley Zoo in Edmonton.

As young children, my brothers and I spent days and weeks at a time on the farmstead every summer in the '70s, climbing barns and buildings, shooting beer cans with pellet guns and becoming well-acquainted with every farm animal on the property.

When September rolled around, we reluctantly left the freedom of the farm for the confines of the city, Mom raising her three boys alone, struggling to make ends meet while working as a certified nurse's aide at the Misericordia Hospital in Edmonton.

After three long years of single motherhood, in the winter of 1978, a grizzly of a man walked into her life. Barrel-chested and bearded, Roy Vahey had once owned nine Doberman pinschers while working for the military police in Ontario. He was a journeyman carpenter, cement worker, general contractor, stonemason, drywaller and jack of all trades. He was also an alcoholic. He didn't play or watch sports of any kind unless they involved hunting, fishing or canoeing.

Roy helped my mom become herself again, and they soon wanted a taste of quiet, small-town life to raise three boys. They found it just west of Edmonton, in a farming community called Stony Plain, where they bought a modest two-storey house in the middle of a cul-de-sac and began a new life together at 78 Umbach Road. The home smelled like fresh carpet when we moved in on a bitingly cold December day. One of the first things Roy did was build his three new stepsons personalized wooden toy boxes emblazoned with our own outlaw nicknames – a black one for "Shady Sean," a yellow one for "Bad Brad" and a white one for "Terrible Todd."

When our new washing machine arrived the next summer, Roy repurposed its wooden crate into a makeshift bike ramp. There was no lip or curve to the jump, just an angled straight shot two feet off the ground. To my 7-year-old eyes, it looked massive. I knew I wouldn't jump it the day he set it up. Clutching the handlebars with white knuckles, Sean lined up his bike (a motocross-inspired BMX with two chrome rear shocks, a long black seat and a fake yellow gas tank) in the middle of the road, ready to launch his helmetless body into our front yard. Mom looked on nervously from the front step as Sean pumped all his weight into the pedals and hit the ramp as fast as he could. It felt like the whole world stopped for those three seconds of air time.

He landed perfectly on both wheels but the impact compressed the shocks and jolted him into the air. He outriggered his legs to regain some balance and stopped just short of the house. With a flick of the wrist he dropped his bike like he meant it, and ran around the yard with a proud smile on his face, high-fiving everyone within reach. Roy had snapped a photo in mid-air, with Sean's feathered hair flowing in the wind, his face clenched tight with concentration and fear – the brave little guinea pig who would start a small-town bike-jumping revolution.

Soon all of the kids wanted to hit the "washing-machine ramp." Those who followed Sean's speedy style found success; those who nervously approached the ramp with insufficient speed "endoed" off the ramp and ass-over-teakettled it into the dirt.

A few hours later, I finally mustered up enough courage to try the ramp at a Sean-approved speed, only to teeter on the landing and crash on my right shoulder. Sean was too enthralled by the atmosphere to let me lie on the ground crying; he picked me and my bike up and coaxed me to hit it again. I landed the second attempt solidly but my flailing feet didn't have enough time to get planted back on the pedals. My sphincter sucked up the landing before the shocks did. Brad was still too small for the big bad ramp, so he rode around the pavement on his plastic Big Wheel, watching in awe as rider after rider laid their tire tracks into the wood. That bike ramp became the undisputed champion of the neighbourhood that summer; our first real introduction to adrenalin.

As we grew older, we returned to the family farm often, helping our grandfather milk the cows and make barbed-wire fences, oblivious to how much backbreaking work he had put into this piece of land, and how fortunate we were to spend our summers surrounded by the spoils of his labour. We ate fresh raspberries, peas and carrots straight from the garden and threw rocks over the wooden fence towards Willy, the rock-eating cattle dog. At night we'd roast marshmallows over a campfire in the birch forest, fall asleep late and do it all again the next day. Then, in December 1982, after 37 years as one of Canada's true immigrant pioneers, John Marchuk lost a long battle with emphysema, succumbing to his one and only vice: tobacco. The epitaph engraved on his tombstone read:

JOHN MARCHUK
1910–1982
A Man who found meaning through the love of nature.

Not long after, in 1985, Sean was hired to work on the maintenance crew at the nearby Stony Plain Golf Course, where his fascination with sunrises began. He'd drive his big powder-blue 1972 Dodge Charger to work at 5:30 a.m. then cruise around the golf course in a rough-mower or trap-rake, the slowest of the maintenance machines. His boss didn't trust him with anything faster, especially after seeing him trying to jump fairway bunkers with the red Honda three-wheeler one day.

Sean had started to hang out with a bad crowd, skipping school to smoke hashish and staying out late every night wreaking havoc in the neighbourhood by egging houses and getting into fist fights. None of which sat well with Roy. At one point Sean's rebelliousness spun so badly out of control that my parents considered enrolling him in military school to "get him on the right path."

Regardless of his path, Sean helped me land my first job, also at the golf course.

"What do I have to do?' I asked, sweating through the ten-minute interview as a skinny 13-year-old kid who had never held a golf club.

"Just keep the carts and clubs clean," said my boss, Gord Brayton. "And don't ever show up late."

The pay was $3.60 an hour.

I had no way of knowing it at the time, but that job would introduce me to a new world and the first true love of my life – the game of golf. I worked at least six days a week during the summer. Mom was happy because I was never more than a five-minute bike ride from home, and I had a free pass to play golf, a full-time job *and* was staying out of trouble. Sort of. My friends and I were a bunch of early-teen rabble-rousers enjoying (and abusing) the freedom of youth on that golf course – our own field of dreams – where we'd play into the darkness almost every night, eyeing down one another's tee shots in the dusky haze while the train rambled along the tracks next to us. Someone taught us that jamming a tee into a golf cart's governor system would open the throttle enough for an extra jolt of unregulated speed. These souped-up carts enabled us to play a 90-minute run-and-gun night golf in the twilight, smoking Colts and drinking Labatt's Lite that we stole from the concession stand on the tenth tee. The bonds of friendship hardened like steel during those endless hours on the golf course, and I understood why the great Moe Norman once said, "Golf is happiness. It's intoxication without the hangover. It's stimulation without the pills. Its price is high yet its rewards are richer. Some say it's a boys' pastime yet it builds men. It cleanses the mind and rejuvenates the body. It's these things and many more for those of us who know it and love it. Golf is truly happiness."

I believed and understood, even as a teenager, that golf lived on the threshold of seduction and addiction. A purely struck golf ball is a feeling that stays with you for life – the elusive combination of sound, feel and sight cannot ever be forgotten. At impact, the magic sensation in your hands flows immediately to your eyes, which track the flight of the launched ball towards the target. It's a majestic reward for perfect contact from a well-oiled swing. From that point on, a true golfer devotes many quality hours to the lifelong endeavour of creating that feeling again and again. The smell of freshly cut grass. The glint of morning sunlight sparkling off drops of dew. Wild animals sauntering through the fairways – Mother Nature's fine work on display in a great green open space.

I was addicted. I remember Mr. Don Walls, the club's grand patri-arch and a paunchy old Englishman, watching me hit a tee shot on the short par-three third hole during the club's annual Junior Open. I had about 135 yards to the hole and pulled out a three-iron.

Mr. Walls eyed up all 90 pounds of me. "You're not gonna get that up and over that front bunker, son, maybe you should pull out a three-wood?"

Undeterred, I struck the ball purely and it flew onto the green, roll-ing to within four feet of the cup. He was elated. I was surprised.

"Nice shot, young whippersnapper. Boy, you sure do have a smooth swing. Keep it up and you'll be winning these tournaments in no time. Now go make that putt."

I walked up to that green feeling like a champion, and poured the putt into the back of the cup for my first deuce ever.

In the summer of 1982, Roy deemed us brothers and our cousins Kelly and Ryan capable of handling a canoe on our first true adventure – a five-day paddle down a section of the Pembina River, two hours' drive north of town. Apart from the five Lawson boys, he'd also bring along Brad's best friend, "Boog," a timid kid who lived across the park behind our house and seemed afraid of his own shadow. We were sur-prised that his parents even let him go. Six inexperienced kids all under the age of 14 were crammed into two 17-foot fibreglass canoes, and by the time we reached the put-in, you could've sliced the nervous ener-gy up like a loaf of bread. Roy's plan was to expose us to a hands-on wilderness experience by easing us into the flow.

The first day went to plan: calm water, minimal current and nice weather. But on day two the river had its own plan. Not even two kilo-metres into the day, a tricky eddy line swept Sean and Kelly (with Ryan crouched in the middle) sideways into two perfectly placed boulders exactly a canoe length apart. In an instant, bags of gear and food began flowing out the gunwales of the capsized vessel. Sleeping bags stuffed inside of black garbage bags floated downstream as panic ensued. Roy swung the other canoe to shore, ensuring the rest of us boys were safe before plunging into the water to swim after every floating bag and piece of gear he could possibly get his hands on. Dozens of pop cans sank to a watery grave, as did a box of Roy's expensive camera equipment. To our surprise, Roy wasn't angry. He knew anything could happen at any time – that is the law of the wild.

As the campfire flickered on the beach, Roy used a stick to trace the entire scene in the sand, showing us what went wrong and how to prevent it from ever happening again. We eventually found our groove, each boy pulling his weight in the canoe and at camp, learning how to build a proper fire, cook over coals, open a can with a knife and make a lean-to shelter.

On the very last day of the trip, we discovered a rotten cow's carcass teeming with plump white maggots, and then, as we were hauling gear up a hillside to the road, Ryan stepped on a wasp nest. They swarmed his body, causing him to scream and run in circles like a cartoon character, his head and body covered in angry wasps. Roy shouted at him to jump into the river, and he finally ran in, dunking his head repeatedly while crying for help. Roy was picking dozens of still-alive wasps from Ryan's hair for two hours while we waited for our mom and Auntie Dee to pick us up.

It was a tough end to an otherwise mostly successful adventure. Sean had recovered from the capsize and earned Roy's Best Paddler award. I won Best Camper and Ryan got the Medal of Courage. The trip taught us how to work as a team and further fanned the flames of an adventurous youth in the outdoors. Although he didn't come to any hockey, basketball or volleyball games and never once set foot on the golf course, Roy taught us how to hunt rabbits, sharpen a knife, gut a fish, shoot a bow and chop and stack a cord of wood.

But outside of time spent in nature together, Sean's rebellious teen years conflicted with Roy's strict, military-style parenting. The two clashed constantly, ripping holes in the family fabric. Ultimately, Roy's temper and alcoholism got the better of him. Mom had no choice but to ask him to leave, and as a young boy I struggled emotionally with that, begging for her to let him stay and for Roy to promise to quit drinking – a promise he couldn't keep. In the winter of 1987, he was admitted to the local hospital with a mild fever that soon became much more. I remember visiting him in the Misericordia Hospital in Edmonton less than two weeks later – his body riddled with jaundice – and I vowed I'd never again go see him like that. Roy died from cirrhosis of the liver two days later, at the age of 47.

Twice widowed before her 43rd birthday, Mom was once again back to raising her three boys on her own.

WAKE UP EARLY,
STAY UP LATE

ROSSLAND, BRITISH COLUMBIA

April 1, 1989: "Terminal Day" at Red Mountain. It was the last day of ski hill operations, and the springtime air rang full of festive energy. Skiers young and old crowded onto the back patio of Rafters Pub, listening to live music, smoking dope and drinking pitchers of cheap draft beer. Amidst the hoopla someone noticed a figure moving in a stand of cedar trees across the road. It was Sean, slowly climbing up the biggest tree of the bunch, a western red cedar almost 60 feet tall that became quite thin and flimsy in the last quarter of its height. Suddenly a branch broke, and Sean dropped a few feet. Everyone gasped, but he righted himself on a lower branch and kept on climbing until he made the top, which he then began shaking wildly back and forth with exaggerated energy, getting the crowd riled up, until he finally snapped off the top of the tree with his hand. A raucous hail of applause followed, and from the look on his face he felt like the king of the world. Descending with the treetop between his teeth, Sean slipped again, this time pinballing quite a ways down the tree until the thicker lower branches broke his fall.

"Holy shit, is he okay?" someone shouted from the crowd. Everyone stopped and stared, waiting in suspense for the outcome. Sean jumped down, emerging from the bushes, his clenched fist raising the tree-top high above his head like a trophy. Adrenaline had outweighed the pain. He was unscathed. The crowd howled in laughter and celebration as he bounced joyfully into the bar and handed the treetop to the bartender, who stuffed it in a pitcher and filled it with beer.

Sean had heard about the town of Rossland through his ski-racing best friend, Ted Funk, who had shown him a *Powder Magazine* photograph of a skier in waist-deep snow breathing through a snorkel at Red Mountain, in the heart of the now-fabled Kootenays region. Sean cut the picture out and pinned it to his bedroom wall, telling Mom he wanted to live there one day.

We'd been introduced to skiing as young boys, thanks to the proximity of a man-made ski resort called Lake Eden, a hidden gem just 15 minutes from home in Stony Plain. Dressed in jeans, toques and goggles, we'd clutch onto the rope-tow with our shitty woollen mittens and flail down the bunny hill, wet and cold from endless wipeouts but laughing uncontrollably from the pure joy that comes from sliding on snow.

Skiing worked its magic into our blood, and we started skiing every single weekend, and most nights after school under the lights. Before long the three Lawson brothers were competing in the local Nancy Greene Ski League, in love with the icy rush of speed, grateful that Mom could scrape up enough money to keep us on skis.

We discovered new meaning on that little hill, racing through gates with our new-found friends, carving turns in the icy snow and freezing our fingers and toes because we never wanted to leave. In the spring of 1982, the Alberta provincial ski-racing championships were set to be held at Marmot Basin, in Jasper National Park, so we packed the family station wagon and drove three and a half hours west to the gateway of the great Rocky Mountains. When we first laid eyes on the snow-covered peaks and herds of elk that surrounded the vehicle on the outskirts of Jasper town, it was as if a new world had risen just beyond the hood of the car.

As a ski hill, Marmot was so big we found it easy to get lost, especially in a murky whiteout. With no night lights lining its slopes, the lifts only turned until four p.m., so we stayed high up on the mountain to ensure one long massive run at the end of the day, skiing right to the car and our mom waiting with hot chocolate and a hug. Linking those long turns together was infinitely more fun than wearing bibs and smashing through slalom gates, and competitive racing soon fell by the wayside. For us, the true essence of skiing was all about freedom. We begged Mom to take us back to Jasper as soon as possible, but she couldn't afford it. We'd have to settle for Lake Eden's tiny hills to feed our fix.

After graduating from high school, Sean worked the summer months at the local lumber mill in Stony Plain, and found out that Red Mountain was hiring ski instructors. With zero experience, he applied and, surprisingly, got the job. Days before his 19th birthday, Sean packed his ski gear and the contents of his bedroom into his beloved 1980 Ford Bronco and headed 12 hours west, with Ted Funk riding shotgun, to the historic mining town that boasts some of the deepest snow in the world.

Like many ski towns, Rossland seemed made up entirely of young ski bums whose sole purpose was to party and ski as much as possible. Sean Lawson fit right in. He quickly found his tribe, a like-minded crew of freaks, hippies, mountain athletes, party animals, ski patrollers, peaceful warriors and full-time fun hogs. People named Dano and Potsy and Goober and Sparky and Swetty and Sarah and Lizzie and Christ-Why and Rachel. Mostly in their early 20s and late teens, these adventurous souls (plus 40-plus more dirtbag characters with enough joie de vivre to fill a stadium) would become his family. The tribe didn't care what you wore or what you drove or how much money you had or didn't have. Frequent come-as-you-are, bring-what-you-can potluck dinners supported a culture where storytelling and shenanigans took centre stage. This family of friends supported one another almost unconditionally, every one of them driven to work a little, play a lot.

Sean adapted well to this way of life, finding ways to earn himself the standard Kootenay diet of weed, beer, Kraft Dinner and Sapporo Ichiban. But Sean and his friends really only cared about eating powder. No matter how hard they partied or how bad the hangovers, true Rossland ski bums were always up at seven a.m., ready to roll. The real hardcores would pass out in their toques and long johns, still drunk from the day's après-ski session and dancing past midnight with ski boots still on. This lifestyle impressed itself upon Sean and first clicked him into the mindset of what would become a personal lifelong mantra: *Wake up early, stay up late.* He would write those six words inside the covers of books, on the tops of party-night pizza boxes, and on the walls of the ski patrol shack, encouraging others to live the same way. Always eager to squeeze every drop of juice out of every hour, he despised idle, stationary pursuits like watching movies or TV. Wasting a day because of a hangover was like hell for him, but booze often got the upper hand. His Achilles heel was rum and coke, and he was a quick drunk, slurring after two stiff drinks and sometimes letting alcohol carry him to the point of blackout drunk. It was a comedy show for those around him, and they loved him because of it, but for a younger brother it could be an embarrassing shitshow to witness. He fed off the laughter, off the cheers, off the peer pressure to do crazy shit like jump out of third-storey windows into deep piles of snow. Making people laugh gave Sean the freedom to be himself.

That life-of-the-party Rossland Sean was an improvement on the one that left home. After Roy died, he had railed against society in a typical Albertan teenaged way, listening to heavy metal, smoking pot and getting out-of-hand drunk. One night after a Metallica concert in Edmonton, he was so dead set on meeting the band after the show that he jumped onto the back of the tour bus as it pulled away from Northlands Coliseum. The driver must have gotten lucky with a series of green lights, because within minutes Sean and the bus were gaining speed on Highway 2, bound for Calgary, three hours south. Sean banged the tinted rear window as loud as he could, but nobody inside could hear him. He had no choice but to jump off the back bumper at high speed, rolling into the ditch. Luckily, he was drunk, wearing a leather jacket, and still young enough to have bones of rubber.

Without Roy's strict parenting, a new sense of anarchy and freedom took hold. The song "Fuck tha Police," by controversial anti-establishment rappers N.W.A., often blared from the ghetto blaster hoisted on Sean's shoulder. The song became his rallying cry in protest, his way of giving the middle finger to the system. It didn't matter that the system, for the most part, treated Sean just fine. He was bothered by the fact that there was a system at all.

Mom hated the direction her son was heading. He had become a cop-hating headbanger with no respect for society. Frequent arguments between the two escalated into shouting and door-slamming, mother-vs.-son fights with no winner except seething anger. Mourning was tearing them apart at the seams. Mom, having lost so much already, felt she was losing her son as well.

Sean's easiest escape was skiing, but moving away from home and family proved more difficult than he'd expected. After a season-ending knee injury the next year, he spent his days inside, drinking tea and writing letters with little of his usual zest for life. As the months ticked by in the mountains and his body healed, Sean's adventurous escapades with the tribe eventually became bigger and bolder. And with the risks came more injuries, and the low-morale cycle would repeat itself. Sean wanted nothing more than the feeling of fresh, cold snow spraying off the tips of his skis and into his face, but an assortment of injuries prevented him from getting the goods. Fear of missing out took a toll – it's hard to hang with friends who've skied deep powder all day while you've been in bed, managing pain. Sean struggled with loneliness and started to feel like maybe he *didn't* fit in. The darkness of depression began knocking on the doors of his psyche. During his third season at Red Mountain, he decided, at the urging of his closest circle of friends, to finally see a doctor about his mental health, and was prescribed oral lithium compounds as an antidepressant, which Sean kept completely quiet about. And when he tore the ACL ligament in his other knee at the beginning of the next ski season, he started wondering if he truly was on the right path, as he wrote in the first of his voluminous collection of journals:

November 22, 1993
Rossland, BC

I can't believe that I'm sittin' in the physiotherapist's office.
FUCK! After all that talk about taking it easy cuz it'll be such

a long winter, I was the one who said "Let's go in" and had a fucked wipe-out, tweaking my good knee. Christ man, what's with the constant stream of bad luck and injuries? Always when things pretty much couldn't be better. Is there some sort of message I'm supposed to get from all of this? Maybe that's the message, the mountains don't want me right now. Get the fuck out... go... follow your heart.

One night over a picnic table strewn with empty beer cans, a Rossland friend suggested a trip to the Himalaya "to see what real mountains look like." Within two weeks Sean arrived in Kathmandu during Diwali, the Hindu autumn Festival of Lights – a time of full-festivity colour and chaos. The vibrant pulse of intense celebration had waned by the time a cabbie dropped him in the infamous Thamel district at a place called Sam's Bar, a lively, multi-ethnic pub with flags of all nations and handwritten felt-pen notes covering the walls. It was the type of place where heroic mountain plans were born after six pints of beer, only to dissipate a few hours later from a high-altitude hangover so fierce it made death seem preferable, and a possibility.

The west-meets-east hippie-travellers vibe felt like a welcome embrace for Sean. The next morning, even a vicious hangover couldn't keep him in bed. He headed to the hotel rooftop at sunrise to catch his first glimpse of a mountain range of incomprehensible scale – the arresting, magical Himalaya, with their peaks shining like a band of white diamonds in the distance.

"It's my soul and spirit to be in high places and empty spaces" was the first line written in his Nepal travel journal.

As the nation's beating, spiritual heart, Kathmandu was also *the* meeting point for mountaineering expeditions of extreme bravado. Since Sean was recovering from his knee injury, he couldn't undergo anything serious and embarked upon self-guided, multi-day treks along the stunning Annapurna Circuit, where the Dhaulagiri and Machhapuchhare peaks stamped their hulking shapes into his brain. Staying in five-dollar tea houses along the route (with food and chillums full of hashish included) helped Sean stretch his finances for weeks. Trekking with a light pack did wonders for his knee.

Soon the peaks, people and philosophy of this huge new world wove themselves into the fabric of Sean's being. He had come a long way from small-town Stony Plain and his years as a snot-nosed prairie kid hanging onto a rope-tow on the bunny hill at Lake Eden. After two months in the country, Sean charted a different approach than most of the backpackers he met, who would follow each other from hostel to hostel, eating at the same restaurants mentioned in the guidebooks, riding the same buses and sharing the same canned adventures. Sean never understood the pack/herd mentality. To him, the adventure wasn't real if you had to pay for it. So, rather than getting drunk in the expat pubs and sleeping off the hangover, he'd rent a cheap motorbike and venture along dusty roads deep into the countryside as early as four a.m. to catch the first rays of light as they bathed the centuries-old rice terraces on both sides of the Kathmandu Valley. Here, surrounded by tiny farms, sacred temples and Buddhist monks, Sean found his own spiritual nirvana, which, for an Alberta boy without a spiritual upbringing, was a big deal.

He loved walking barefoot through the maze of rice terraces, randomly encountering poor subsistence farmers who had spent their entire lives traversing the same footpaths. These rural folk peasants possessed little and lived simply, knowing that a happy heart could overcome a hungry belly during the hard times. In Sean's mind, these were the real heroes of Nepal. During his visits he had only ever seen the rural locals eating *dal bhat*, the Nepalese staple of rice and lentils. Knowing that everyone appreciates an unexpected treat, Sean bought a few family-sized portions of *momo* (steamed buffalo-meat dumplings packaged neatly in little bamboo baskets) and hand-delivered them to a family of new-found farmer friends.

"Namaskar," he said, greeting them with a smile, the gift of food presented in his cupped palms. At first the family was reluctant, shocked that a white man who spoke hardly any Nepalese would do such a thing. Accepting a meal from a strange foreigner wasn't

a common occurrence in rural Nepal. After an awkward moment, however, they put down their sickles and enjoyed lunch with the white guy on a motorbike. Few words were spoken, but their faces stretched with toothless smiles. Sean was no longer the loud, rebellious teenager with a reckless fuck-you attitude. Travel had become his mentor, and he began carrying a new, benevolent attitude into the far reaches of the world.

VAGABOND SEAN

"Todd, Father Patrick is here," says Dr. Debbie, who has come outside to find me. A look of grave concern covers her pretty face. "He would like to know if you want to have a blessing said in case Sean doesn't make it much longer."

Although a young doctor in just her first year in the intensive care ward, Dr. Debbie is no stranger to hospital tragedies. She lost her younger brother a few years ago in a freak cycling accident; he was hit by a drunk driver while out on an afternoon ride. She seems to have taken a special liking to Sean and has no intention of giving up on him. Neither do I. *Of course I don't want to have a blessing said. That feels like we're pulling the plug.*

"I can call him in at any time, just let me know."

I gather my thoughts and agree for my grandmother's sake. Knowing her grandson was blessed by a Catholic holy man in his final hours will comfort her as she mourns. Father Patrick hovers over Sean for what seems like forever, splashing holy water and quietly muttering prayers while moving a pewter crucifix around his body in a slow-moving circle. I keep my distance, my head downcast in disbelief, watching closely, praying. *Please hang on, Sean. Maybe Father Patrick's words will infuse a miracle into your battered body.*

Three months ago, we consulted with a travel health nurse in downtown Cape Town and told her of our plans to ride motorcycles throughout Southern Africa for a few months. In a clean, bright office, she squinted through a pair of wire-rimmed glasses and told us that Lariam was the only anti-malarial prophylaxis being prescribed at the time; it was known in travellers' circles as "Scariam" due to a wide array of side effects, including sudden headaches, dizziness, loss of balance, paranoia, extreme rage, suicidal ideation, depression, confusion and "unusual" behaviour. We weighed our options carefully. Take the pill daily and deal with any or all of the above, or be as vigilant as possible, wear long-sleeved clothing and pants at night, use plenty of insect repellent and always keep the tent zipper closed. We chose the latter.

Sitting at Sean's bedside, I question that decision. Still, his breathing seems to be getting more consistent, and the beeping machines show no signs of urgent warning. Heavily sedated with a cocktail of quinine and morphine, his body has once again fallen into a deep sleep.

He's resting now, let him be. I better go call Mom and see how she's doing.

"Oh, Todd, how are you, my son? How is Sean doing?"

"I was just with him. His breathing is steady, and I don't think he's feeling any pain. I'm sorry, Mom. I'm so, so sorry. I could've done something sooner, but we just didn't know. He's still hanging in there, Mom... he's so strong, he's gonna make it."

"I know, sweetheart, I know. We are all praying for both of you. Just stay strong and be with him. We're on the way. The flights are booked and we leave in a few hours." I can hear the sobs in her voice, but also her resilience and strength in the face of despair. We say goodbye, and I take some time to write a few thoughts in my journal.

My eyes are sore and tired from crying... nothing could have prepared me for what I am feeling and what I have been through the past few days. I am so very scared for Sean, my blood – a courageous man who I am proud to call my brother. I'm scared but I know deep down in my heart that he is going to pull through this. We had such an incredible time on our journey and to have it end like this! But he's strong and his insatiable zest for life is going to bring him over this disease. He's in very good care and in very capable hands which allows me to breathe a little better.

After Sean returned to the Kootenays from Nepal, rumours swirled through the rock climbing community about a climbing mecca in the south of Thailand, a tropical paradise teeming with pocketed limestone walls and thousands of unclimbed routes. Introduced to climbing the previous summer, he became immediately interested in this place known as Railay Beach, and started searching for the *Lonely Planet Thailand* guidebook. Within ten days he'd stuffed a small brown travel pack full of climbing gear and very few clothes, hitchhiked to Vancouver and boarded a plane to Bangkok.

Stepping into the chaos of Khao San Road, Bangkok's infamous backpacker's strip, Sean felt as though his body had been transported to another dimension – not unlike that first ski trip into the Rocky Mountains when we were kids. The neon sensory overload hit Sean like a drug, his first true taste of the world beyond, an uppercut of culture shock that landed with a hard thud.

Known as the travellers' hub of Southeast Asia, Khao San Road is a quarter-mile stretch of Bangkok in all her dynamic, no-holds-barred glory – packed on both sides with raucous bars, cheap hostels and brightly lit street food stalls serving everything from fried crocodile to heaping plates of peanut-sprinkled *pad Thai*. All along this infamous strip, rowdy backpackers cram handfuls of fried bugs into their drunken mouths and Singha beers down their thirsty gullets. Action-packed at any time of day or night, Khao San hums with enough stimuli to fill a lifetime. It was a fresh new buzz, and Sean was digging it.

After a few hours, he hopped in a tuk-tuk with two new-found Aussie friends and headed to Patpong, the seedy underbelly of Bangkok. There, under a canopy of red neon lights, the three travellers were rustled off the street by aggressive touts and led to an upstairs bar. Sean bought a round of overpriced beers and sat in the front row with his new mates as the most bizarre show they'd ever seen started to unfold – the infamous Thai live sex show. Bangkok is one of the few places on the planet where watching two people fuck in front of a live audience is not only possible, it's hard to avoid. More drinks kept coming as a rotating procession of young women took to the stage to wow the crowd with bewildering vaginal mastery featuring ping pong balls, feathered darts, razor blades and felt pens. Then, the pièce de résistance: a man and woman walked onstage hand in hand, looking completely detached from the situation. He took off her bikini, laid her on the stage and went down on her for a while. She took off his underwear and went down on him. Then he climbed on her and fucked her right there in front of everyone, missionary style. After a half-dozen position changes with a few thrusts for each, they finished and walked off stage nonchalantly. The lights came on like at the end of a play, revealing a room full of dropped jaws.

Climbers were a tight bunch back in the early days at Railay Beach, and Sean quickly found another tribe amongst a ragtag crew of Canadian climbers: Trevor "T-Mac" McDonald, Mike Tyler, Angus Maxwell, Glen Harris and Mike Strimas – all equally buzzed about life in their new mango-lassi'd world.

For Sean, Railay offered the perfect change of scenery, alight and alive with strange sights and sounds, tastes and smells, everything heightened by a backdrop of unrivalled paradisiacal beauty. Towering limestone walls and white-sand beaches framed a setting of such enchanting allure that many who came never left. Dotted amongst the stalactites and stalagmites existed the ultimate vertical playground – hundreds of climbing routes bolted into exquisite pocketed limestone, with new routes begging for discovery every day. For a climbing junkie, Railay Beach *was* paradise on earth. Sean learned fluidity and finesse, energy rationing and footwork, mental focus and physical prowess. He got stronger, more agile, and climbed his heart out. Wake up early, climb until late. Sometimes the climbs were straightforward with the reward of stunning scenery at the top. Other times...

October 12, 1994
Railay Beach, KRABI

Angus and I left one afternoon for a 4-pitch rock climb that
turned into an epic. The first pitch was sketchy and had some
loose rock on it, the 2nd and 3rd were more difficult with a
strange line that was hard to stay on-route. The 4th is where a
paperback-sized hold came loose and smacked me in the face on
lead causing some blood and a bump yet I didn't fall. So there
we were at the top with sunlight dwindling by the minute and I
knew that we had to hurry. I started to rap down and was pretty
stupid actually... just because we had a long rope doesn't mean
that you can make it to the 2nd station. I jumped the gun cuz of
the rush and lack of light and went too fuckin' far man and was
suspended in mid-air, unable to come in contact with the rock.
SHIT! At first I was quite pissed off that I made such a stupid
mistake and immediately realized that we were probably stuck
for the nite. So there we were having to wait 11 fucking hours
for the sun to come back. Talk about uncomfortable eh! No
water, just T-shirts and shorts and not even smokes. Checked out
the stars and the lights all over Sunset Bar thinking about our
friends who didn't know where the fuck we were. What a grand
view though eh! We didn't talk much and I caught some piss
drizzle from above a couple times. That climb really took a lot
from us. I'm hoping for a safe couple months ahead of me.

Of course, with Sean's track record, "a safe couple months" required
heavy optimism, more so when alcohol was involved, of which there
was always plenty to go around. The Sunset Bar was *the* place to be
in Railay, an open-air, thatched-roof melting pot of hippie travellers,
backpackers and climbers who all came together nightly to witness
mind-blowing sunsets on a pristine beach. When the sun went down
the music went up and everyone got loose, especially during the epic
full-moon parties where wasted foreigners danced to trance music and
tripped out on LSD until sunrise.

Aside from drugs and glow-in-the-dark face paint, fire-spinning became the showpiece attraction of any good full-moon shaker. On Friday, November 18, the night of a penumbral lunar eclipse, two locals were hired to dazzle the partygoers with their fire-spinning *poi* (balls of fire on the end of a chain) performance. Dreadlocked and dripping with sweat from twisting and twirling flames around their chiselled bodies, the spinners soon had a crowd of 200-plus gathered in a giant circle at least two or three bodies deep. Like most of the drunken backpackers, Sean had never seen fire-spinning before. He sat in the front row, silently transfixed, studying the moves and the momentum of the flames. In the pitch black of night, the dancers controlled their *poi* with such precision and control that Sean knew he wanted to be one of *those* guys. As the show progressed, the crowd swelled even more, drawn by the wow factor and the whoosh of spinning flames. Fuelled by liquid courage, Sean decided it was his turn to have a go. He'd been at Railay long enough that it wasn't a huge surprise to see him walk confidently towards the Thai performers with an eager look in his eyes. They assumed he had spun fire before, and thus trustingly relinquished the chains.

At first Sean handled them with surprising competence. The crowd cheered him on, and he spun the *poi* faster and faster. For a rookie he was holding his own… until he got cocky and tried spinning the chains behind his back. Instead of an impressive flurry of light and rhythm, Sean's back caught fire when kerosene from the fire balls spilled onto his cotton T-shirt. The crowd began to yell warnings, but the music was too loud. In the frenzy, Sean thought they were rooting *for* him, not screaming *at* him. Back in his familiar element, making people laugh while doing something stupid, Sean jokingly tried to fend off the Thai spinners who rushed to help. He spun and parried as if he were Bruce Lee holding a pair of nunchucks. The crowd went wild with laughter. Swept away in the euphoria of the moment amongst a swirling chaos of pumping music and flickering flames, Sean kept swinging the chains at the very people who were trying to help him, until they finally tackled him to the ground, dousing the flames in the sand. The next day he was the talk of the town, whether he liked it or not.

Six weeks later, he played with fire again, as he relayed in a letter to friends:

December 31st, 1994
Andaman Beach, Thailand

I've been here at Railay for almost three months this time. Love the place! The climbing is spectacular. A couple of friends and myself rented DT200 dirt bikes for a few days and it was the best time man! It was hilarious, you should've seen us getting lost, wiping out, having some pretty close calls on the highway (the driving is intense here and of course we had neither helmets nor shirts). On the 3rd day Tyler and I found endless singletrack thru coconut and banana tree plantations, criss-crossin' up-down and around the valley surrounded by limestone cliffs and lush mountains. WOW, what a rush man. Gotta do it again someday eh but the night we got back to Railay I fucked up man. It should be no surprise though and you people warned me to take care of myself. I had better watch if I happen to be in Karachi or near the Afghanistan border eh. Don't worry. So... I was stoked for climbing the next morning but wanted to socialize over a few drinks. You know how that saying goes eh "Just one more." Ya right. I was on the second floor overlooking the scene and simply decided to jump off into the sand. Anyways, when I landed I lost my balance and rolled over backward into the burning hot fire full of glowing coals! There I was on my back wriggling and twitching for a full long four seconds until finally rolling into the Andaman Sea. Thank God it was high tide eh. Everyone was starin' at me like "What the fuck did you just do Sean? Jesus Christ!" It wasn't until I fully emerged from the ocean that I realized the magnitude of my burns. With burns the pain comes afterwards man and it really hurts a lot sometimes. Keep out of the sand, sea and sun says the doctor. I live on a beach in a bungalow in the jungle man, fuck. I can't do anything. It sucks, but it could've been worse.

Sixty per cent of his back and legs were covered in second- and third-degree burns – a hard pill to swallow in the tropical heat, with no hospital for hours in either direction. The damage was extensive, and gruesome to see, especially after Sean slathered on a local molasses-like jungle-potion paste that made his burns look "like some sort of Cajun chicken dish," as T-Mac would later remark. With these new burns inflicted less than a month after his fire-spinning incident at Sunset Bar, T-Mac and the crew couldn't resist branding Sean with a new nickname, Fireshow Sean.

Then something magical happened that swung the pendulum in a positive direction: a chance encounter that Sean deemed "the ultimate moment in my travels." Her name was Sarah Peterson, a friendly, blue-eyed, solo-travelling 26-year-old from San Francisco. They immediately fell into a warm, sexy connectedness, something Sean had never experienced before. Contradictory to his often rowdy ways, the two developed a relationship of "quiet radiance and truthful light," as Sarah described it. She took an instant liking to Sean's authenticity and childlike wonder about the world. Having finally found someone to share his experiences with, Sean fell head over heels in love.

Sarah let him be himself – a quirky small-town kid with big dreams and a wild heart ready to explore the world his own way. For the next six months, they journeyed to the most magical of places, including the ancient city of Bagan in Myanmar (arriving shortly after a strict, nation-wide curfew had been lifted, Sean and Sarah were two of just 20 foreigners in the whole country). They camped in the snow and fired AK-47s in a gun-making town in Pakistan, visited Buddhist monasteries carved into mountains, climbed temples on acid under the full moon, ran down mountain paths in the Karakoram range, and completed long-distance treks through the mind-blowing Hindu Kush Himalaya. Unfortunately their six-month whirlwind fling came to a heartbreaking end when Sarah chose to go back home to San Francisco. Sean was crushed, but his quest for travel culture shock led him to the slums of Delhi, where the doors of his mind were blown off once again. The constant mayhem and abject poverty forced him to adapt to an overwhelming new environment, where shitting in the streets was as common an occurrence as bloated human carcasses floating down the Ganges River.

Sean revelled in the newness of it all. In Calcutta, he would frequently turn the tables on the city's rickshaw drivers by running their rickshaws *for* them, forcing the drivers to sit in the customer seat behind, persisting through their confusion.

"My friend, you have spent your whole life running these wheels through the city streets, why don't you let *me* run for a while. I want you to experience what it's like to be a passenger."

"Oh no no no sir, this cannot happen. You cannot take my rickshaw. I need to make the money for my family."

"You sit, I pay," he'd tell them, treating each driver to lunch and cold drinks after an hour pulling them around the city.

Some were embarrassed to be seen sitting in the seat of the rickshaw with a foreigner up front, but everyone on the streets stopped, stared and laughed. A lot. Sliding that fleeting moment of comical joy into the lives of strangers was his way of making the world a smaller place.

March, 2, 1995
Varanasi, India

Hey Graeme,

Varanasi on Holi Day was absolutely crazy man. A water war of color and tomatoes and balloons and squirt guns. Vivid blues, reds, greens, pinks and more. Total chaos in the streets in the early morning and they (Indians) were all pretty drunk and riled up man! Women were advised to stay indoors cuz they will get hassled and grabbed by the drunkard mob. But Sarah and Anna didn't wanna miss out, so Wolfie and I went along with them. It actually started right at our hotel as the water pump guy started dousing liquid and chanting "Holi Holi Holi" then kids ran out of ammo and resorted to hucking damp cow shit on us. I took a bit in the face but got shelter and loaded up with some ammo of my own. Haha! Then shit started to get real out of control man. As soon as we hit the main streets there were adolescents and young men, LOTS of them. We were still water fighting and everyone had the most amazing designs on their faces and clothes. It started to get eerie as they got more aggressive and started walking behind us and grabbing the girls. The pace quickened and some of the fuckers really grabbed and surrounded the girls. They fought back and of course Wolfie and I were defending too. It was quite an intense scene. There were a couple nice Indians helping us too and it was still a fun paint war in the middle of the serious fighting. Those dudes took some pretty hard blows though. India is excellent.

For Sean, travelling the world for as long and as cheap as possible had become a game, an adrenalin-filled wonderland full of opportunity and wide-eyed exploration. He'd often pay for his accommodations at guest houses by landscaping, working shifts as night security or waking before sunrise to rake the beach clean of seaweed that had drifted ashore overnight. He'd intentionally ride third class on trains and buses, or hitchhike across entire countries just to stay on the road one more day. But Sean's voyages were never so deep that he lost sight of home. The rift between mother and son had long since healed, and the family fridge in Alberta was adorned with postcards from all corners of the globe, packed with so many words that the margins were full of his scribbled ramblings. As he navigated, and relished in, the mind-altering experiences in one country after the next, Sean's struggles with loneliness and depression began to disappear. And although Mom missed him dearly and knew he was likely up to no good most of the time, she was proud of the young man he was becoming. That made her the happiest.

BROTHERS IN ARMS

CAPE TOWN, SOUTH AFRICA

Sean and Brad had grown apart after high school, each becoming a radically different product of their environments in two completely different places in North America – Sean in laid-back Rossland, BC, and Brad in redneck Houston, Texas. Aside from skiing, motorcycles and drinking, they had very little in common. Sean had become a world-travelling hippie dirtbag mountain man who found his freedom ripping up dusty roads on a dirt bike, while Brad, a city-slicker bartender with a model's handsome looks (and a legit black-and-white photo portfolio to back it up), raced around on a Kawasaki Ninja sportbike, chased fast women and wore cologne that matched his fancy black-and-white wingtip shoes.

After not seeing each other for six long years, Sean and Brad finally met in Tulum, Mexico, for a long-overdue reunion. True to form, after swilling a few strong Cuba libres one evening, Sean began swinging from the rafters – literally, climbing the interior bamboo frame of their rented *palapa* – when his left arm slipped off one of the beams, sending him crashing onto the tiled floor, separating his elbow on impact. The planned camping adventure in the coming days was over in an instant, replaced instead by an expensive trip to the doctor (with Brad footing the bill). With Sean passed out from pain medication, Brad made plans to head back to the US. It had been a fun-filled party weekend, but the subcultural divide proved too vast – there just wasn't enough common ground for the brothers to continue to travel together.

"Fuck I was mad at myself for climbing around when I was drunk," Sean later wrote in his journal. "I wish Brad would've stayed longer but I didn't expect him to sit around in a hammock all day long either. With my arm in a sling I couldn't do much. At least we got to spend some time together. He's a good dude."

Sean spent the next three months with a Rossland friend Sarah Weinberg, traipsing around the ancient Mayan ruins of Palenque, Chichen Itza, Tulum and Tikal while waiting for his body to heal so he could come back to Canada for another climbing season. As his travel funds dwindled, Sean heard from some climbing buddies that the ski resort in Whistler, BC, was in the midst of a construction boom, with lots of labourer work to be had. That was all Sean needed to hear. He spent the summer of 1996 framing houses and banking enough money to buy a two-tone blue Dodge camper van, complete with a megaphone rigged to the roof so he could heckle and blast music at unsuspecting pedestrians. A dog-eared copy of Robert Young Pelton's *The World's Most Dangerous Places* held a permanent place on the dashboard of his new home-on-wheels.

After surviving the summer in Whistler relatively unscathed, Sean returned to Rossland in the fall to discover that someone had bestowed upon him the nickname "Knuckle" – an apt but unwanted moniker to describe his klutzy, accident-prone character; a knucklehead. No matter how calculated Sean tried to be, there always seemed to be a missing link between victory and defeat. He would take things too far, too fast, sliding along the fine line between bravery and stupidity and too often falling off the wrong side. Even though the nickname was intended as a funny jab, Sean hated it. He wanted to be simply known as Vagabond Sean, or just Lawson, as most in town had previously called him. To his credit, Lawson/Knuckle made it through the ski season without any major injuries, and by the following spring he was ready to get back on the road.

May 21, 1997
Airport Hotel, Kuala Lumpur
Malaysia

Dear Todd/Brad,

AFRICA...oh yeah, I totally wanna go. Wouldn't it be amazing for the three of us to be together again someday?! I love my free time and need to concentrate on sports and want to explore new places. People think it's crazy that I worked in Mexico for pesos, and even I didn't believe it happened, but it just did and I loved the remoteness of the area and simplicity of life, the Caribbean sea waves lapping up at the beach with that landing strip carved outta the palms for the drug cartel to land their coke planes made things pretty interesting too. There are so many other experiences to find in life that can't even be looked for, they just happen sometimes, you know? Anyways, I look forward to the same for you guys, my brothers. Let's get closer and tell all, okay!

Love, your big bro,
Sean

In the heyday of '90s travel, when pen-and-paper communication was the only way of keeping in touch with anyone, visiting the post office in a far-flung town or capital city to receive mail became a real event, almost like Christmas morning. Who knew what would be waiting, or which friends or family had timed the connection correctly?

Sean would anxiously plan itineraries based on where he could pick up mail at the various GPO Poste Restante or General Delivery boxes. As his list of countries grew, so did his legion of worldwide friends, many of whom were beneficiaries of his letters and unique DIY post-cards featuring one of his own printed photographs (he had purchased a Canon SLR From a Singaporean backpacker and began shooting in earnest) glued onto a random piece of cut-out cardboard. He treated photography like another outdoor sport, chasing early-morning and evening light, which worked well with his mantra. The postcards had hand-drawn address lines and a little box for the stamp on the back, along with his purposely misspelled return address:

Vegabond Sean
NFA – No Fixed Address
The World

He would send candid portraits of villagers and drunk locals or his favourites: macabre black-and-white photographs of bloated corpses floating in the Ganges or blood-stained vultures pulling the flesh off of dead alpacas in the Peruvian altiplano.

Sean's images reminded me of the stuff in *National Geographic* magazine: raw, real, well composed. Keeping in close contact with his worldly friends, especially those who filled page after page with notes and quotes and scribbled sketches in his ink-stained journals after having spent some time with him, kept his spirits high.

Sean. Definitely out of this world. If you pulled out a ray gun I'd believe it. So if you make it to the mother country sometime man, call me.

—JUSTIN EXLEY, UK

Sean, I used to keep a book like this. The difference between yours and mine is that more than 2 people have written in yours. Says a lot doesn't it.

—LORI HANNA, PERTH, ONTARIO

Spend a few days with Sean… you'll seem more open-minded and a hell of a lot more friendly. What a bloke!

—MARK SUMAS, COLORADO USA

Okay, Sean! The man with a thousand cuts and bruises. Stop picking them! You remind me of a poem actually. Strong as the

desert, soft as the sea, moving like the wind, forever free. See
ya next time. Stay gold

—HEV, ISRAEL

Today is my lucky day. I see the good man. He is Canadian. So nice
to meet such a kind man foreigner. You give me a photo of you. I
like it too much. Please be safe and perhaps see you in Canada.

—MY NAME IS AGUNG, JUST CALL ME AGUNG.

Sean Fucking LAWSON! What the fuck... there aren't too
many like you out there. Just fucking stay real mate, you're
choice as you are. Come to New Zealand mate!

—"BIG" WILL. CHRISTCHURCH, NZ

I admire a person, not plastic or hypocrite. I hope you can
maintain your attitude greatly and I like you so much.

—YOUR FRIEND, JUDITH MAGUDDAYO

Much like the way they'd entangled my older brother, the tentacles
of backpacker culture had wrapped themselves tightly around me in
my 20s. While Sean had been on the road almost continuously, bas-
ing himself out of dirt-cheap Southeast Asia and its smorgasbord of
cultural highlights all within a five-hour flight of Bangkok, I had also
travelled every winter for four to five months, and always alone. I'd
explored New Zealand, Australia and Indonesia one year, Western
Europe the next, Mexico and Central America after that, leaving the
world of professional golf behind and out of my mind. Instead, I filled
it with the intoxication of travel itself; of long-distance chicken buses
and sensory-overload markets, of multi-day volcano treks and hitch-
hiking through entire countries, of scuba dives and rowdy hostel
parties full of exuberance and international flair. Even the non-
glamorous realities of Third World travel, like suffering alone in a
cockroach-infested beach hut while a food-borne sickness ravaged

my body in fever-ridden waves, wasn't enough to veer me off the path
of wanderlust. Travel had taught me to judge less, to smile more, to
accept things the way they are, not to take one single day for granted.
Most importantly, travelling taught me not to judge anyone. Through
it all, I had amassed a modest travel education, but I knew it paled
in comparison to Sean's immersive globetrotting master's degree.
Collectively, we had set foot on five of seven continents, but not once
had we travelled together. We chose Africa to change that. I'd go first
and roam around South Africa alone for a month while Sean finished
exploring Cambodia on his dirt bike. The plan was to meet in Cape
Town on New Year's Eve, 1998.

When my feet touched African soil, I felt an instinctual freedom
I'd only ever felt once before in my life: back on the farm, running
through wheat fields with my brothers. I had heard of people saying
that Africa has a strange way of creeping into your skin, but *already?*
I bought a ticket on an organized mini-bus tour around Soweto, five
backpackers and a guide driving through the biggest township in Africa – a massive melting pot of Black South African cultures with more
than a million people crammed into 200 poverty-ridden square kilometres. SOuthWEstern TOwnship was created in the 1930s, when the
colonial South African government began separating the Blacks from
the whites, and the struggle against apartheid became central to Soweto's identity. I had seen poverty before, but never on such a scale or in
a monstrous slum like this. Every house and building was surrounded
by broken-glass shards cemented into cinder-block fences. Razor wire
covered the roofs and thick steel roll-down doors kept the occupants
safe inside at night.

At one of the illicit *shebeens* that dot every corner of the township,
our small group drank a frothy sour-corn beer called *umqombothi*,
poured with a ladle from five-gallon buckets by big round ladies
layered in aprons. It tasted nothing like beer to me, and I nearly puked
on the dirt floor between my legs after the first swig. The half-dozen
men seated at the next wooden table glanced over and laughed hard.
Breaking the ice never felt so awkward. As it was only 25 cents a
mug, I bought a round for all, and we sat together between rusted

corrugated-metal walls, illuminated by a single light bulb dangling from the ceiling. We passed an hour together in perfect harmony clinking mugs and listening to stories of Soweto's most famous resident, Nelson Mandela, one of my heroes in life. An hour later, we strolled through the humble house he grew up in on Vilakazi Street – as close as I've ever got to brushing against Mandela's greatness. Desmond Tutu's home was on Vilakazi too, making it the only place in the world where two Nobel Peace Prize winners grew up on the same street.

As I made my way west across the country by bus and thumb, I kept thinking of how Sean and I had grown apart over the last decade. Aside from a couple of visits here and there, we hadn't seen much of each other in the last 10 or 11 years, and some of my memories of our teenage years weren't good – Sean could be a bit of an asshole at times, always trying to exert his older-brother powers. He'd constantly try to punch me and Brad and bully us around. I wasn't sure our old dynamic would work for four months in Africa, especially since both of us were lone-wolf travellers. But we were still brothers, and I loved him as such. I hoped that would be enough.

When Sean arrived in Cape Town I almost didn't recognize him. Gone was the awkward, round-glasses John Lennon look that he carried through most of his 20s. The lean, wiry body I remembered was replaced with strong muscle chiselled from thousands of hours of climbing rock and riding motorcycles. Even the timbre in his voice had changed; the enthusiasm was still there, but it seemed more measured. He was a changed man, and I liked it. I could somehow sense that I was in for a wild ride.

Almost immediately after hugging me hello, Sean dug into his travel pack and pulled out a bundle wrapped in a colourful red blanket – a heavy load of ropes, carabiners and tinkling equipment called cams and nuts and hexes.

"The blanket I bought in Mexico," he said, poking his head through a hole in the middle. His radiant smile had definitely remained the same. "I had a zipper sewn into it so you can also wear it as a poncho. I call it the Mexi-blanket." The patterned blanket also bore a Coca-Cola patch, in homage to Sean's favourite beverage.

Our first night in Cape Town we ventured out into the city on a backpackers' roofless-bus booze cruise, and ended up at an all-night rave called Synergy. With pulsing lights, electronic dance music, and 2,500 party-goers, I lost Sean almost immediately, eventually surrendering to the party in hopes of either bumping into him at the front of the dance floor, or at the hostel the next morning. The latter proved to be the case. Sean rolled in around ten a.m., charged and excited for the day ahead. I just wanted to sleep. After a few days, I quickly fell into the folds of Sean's intoxicating quest for adventure and fun. Wake up early, stay up late. We soon connected with a friend-of-a-friend named Garrreth Bird, who led us into our first forays amongst the stunning cliffs of Table Mountain, Cape Town's iconic shining jewel. While easily accessible from the city's downtown core, the mountain – immersed in walls of hard sandstone speckled with the bright crimson red of the king protea, South Africa's national flower – felt worlds away. After spending a month with that mountain, box-ticking climbing routes and reforging the unspoken bonds of brotherhood and trust, Sean deemed us ready for a multi-pitch mega-classic, a steep traversing route known as Jacob's Ladder. Although Sean took on most of the danger by leading every pitch, I felt proud of myself for keeping pace. The route was airy and scary for a novice climber, with exposure that pocked my arms with goosebumps. As I mantled over the final ledge, waves of white clouds washed over us, and a fine mist soaked our faces within minutes. We stood in silence, slowly turning in circles, lost in our own worlds.

"Nice climbing today, Dr. Toodwad," Sean said with nostalgic mirth. He had come up with the nickname when we were kids. (Brad was, inexplicably, "Odja Odja," and he often, strangely, called Mom, "Put".) Starving, we walked into the mountaintop restaurant and ordered a pizza and two cold beers.

"Hey, man, why don't we just take the bikes and go," Sean said, taking a gulp. "Maybe make it all the way to Kenya or something?'

I stared at him for a while. It was a big, bold idea, and I didn't really know how to answer.

Two weeks previous, we had become the proud owners of a pair of used Honda XLR250s, and I was just getting the hang of riding. Little did Sean know that a paradigm shift was happening inside of my soul. I was ready for a big life change and had thrown that out to the universe, but I didn't expect the answer to come from my brother, and not so soon. The unbridled freedom of such a trip was undeniable. I pictured a magazine photo we had pinned up on our wall in our rented loft: a shot of a lone elephant standing in tall yellow grass, silhouetted in front of a bright red African sun. I imagined Sean and I at the side of a dusty rural road, staring out into that very same brilliant blazing ball of fire.

It wasn't an easy decision to come to. I liked my job and the people I surrounded myself with on a daily basis, but dedicating eight months of my life every year to golf seemed a hollow pursuit – it wasn't feeding my soul like Africa had been so far.

"I guess I'll have to call my boss and tell him I won't be coming back in April, then," I finally responded. The call of our names from behind the counter interrupted the moment. Sean retrieved our meal, spinning the pizza box off the edge of the stainless steel counter for me to catch.

"Really?!" he said, surprised at my lack of indecisiveness. "Wow, when you wanna leave?" he asked, a chunk of hot pizza bobbling around in his open mouth. He didn't wait for me to answer. "Let's buy a map today and start to suss out where we … fuck, I think I burnt the roof of my mouth!"

"Where do you think we should go?" I said, "You think it will be dangerous?"

"Yeah it might be, eh," he said, clenching his teeth while inhaling quickly, a signature Sean expression. "Shit, we better think about all this stuff."

The excitement level dropped a few notches and we sat in silence, eating the crusts of our pizza. On the way home, we hit a gas station, bought a Rand McNally Southern Africa map and a six-pack of beer, and spent the evening sunk into the grubby couch on the balcony of our rented room in Sea Point, investigating our options.

"We'll go up to Namibia and check out the dunes."

"What dunes?"

"My buddy Jimmy that I rode with in Cambodia told me about these massive sand dunes in Namibia. He said they're the biggest in the world."

"When I was in Kruger National Park, I remember someone talking about Etosha," I said. "It's supposed to be one of the largest and best game parks in Southern Africa."

We were both sliding our index fingers up and down the fresh new map, seeing where each little red line would take us.

"We'll stick to as much gravel as we can," Sean said. "It's way easier on your tires and the scenery is always nicer on country roads. *And*, there'll be less traffic, so less chance of accidents."

His logic sounded good to me. After all, when it came to experience behind the handlebars of a motorcycle, Sean certainly held the advantage...

November 23, 1998. For thousands of people in the small city of Battambang in northwestern Cambodia, watching live motocross inside the soccer stadium was akin to having front-row seats to see the Rolling Stones. The deafening combination of man and machine, high-pitched engines and two-stroke fumes whipped the crowd of 3,000-plus into an intoxicated ball of frenzied energy. Kids scurried and bounced all over the place; some climbed trees to get a better look at the racers, especially the blond-haired *barang* (foreigner) from Canada. It was an intense environment, even for Sean. He thrived on the attention but tried hard to remain calm at the start line, repeating the words of his coach and motocross mentor, Vay Than. *Head down, stay focused on the first corner. Snap the throttle and breathe.*

Sean's interest in all things motorbike had been piqued by the Crusty Demons of Dirt action-sport film series of the early '90s, in particular a segment from Swakopmund, Namibia, where riders launched themselves off massive "step-down" sand dunes in fifth gear, fully pinned. "Ling, deeedaaaaa," he'd say, mimicking the sound of a two-stroke engine.

Sitting atop a machine with serious horsepower – a finely tuned 1998 four-stroke YZ400F, the first of its kind in all of Cambodia – Sean knew he was dealing with more raw power than his experience warranted; too much throttle on a bike like that, and the race is over before it even begins. He steadied himself on the far right side of eight other riders – elbows up, eyes ahead, feathering the throttle as the bike thumped and thundered between his legs. A lifetime of outdoor-sports experience had boiled down to this crucial moment: *Breathe and focus. When the flag drops, keep your chest over the bars and hammer on the throttle. Look only at the first corner. Be the first one there...*

Two hours earlier, an aspiring Canadian photojournalist named Rita Leistner had been trying to get into the stadium. With two camera bodies draped around her shoulders and no ticket to the race, Rita was the only female foreigner for hundreds of miles, so it was clear that she must know the only foreign racer in the stadium. Escorted into the athletes' area, where Sean was watching the professional riders' heats intently, Rita tapped him on the shoulder. Sean spun around to see the smiling, dusty face of the woman he was madly in love with; a woman who had just spent eight gruelling, bumpy hours in the back of an old pickup from Phnom Penh, sardined with a dozen other passengers, to come see him in the race he'd been talking about for months.

"I can't believe you made it!" Sean exclaimed, picking her up off her feet and twirling her around. "I wasn't expecting you to show up! Holy shit! Thank you, this means a lot to me." Sean carried that unexpected emotional support right out to the start line.

Head down, stay focused on the first corner. Snap the throttle and breathe. Through the stadium's crackly sound system, the announcer shouted each of the nine riders' names as they redlined their engines to the crowd's delight. In typical Cambodian fashion, there were no rules for the open-class amateur division; anyone of any level of experience using any kind of bike could enter; more than half of the racers didn't even have helmets. The flag dropped. The crowd went ballistic. Sean snapped the throttle but flicked the clutch too quickly with his weight shifted slightly too far back. A rookie mistake. His front tire popped up for a split second, and by the time he settled into a proper position, it was too late. He missed the holeshot and reached the corner in third place.

Just stay patient and ride a good race, he remembered Vay saying during training sessions. *You never know what will happen.*

Sean held pace and kept the two lead bikes in his sights, finally passing the rider in front of him halfway through the race. One down, one to go. He tried everything to gain ground, but the window closed further with each passing lap, and only two laps remained. Then he caught a break. For once, it wasn't Sean Lawson who fucked up. The rider in the lead held too much speed into the last corner and was forced to run it wide. Sean pounced on the opportunity, hammering his throttle and barely edging past the lead rider on the inside before accelerating quickly through the corner and blazing past the checkered flag.

The crowd erupted in a thunderous roar as Sean pumped his fist into the air. And for the first time, an underdog foreigner, proudly wearing the number 47, was crowned the 1998 Mild Seven Cambodian National Supercross Amateur Open-Class Champion. Rita captured a heroic post-race image of Sean with the big, shiny two-foot-high winner's trophy. Celebrations continued until sunrise, with rum and coke flowing continuously from the silver bowl of Sean's trophy. Nobody was calling him Knuckle anymore.

Sean's Cambodian moto adventure had truly begun a month before, with a random encounter outside a guest house that wasn't even his. Jimmy Martinello, a fellow Canadian and kindred soul from Whistler, had journeyed to Phnom Penh to meet his buddy Sean – the two had connected in Railay Beach and gone hunting for new climbing routes using longtail boats to access climbs on limestone karst towers so impressive they looked like they had melted into place like dripping wax. The problem was, Sean had no idea he was coming, and Jimmy had no clue what part of the country to start his search in.

But after just a few days getting his bearings in Phnom Penh, Martinello suddenly heard a familiar voice and a wheezing cough. There was Sean, smoking a joint with another backpacker just steps from the very accommodation he was set to leave the next morning.

"Holy shit! I had no idea you were even in the country," said Sean, completely surprised.

"And I can't believe I actually *found* you!"

Within 48 hours, they were clutching the handlebars of rented Honda XLR250s, leaving the city for the wilds of the Cambodian countryside, each carrying just a small backpack of clothes and a thin nylon hammock made by local landmine victims. Adventure awaited – a new country, new culture and the road less travelled. A rugged, laugh-filled week later, as they approached the northern border, some troubling news sent a loud and clear message that they should start sticking to the road *more* travelled. Nine foreign travellers (whom Sean and Jimmy had met previously in Phnom Penh) had been kidnapped and held hostage by the Khmer Rouge militia. Tied by the wrists and ankles and laid face-down in the forest, the tourists believed they were awaiting sure execution. But an elderly Cambodian woman had begged the soldiers to spare their lives and instead take all of their personal possessions, which the foreigners were more than happy to relinquish in order to see another day. With this harrowing tale in their minds, Jimmy and Sean carefully ventured northeast to Siem Reap atop roads lined with ubiquitous red-and-white skull-and-crossbones warning signs: *Danger!! Mines!!* After successfully evading any explosions and run-ins with the Khmer Rouge, Sean was about to explore another of his dream destinations – the ruins at Angkor Wat, all their majestic grandeur in front of his dazzled eyes.

With many tourists present, the ruins felt a much safer place to camp than the bush or roadside, so Sean and Jimmy took their chances and found a place to string up their hammocks within the boundaries of the hallowed, ancient grounds. That night, they spent hours wandering the ruins on foot, avoiding the night watchmen while absorbing the aura of spirituality emanating from the hundreds of temples that make up the world's largest religious monument. It was an experience even Sean had trouble putting into words, though he certainly tried a week later, safely back in Phnom Penh, on his first date with the woman who would later cross the country herself, by bus, to witness Sean's victorious moto mayhem.

Sean and Rita met at the Freedom Bar in Phnom Penh, an expat gathering place known for its communal dinners, which was what Rita had come for that evening. She sat down at the only empty chair at the table, across from Sean, and quickly learned they were both from Canada, both loved skiing and the mountains, and both loved to take risks. It was settled: Sean was in love. Even her name, Rita Rosemary, was eerily similar to our mom's, Rita Marian Rose Marie.

Cambodia in the 1990s was an intense place for foreign travellers, dangerous but alluring in a Wild West kind of way. Decades of suffering under the Khmer Rouge had given the Cambodian people an incredible resilience and gratitude for life. The vibe was infectious. One couldn't help but feel grateful for every minute of life, and Sean and Rita – both already bold souls – were emblazoned to live each of their moments together as fully as possible. Intrigued by documentary-style photojournalism, Rita had chosen Southeast Asia to start her budding career. Sean was keen to keep learning the nuances of travel photography and started working as a freelance photographer/ writer at *Bayon Pearnik*, an English-language newspaper owned, ironically, by two French expats. The freedom of Cambodia seduced the couple, who became what Rita would later call "as reckless as hell." While she sought out conflict zones to photograph, Sean explored the remote countryside on his dirt bike, lighting a passionate flame for two-wheeled travel that he intended to keep burning no matter where the world took him.

December 12, 1998
Siem Reap, Cambodia

I'm going to see my brother soon, Dr. Toodwad. AFRICA, finally! The only continent I have yet to set foot on (except Antarctica). We're pretty different too but he's been living in Jasper for a few years now and he travels a lot also so I think it will be good for both of us. Hopefully he'll be into buying a dirt bike so we can explore together. I love it so much. I will miss Cambodia though… it's been a good few months here.

While Sean had hoisted trophies and dodged the Khmer Rouge, my one and only moto experience had been a three-day stint through the jungles of Koh Phangan in Thailand, five years prior, with my buddy One-Eyed Mark.

Poring over the map of Southern Africa, I still had so many reservations beating in my heart. I knew it wasn't an adventure to be taken lightly, but Sean was not about to start letting me make excuses.

"This will be the best adventure of our lives, man!" he said, his voice gathering steam as he cracked open a couple more beers. "I've met people who've done similar trips and every single one of them said it's *the* best way to travel. No buses or trains, no walking for miles with packs on. We can go pretty much wherever we want. Holy shit, Todd, this is going to be fucking *awesome!*"

A sense of pride swelled deep in my chest. I smiled on the inside, thinking about the situations we would find ourselves in: random encounters with strangers, camping under the stars, elephants and ostriches and hyenas in the wild. I knew I could rely on Sean in case anything went wrong, but I still had many fears. *What will the roads be like? What about heat and wind and fatigue? What if we ever get separated from each other? What about violence? Are we going to experience any hostility or racism?*

"I wish Brad could come with us," he said, interrupting my thoughts.

"I know, that would be the ultimate. But even if he was here I'm not sure he could ride, his back is pretty fucked up."

"Hey, let's send him a little care package before we leave. Keeping him with us on this journey will be important."

To save funds for the impending journey, we soon found jobs as bicycle couriers, pedalling our way into the best shape of our lives, riding some 60-plus kilometres a day into the hills and headwinds of Cape Town. Sean added to the travel fund by delivering takeout food on his motorbike in the evenings, then by selling ice cream "lollies" to beachgoers at Clifton Beach on weekends. He knew there wasn't much money to be made but didn't like how many of the whites treated the Black ice-cream sellers on the beach, so he said, "Fuck it, I'm going to do that too."

He spent several Sunday afternoons walking around the white sand of Cape Town's swankiest beach, shouting *"Iiiice* cream... to make you have *niiiice* dreams." Meanwhile, I found myself falling in love with Samantha Engel, an outgoing, olive-skinned beauty I had met at the Purple Turtle, a live-music venue on Long Street that often featured Hog Hoggidy Hog, a thrash-punk band Sean and I rented a house with. We often showed up to support them, and I navigated the rowdy mosh pits well enough to impress Sammi, who then introduced me to the wild rave clubs of Cape Town, where a little white pill called ecstasy fuelled all-night electronic-music dance raves.

Within 20 minutes of swallowing my first "E," I slipped into an otherworldly realm that heightened all of my senses to the peak of bliss. For hours on end, we'd dance and talk and hug random strangers because of an accepted mindset built from instant respect and friend-ship. Ravers on E naturally spread the vibe of honesty, acceptance and admiration towards one another. Holding hands or kissing felt almost orgasmic. All I wanted to do was dance and connect with people. Then, from out of the thumping cave, we emerged into the reality of blinding eight a.m. sunshine that tinged it all with a hint of shame.

I started to sense some jealousy from Sean about my newfound nocturnal habits and friends, and a hint of disappointment as well. He would have plans to go climbing every Saturday morning while I was just getting home and wanted to sleep all day long. Luckily, he and Sam got along famously, and I decided to alternate my weekends: party and play with Sam one weekend, adventure with Sean the next – sunset scrambles to the top of Lion's Head, high-speed rollerblading behind pickup trucks to Camps Bay, weekend sojourns to climbing crags in the Cederberg and lots of riding our beloved new bikes. Mean-while, plans for our epic adventure were full steam ahead. We set our departure date for April 20, 1999.

THE SANDS OF NAMIBIA

MAY 1999

Like all good boys before a grand adventure, we first needed to make a promise to Mom. Freewheeling side by side with the red earth of Africa flying past our heads was something we'd never done before. We knew she'd be worried, even though we'd be travelling together.

"We'll be back in time for your wedding to walk you down the aisle," we assured her on the phone at sunrise before hastily packing our bikes.

"Be careful, my sons," she said. "You're in Africa – anything can happen."

"Don't worry, Mom," said Sean. "We'll take good care of each other. We're brothers. Remember, I'm going to be your official wedding photographer, right?"

"Yes, of course, Sean. I know you'll both be there. I'm so excited."

When we hung up the phone, Sean breathed a sigh of relief. He'd been travelling non-stop for almost ten years and knew it always made Mom concerned. To his credit, some of Mom's lifestyle choices concerned him as well.

"I still can't believe she's marrying a fucking cop, ha! But I'm glad she's found real love again. She deserves it."

On the northern outskirts of Cape Town, a straight-shot gravel road stretches for miles in front of our handlebars, like peering through the sight of a rifle. After three solid months of working, saving, planning and organizing, the fact that we're about to embark on the adventure of our lives begins to sink in. At a roadside gas station we re-tighten the straps holding our packs onto the jerry-rigged wooden racks behind our seats. Ripples of anticipation course through our veins – the sparsely inhabited Western Cape is sprawled in front of us for the taking. After an enthusiastic high five, we mount up and peel off into the headwinds of adventure with not a car in sight. Unaccustomed to riding the bikes with any weight attached to the back, I almost go down in the loose gravel before the trip even begins; the front tire feels like it's floating an inch off the ground. Once we plane out, a pair of ostriches on the other side of a barbed-wire fence start sprinting alongside us at full stride, clouds of dust billowing from behind their gigantic, two-toed feet. Their velocity is astonishing. My speedometer reads 50 kilometres an hour, 55, 60. *Whoa! Are they actually racing us? Or scared that we're trying to mow them down?* In this precise moment, the epitome of true freedom grabs hold of my being and pulls me out of the real world and into this one. In an instant, it all changes. Africa has definitely crept into our skin. I open up the throttle. Nothing else matters.

Two days later, we roll into a sprawling thousand-acre cattle farm on empty stomachs and one flat tire. Gert and Jony, two Coloured farmhands, greet us in Afrikaans and set about taking my back tire off, unveiling a huge rip in the tube by the valve. Stupidly we don't have a spare, forgotten in Cape Town along with other key items like tire irons and an inflatable sleeping pad for myself. Sean has to return to Vredendal, a 200-kilometre round-trip journey in the dark, to buy spare tubes for both bikes while I set up camp next to an old barn. Gert and Jony bring over a foam mattress that fits snugly inside the tent – a nice gesture, as it means I won't have to spend the night sleeping on top of my clothes again. After Sean returns with a new tube, we sit around the fire, drinking instant coffee, eating rice soup and attempting to play the harmonica with our new friends. The owners of the farm, Alby and Adele, catch wind of the two Canadian strangers on bikes after returning from church and invite us into the house for a *braai* (barbecue). They butchered a sheep that afternoon and are delighted to have unexpected guests. Upon entering the house, Sean glances over his left shoulder to look at me, smiling but not saying a word. I know exactly what he's thinking: *How is it possible that we're staring at the exact same doilies and crocheted blankets that my grandparents had in their house on the farm?* We're 10,000 remote miles away and it feels like we've been here before; 1978 all over again inside John and Helen Marchuk's farmhouse. Even the furniture and clocks and lamps all look the same.

"My dad was born on this farm in 1920," says Alby, roasting fresh meat over a hand-welded grate that he raises and lowers on a chain depending on the heat of the coals. "This is what our family knows. There is nothing around here for miles. Our closest neighbour is ten kilometres north. It gets very lonely sometimes, but we are one family, and we all enjoy it out here. We do what we want."

Everything reminds me of my grandparents. Their hardened farm hands, their simple way of life, even the patterned dinner plates are exactly the same. We let the night carry on, drinking brandy by the fire until the bottle is empty. Our hosts want Sean and I to stay longer, but we're only a few days into this journey, and it's time for us to run wild. In the morning, the guys help fix my tire, and we're off again, headed north through a landscape of sprawling acacia trees along the best gravel roads I've ever seen.

A few days later, just across the Namibian border, I see motion in my cracked right-side mirror and catch a glimpse of a speeding vehicle dodging potholes in the distance. Dodging potholes on a motorcycle is fun, like a game almost, but this guy isn't playing around and seems hell-bent on getting somewhere, fast. We pull over to let him pass but, surprisingly, he stops abruptly, music blaring and the smell of cigarette smoke wafting from the open windows of his white Toyota Land Cruiser, Africa's ubiquitous overland adventure vehicle. He's rocking a full blond mullet flowing out from underneath a John Deere trucker cap. I'm not sure what they call a Namibian redneck, but this bloke could surely be the poster boy.

"Whey you okes coming from aye?" he says in a thick Afrikaans drawl, accentuating the *r* with a drumroll accent. I notice two rectangular bumper stickers on his back window: *NO MUFF TOO TUFF, WE DIVE AT FIVE* boasts the right side. On the left: *Life is like a dick. When it's soft, you can't beat it and when it's hard, you're getting SCREWED!*

"Be careful at night, aye," he warns after hearing our plans. "They still lions 'round here, roaming 'round, looking for prey."

And then, with a nonchalant two-finger wave, he's off, leaving a rooster-tail of black fumes and dust in his wake. We take the encounter as a good sign to rest for a while. Even on a good day, it's tough to cover more than 300 kilometres. Under the dappled shade of a lone acacia tree, Sean lays out a picnic lunch on the Mexi-blanket – cheese and crackers, slices of apple and sun-warmed water to wash it down. While we rest our dust-caked bodies on the earth, a massive bull elephant saunters out of the bush, too close for comfort, but he doesn't see us at first. His hulking body is covered with a fresh coat of fine red African dust, and though his left tusk has broken in half, the other nearly touches the ground. Turning and noticing us, he flaps his ears and stares intently for an uncomfortably long but mesmerizing moment. A true gentle giant. He then releases a trumpeting wail in our direction that punctuates the encounter like a clap of thunder. We know who's in charge. Goosebumps speckle my arms. I'm terrified but want nothing to come between us and this moment of pure African magic, actually living the kind of wildlife encounter I've only ever seen before on TV, as a child. Just in case this enormous animal *does* decide to charge, Sean and I stand slowly and move behind our bikes, foolishly thinking that some kind of barrier is better than no barrier at all. Then "Big Red," as we call him, takes one more look and vanishes silently into the veld, leaving us with racing hearts and a memory seared into our brains for the rest of time.

As Sean unzips the tent, in pours the biting cold. It's just past four a.m., and the thought of hot coffee is the only thing that can coerce my shivering body out of a thin sleeping bag not nearly warm enough for the unexpected cold of the African desert. Soon we'll be witnessing one of Mother Nature's greatest spectacles: sunrise in the great red sand dunes of Sossusvlei. Sean has been talking about this place for months, and he wanted, almost needed, us to be the first ones to leave the Sesriem campground – hence the alpine start. The campground is completely silent and pitch black as I hastily dress myself in every stitch of clothing I own – long johns, two pairs of socks, jeans, T-shirts, long-sleeved sweater, fleece, jacket, gloves and toque. *Isn't this supposed to be Africa?* We packed our lunch last night: tuna sandwiches, cheese and crackers, two chocolate bars, two cans of Coke and two beers are stuffed into a small blue cooler bag that, miraculously, has kept a grapefruit-sized chunk of ice still frozen.

"Hey, let's go before someone busts us for trying to leave too early," I loud-whisper at Sean as he's taking a leak.

Under the cover of darkness we sneak out of the campground, pushing our bikes in neutral until we're well clear of the gate. When we arrived yesterday, we'd asked the security guard when the gate would open the next morning.

"Sunrise to sunset are the hours," he replied, somewhat surly.

Getting busted by the guards now would ruin our grand plan to arrive at the dunes before anyone else. Safely outside the gate, I pause before kick-starting my bike to look up at a trillion stars dotting the huge black sky, so magical in scope and scale it feels like I'm witnessing my life changing in front of my own eyes. Twenty minutes into the ride, my fingers are so cold I can barely pull in the clutch to change gears. I want to stop to warm them up, but Sean is too far ahead of me, so I keep pressing on, knowing that we're in a race against the magic morning light that waits for no one. At least the four-stroke engine between my thighs provides a sliver of warmth. We arrive at Dune 45 in the silver-hued purgatory between night and day and start walking briskly up the ridgeline, hoping to get some blood flowing into our frozen bodies. No words are spoken for many strides. Nothing matters but reaching the top as the sun's rays awaken another day in the Namib Desert, the oldest on earth. As we reach the summit of the shark-fin ridge, Sean reaches into the top pocket of his dirty daypack and pulls out an old bicycle-tube patch kit. I notice him fumbling around with the little green case, his headlamp perfectly illuminating the plastic in his cupped hands.

"Hey, I didn't tell you this, but I have these. Should we take one each?"

In the palm of his hand, he presents two tiny pieces of paper... if there was an ideal time to take a tab of LSD, this is probably it. We dab it onto our fingers, place it gently on our tongues and sit down in sand so deep and fine it flows like water. The silence of darkness fades into dim light as the sun sparks up the surrounding landscape in a warm orange glow; light so incredibly pure it's almost tangible. Mountains of red sand, blown by the winds of time, slither for miles in the distance like the backs of a thousand dinosaurs poking through the desert. The play of light and shadows grips us in a silent trance. Time stands still, but the dunes keep moving, and we can't stop smiling.

"Holy shit this place is *insane*," Sean says, his eyes bulging in awe, as he casually passes me a joint. "So remote. I mean, seriously... look at these fucking dunes! They're massive. And we're the only ones here!"

"It really is incredible," I say, trying to comprehend the spectacle. "Apparently these dunes stretch all the way to the coast, like 60 miles or so. I was reading something last night abou—"

"Let's go!" Sean interrupts. "We can totally make it. This is like sand mountaineering. I even have my tiny compass in my pack."

"Dude, we have two litres of water and you want to hike 60 miles through this desert?" I say, pointing with outstretched arms at the thousands of dunes in front of us. "Are you fucking insane?"

"Maybe we can come back tomorrow and try?" he says, half-joking but also somehow totally serious.

The few tokes we've just had are starting to accelerate the effects of the LSD. The shadows are darker, the wind seems stronger and our faces are lit up with bewilderment. We've only climbed 500 vertical feet but it feels like 5,000, and the sand beneath our toes is more than 55 million years old. Lying down for a rest, the only living thing we see, aside from a few tufts of vegetation growing along the lower slopes of the dunes, is a big green grasshopper that lands one foot in front of my face. I can see every miniature detail of his pulsing body: his big purple eyes, his tucked-back wings, his powerful legs. He doesn't move at all, letting me creep within inches. Atop the next crested peak, Sean holds up two ceremonial beers directly into the sunlight like a victorious warrior holding his sword to the sky, ensuring we don't take the moment for granted.

"Here we are, in the oldest desert in the world, surrounded by mountains of sand with the sun blazing down, and in my hands I'm holding two ice-cold beers. I think that in itself is pretty damn cool. So cheers to us, cheers to Africa, and cheers to being together as brothers."

I close my eyes, feeling the cold can in my hand, and take three meaningful gulps. The carbonation sends an invigorating rush rippling through my body. I open my eyes, and all around me the blaze of glory is still in full swing. A powerful sensation sweeps over me – I can *feel* the landscape around us, alive, shifting in a constant flow of movement; dunes growing, forming anew, snaking their way into the desert horizon. The scene is otherworldly, what I imagine heaven might be like. Not a single cloud in the sky, just a brilliant blue eternity adding another element of contrast to the landscape. I look over at Sean, who appears to be on the same wavelength, savouring the moment. Elegantly shaped dunes of caramel brown, plush orange, burnt red and every shade of a rooster's plume are showing off their perfection under the radiance of the powerful desert sun. It's the ultimate photographer's dream.

"Fuck, this is excellent eh?!" Sean asks. "I just really can't get over how incredible this is. I mean, I've been to a lot of places – and you know me, I really dig sunrises – but this blows everything away. It's so goddamn *huge!*"

Laughing hysterically as the hot sun blazes punchy colours into our bloodshot eyes, Sean suddenly stands up, leaping from the crest of the dune with a cartoon-character expression draped across his face. He lands silently in deep sand that swallows his feet, but the momentum keeps him barrelling downward. His legs are no match for the steep angle of the dune, and he tomahawks all the way to the bottom, limbs flying, sand spraying high into the sky. I jump next and soon my legs are sprinting in giant strides down the hillside. It's impossible to contain my glee, and it's too much for my motor skills to comprehend.

All I hear is laughter as I rumble past Sean, coming to a stop near the dry, baked surface at the base of the dune. My mind feels exhausted from trying to process so much exhilaration. We shoot several rolls of film before eventually realizing we have to face the grim reality that this day is almost over. Soon the sun will drop behind the dunes and a blanket of cold will sweep across the valley, putting the desert to bed for another peaceful night in a sequence that stretches to the beginning of time.

SWIRLING MORTALITY

LIVINGSTONE, ZAMBIA • June 1999

The Victoria Falls adrenalin dream appears to be alive and well, at least according to the adventure-spewing billboards we pass on our approach into Livingstone. *Bungee Jumping... Whitewater Rafting... Helicopter Tours... Elephant Rides... Abseiling... Zip Lines.* If there was a place built for backpackers, this is it.

"Let's go rafting here for sure," says Sean at a campsite on the edge of town. "This is supposed to be *the* best place in the world for it."

The next afternoon, we're staring up at the massive canyon walls of the Zambezi River, sitting on the bouncy front stanchion of a 16-foot yellow raft, our feet firmly planted into the foot cups. The roaring sound of whitewater ratchets up the nervous energy buzzing inside of us. Our crew consists of four other tourists and our guide, Moses, who guides us off of the bank, our motions synchronized to his commands. As we plunge our paddles into the brown water, the river soon sweeps us towards a frothing mess of rapids, jolting us into full attention as Moses yells out, "Paddle forward, HARD!"

A massive wall of churning whitewater looms ahead as I pull on my paddle with all my force. A storm of adrenalin narrows my focus to a blinding pinpoint just before the raft meets the force of the wave, ejecting me and Sean backwards like kids bounced off a trampoline. The next thing I know we're getting flushed inside the gaping maw of a rapid called the Devil's Toilet Bowl. Moses scoops us up one by one and we rage happily on for another two hours, shit-eating grins smacked across our wet faces. The raft trip is a rare "paid" luxury for us, and it has not disappointed.

As the post-river beers flow freely in the bar, Sean and I find ourselves in the crosshairs of two young local ladies. Smooth black skin, curly black hair and smiles as bright as the light bulb shining above their heads. At the first hint of flirtation, Sean makes his way to their table with fresh drinks in hand. One thing leads to another, and soon our two-man tent is a two-couples tent. While the petting is getting heavy on Sean's side, my new friend comes at me with passionate force, ramming her tongue down my throat and her hand down my pants. All I can think of is the rampant spread of AIDS in Africa, and no goddamn way I am going there without a condom. It's freaking me out to have Sean getting busy one foot away from me inside the tent while this African vixen (whose name I can't even remember) is trying to rip my clothes off. I'm horny as hell, but the angel on my right shoulder starts talking to me: *You told Sam you'd be faithful on this trip. You love her, don't fuck it up and be an asshole and cheat on her.* But the devil on my left keeps saying, *Fuck it, man, you only live once. Look at this woman in your hands... Just leave the tent, get a rubber from Sean and go fuck her outside in the grass.*

The tent proves to be an uncomfortable endeavour for four drunken adults, so I scramble outside with my cute new friend, pants still around my ankles. She keeps coming at me with her tongue, mouth, hands. Her plump lips and dirty talk are too much for my two months of pent-up sexual energy, and I cum all over her hand as she strokes my cock while I'm still standing. Pleasure and guilt wash over me at the same time. I'm embarrassed that I came so quickly, and stricken by my conscience for not being entirely faithful to a woman I love, but somewhat relieved that I have not penetrated this nubile woman whom I have just met. I still feel ashamed for cheating on Sam. "Just two people attracted to each other," I say to myself to justify my actions. At least she isn't asking for money, which makes me feel good it wasn't two prostitutes who pounced on fresh meat in town.

After nursing a nasty hangover with a pleasantly surprising round of golf at the 100-year-old Livingstone Golf Club, complete with alligators, warthogs and elephants crossing the fairways, we make our way to the general post office, where a surprise from Brad awaits.

Hey Guys... thanks for the postcards. South Africa looks amazing! Wish I was there. I hope y'all are creating more memorable experiences in Zimbabwe. You two be careful and watch each other's backs."
P.S. Did you know Wayne Gretzky retired?

Love, your little brother,
Brad

Sprawled in front of our bewildered eyes, everywhere in all directions, lies a mist-drenched world full of such rainbow-tinted realism I think my heart might explode into the sky. Victoria Falls, in all its sopping-wet grandeur. Avoiding the hordes of poncho-wearing tourists shuffling themselves to all the same lookout points, Sean and I come upon the ultimate rush – bridge sliding. Connecting other viewpoints and waterfall drops are a series of long, strong metal bridges, drenched by a thousand cubic metres of water falling every second into the basalt gorge 300 feet below. On the floor of the bridges lies a continuous, seamless carpet of black rubber, perfectly smooth and slippery, with rounded metal handrails on both sides to offer a bit of balance. The bridges are all built with a slight arc, allowing Sean and I to run as fast as possible to the apex, then skim-slide down the other side in a gradual, rapid descent, applying pressure with our hands on the rails to control our speed. The result is an exhilarating, frictionless experience with zero chance of falling over the edge.

"I feel so *alive* right now!" I shout loudly over the deafening sound of water. Our hangovers vaporized, we spend the next hour running and sliding barefoot in our boxer shorts again and again, exploring every inch of this invigorating realm. Livingstone is living up to its reputation. We emerge from the watery playground as rejuvenated souls shivering under wet clothes. My previous worries of sibling tension have long fallen by the wayside. We're clicking as brothers more and more each day. After ten years, we're getting to know each other again, riding together on the wings of true freedom.

Dear Ambassador to the City of Rossland
City Hall
Nyanga, Zimbabwe

How's it goin' eh? My name is Sean Lawson and I have been living in Rossland (Nyanga's sister city in Canada) on and off for nearly 10 years. I love it! Now, my brother and I are travelling through southern Africa on our dirt bikes, bound for Mozambique. We plan to come down to Nyanga soon and spend some time there visiting some of the sights. I want to meet people who have been to Rossland. I can guess that we'll be there at the end of June. I would appreciate it if you could write to me and let me know if there are any festivities or special occasions during that time. My email is: yz400@yahoo.com

Thank you and I look forward to meeting soon,
Sean

After almost 7000 kilometres of Southern Africa travel, the landscape that welcomes us into Zimbabwe's Eastern Highlands seems refreshingly similar to the Kootenays of BC: crisp mountain air, pine forests and waterfalls. This world of motorcycle travel that was so unfamiliar to me just a few short months ago is now changing the entire makeup of my being. My golf-professional life in Canada seems a distant reality, a world so far removed from the dirt under my fingernails that I can't even be sure I remember it correctly. For the first time in my life, my hair is past my shoulders, and I don't give a shit about anything except how smoothly my bike is running.

A field of a thousand quartzite boulders will always cast an alluring spell over a rock climber, so we don't plan to make much headway today. Sean seizes the opportunity to unpack our climbing shoes and explore the boulderer's playground in front of us. Just a quick jaunt up the hill from the roadside lies a perfect spot to pitch camp for the night – safely hidden between a labyrinth of rock with no wild animals in sight, no humans and little risk of malaria at this elevation. Just another beautiful night under the African sky.

"Todd, we can totally do this at home."

"Do what?"

"Buy a couple of dirt bikes and ride them down to Central and South America."

"Yeah, I guess we could, hey?"

"That would be *another* ride of a lifetime. Just think of it, man, nothing compares to being on a bike. Nothing. Now you know the feeling. We could just start riding south. Peru is amazing, and Bolivia. We could go all the way down to Patagonia, even."

"I think I'm sold now, Sean. I can't believe I didn't have a motorbike until now. I can't even describe these last two months."

I realize that it isn't really the adventure part of our journey I love most, but the immersion. We're sinking our teeth into the continent, its people, its places. And nothing brings us into this state of immersion quite like the motorcycles themselves. At times, I have envied other hardcore travellers who chose bicycles as their mode of transport. With a slower pace, they can *really* immerse themselves in the landscape. What I don't envy is pedalling uphill for 100 kilometres under the mind-melting African heat. That means of transport might have very well broken me; at least on a motorcycle we have a steady breeze to cool us down. That cool breeze carries us into Nyanga, the "sister city" of Sean's beloved Rossland. The quaint town is surrounded by forests and waterfalls and typical cement buildings with their brightly painted storefronts. Directions to the Nyanga Town Hall instead lead us to Nyanga Rural District Council, where we meet Phillip Ngazi, the distinguished chief executive officer. He's wearing pressed brown slacks, a cardigan with big brown buttons and thick glasses that magnify a big pair of eyes.

"Please, welcome to Nyanga," he says, standing on the steps of a stone building that looks like it could withstand a hurricane, "I am the one receiving your letter, thank you. You may call me Mr. Phil. I know that here you will find much adventure for your bikes." He spreads his arms out wide. "You must enjoy it. You will be staying with my family. Please follow and we will reach soon my house – before dark, I wish."

Inside their modest brick house perched on a hill, Mr. Phil's wife, Loveness, has a crackling fire burning inside a stone fireplace, something I thought I'd never see in Africa. It's the only way to heat the home during the cold winter nights at 5,500 feet above sea level. Tonight, temperatures will drop to five degrees Celsius. After a day spent behind the handlebars, climbing into the mountains, it's nice to sit indoors next to a fire with a hot cup of tea pressed between our palms.

"When I visit Rossland, it has always been in the month of June, like now," Mr. Phil says, leaning back on a comfortable couch in the living room. "I have been three times now, and always it is warmer than Nyanga. The people I love so much. And also I enjoy very much when they take me to hike up KC (Kootenay Columbia)... I think that is the name of the small mountain at the back of town maybe? From the top the view of town is so nice, like a jewel hidden in the hills. I can feel good energy in that place."

"That's my favourite place to go," says Sean, wide-eyed and smiling. "I can't believe you've been there! In the summer, I go there almost every day with a pack of friendly dogs."

We share stories well into the night – Sean and I of our adventures in his home continent and Mr. Phil with his tales of Canada. They have no spare rooms but two foam mattresses, so we sprawl out next to the fireplace on the living room floor, content as can be. Under his roof, the world feels a little bit smaller and more connected. A crisp, clear morning reveals a broad landscape with a stunning rock escarpment divided into sections by a series of long, thin waterfalls. Sean inquires about a mountain looming behind us in the distance.

"You can climb to the top," Mr. Phil says. "Its name is Mount Nyangani. The Nguni People call it the roof of the world. They have a special relationship with this mountain. Snow has even fallen once, in 1935. It is written in our history, you know."

A sign at the trailhead says:

MOUNT NYANGANI
2593 metres
8508 feet
Highest Peak in Zimbabwe

WARNING
Do not attempt to climb after mid afternoon or if mist or cloud
in area.
Follow cairns, arrows and track to beacon at summit
Minimum time required to beacon and return 3 hours
Leave no litter
Climb at own risk.

Two hours later, on cue, a warning mist creeps in over the roof of the
world. It reminds me of the day on top of Table Mountain when Sean
planted the seed for this journey, and I take some time to relive the
memory in my head. *We've come a long way since then, and still have so
much more to go.* The thickening mist wraps us in a total whiteout, and
we quickly become lost in a soup of clouds that eventually dissipate,
revealing a sweeping view of the valley that brightens our moods and
warms our bodies as we descend. Phil, Loveness and their twin daughters, Hope and Grace, are waiting by the fireplace with a hot meal of
chicken stew and *sadza* when we return.

"Tomorrow you will ride through the forest to see Mutarazi Falls,
and also many others," Mr. Phil says, toasting us with a ceramic mug
of frothy beer. "It is the highest in Zimbabwe. Very impressive. One of
the highest in the world."

Phil is a breathing rendition of *hakuna matata* – the laid-back African attitude popularized in *The Lion King* and something I'm starting
to understand more deeply each day. He never yells at his children,
never seems in a hurry to get anywhere, and when he speaks he is
thoughtful and precise. The generosity shown to us by Phil and his

family has been boundless. He even helps us make a call to Mom, who sounds happy and relieved to finally hear our voices. It's been almost a month.

"Where are you going next? she asks. "Everyone has been asking me."

"We're not far from the border of Mozambique, so we'll be there soon and should be on a beach by the Indian Ocean in a few days."

"Okay, thank you, my sons, for staying in touch. I love you both so much."

"It will be nice to make a story about Nyanga for the Rossland newspaper," Sean says to Mr. Phil at breakfast the next day. "Let's take some photographs so people back home can see who you are. It is my way of thanking you and your family."

"That will be delightful. My friends," he says, pausing for a long while as we strap the last of our belongings onto the bikes, "you have enjoyed your time here in our town, I can see. That makes me happy. I hope I will see you in Rossland if I am able to come again."

Descending from Nyanga's crisp mountain air, we head east, dropping down into the steamy tropical jungles of Mozambique a few days later. An idyllic riverside campsite draws our eyes and tires off the gravel road, and we pitch camp before anyone shows up. Watching Sean set up the tent, almost instinctively by now, I take some time and space to reflect. We've been on the road for only two months, and already I can feel a seismic shift in our overall psyche – a tranquility in our brotherhood that didn't exist before. Our days are spent riding and camping, punctuated by close encounters with rural Africans whose warm spirit leaves us feeling welcomed without prejudice. Sean joins me, our backs resting against the trunk of a mammoth baobab tree, and says, totally out-of-the-blue: "Hey I guess we should talk about this, eh… just in case something *does* happen?"

"Talk about what?"

"Like, if anything happens, do you want to be buried or cremated."

"Cremated," I say after a thoughtful pause.

"Me too. I want to be cremated and to have my ashes spread in as many places as possible… but for sure at the top of KC in Rossland… and at Railay Beach."

We take a few moments for the thoughts of our own mortality to swirl amongst the impressively huge boulders stacked in piles around us.

"What made you think about this?" I ask.

"I don't know, I guess I just thought we should talk about it."

"And if you could be reincarnated, what three animals would you choose to come back as?" I ask.

"An eagle, for sure. Imagine soaring above mountain peaks and swooping into a valley at top speed to catch dinner in the river with your super-sharp talons!" Sean responds, his fingers curled like claws. "Second would have to be a dolphin, maybe even a shark. Such a different world that would be. Free like a bird, but flying underwater. And I'd also want to be an elephant, roaming around this continent... the king of Africa."

The hint of death remains the next morning, lingering inside my helmet as we start to ride. I hadn't thought of death or dying since we left, not once. Now, as fast as the rocks and boulders are flashing past us, my mind reaches into memories of deceased friends and relatives. My grandfather John; our stepdad, Roy; the inspiring spirit of my dear friend Dennis Buerger; and my real father, Michael. The road is a chattery washboard, and I'm careful not to get too lost in thought.

As the stunning landscape flashes past, the dark thoughts slowly dissipate. Africa's sun massages my mind back to the present, the adventure and beauty all around. Soon our bouncing shadows tell us it's time to find camp, which we do underneath a leafy tree near a shallow river as the last of the day's light gets sucked into night. A tranquil scene greets us in the morning; a mirror-flat river reflecting marshmallow clouds in a warm summer sky. A handful of ladies are washing clothes and pause to look at us as we emerge from the tent. It's already hot and not yet seven a.m., so we head for the river's grassy edge and jump into a sandy pool. The ladies laugh in approval, watching us with fixed eyes as they scrub their clothes together, puffs of lathered detergent flying from their hands.

"Ah, we are just workers," one of them says with a shy smile. "We want to see if we can find some money... maybe there is someone wanting to hire us." She delivers the statement with no undertones of desperation or other familiar "poor-me" stories that many of the fast-talkers in some African cities have honed to works of crooked art. I mount my bike, but something distracts me before I throw my leg over the seat. Loudly I hear one of them shout, "Sir, you have punksha, you have a punksha!"

The others laugh at her over-excitedness, but I'm not smiling. We're down to the last patch. Puncture number seven, and *all* of them on my bike. We set about repairing the tube while the others help and hang about, picking away at the green grass they're sitting on. A nearby stump serves as a sturdy, balanced block to prop my bike upon, and for once the patch job goes quickly. Gearing up, I swat a mosquito from my arm and make a note to keep the repellent in the top of my pack. There will be many more bugs here in the lowlands. We would be content to stay another night in the embrace of these surroundings, to swim and bathe and camp under the sparkling brilliance of the black African sky, but time marches on. Mom is getting married in two months' time...

– 7 –

GOODBYE, DEAR BROTHER

SOWETO, SOUTH AFRICA • July 19, 1999

A yellow, mucus-like discharge keeps building up in the corners of Sean's eyes. I hate it. I hold a wad of tissue in my hand, constantly clearing his eyes of this ugly pus. I want it to go away. *If he dies, at least let him see clearly into heaven.* Every time I speak to him, he responds by slowly blinking his eyes, which brings a sliver of momentary calmness to the situation. He knows I'm by his side, or at least I'm holding on to the belief that he does. It's my one and only hope. But he's beginning to show signs of jaundice, and a memory creeps in of my darkest time as a teenager: watching that deathly shade of yellow pass through Roy's body in his final days. I can't handle the sight of Sean like that. Until now, my utmost faith in a medical miracle wouldn't give in to the thought of him dying in my arms. *I know he will pull through. He has to, right?* I leave him to rest and head back to the telephone.

Suddenly I realize that *I* could also have been bitten by a female *Anopheles*, the genus of mosquito that transmits the deadly plasmodium parasite only at night. *Both of us could be dying right now. But why him and not me?* I wrack my brain to figure out where he could've been infected. I remember Dr. Debbie telling me that cerebral malaria incubates in your liver and can take up to five weeks to emerge. *It must have been in Mozambique.*

Two places come to mind. The first, on an island called Bazaruto in the Indian Ocean. After eight months in Africa, I felt the continuous movement of life on the road starting to wear me down and was craving a bit of soulless convenience over non-stop cultural immersion. I could have easily holed up in an air-conditioned hotel room, plugging into the banalities of American TV entertainment for hours on end, eating pizza and downing glass bottles of ice-cold Coca-Cola rushing effervescent down my gullet. Instead, we left our bikes chained together inside the thatched hut of our friendly dhow captain and set sail for a week of tropical Africa in all its postcard glory: slivers of white sand ringed by palm trees swaying in the breeze, gin-clear scuba diving, iceless coconut cocktails and bonfires on the beach. Pelted by thick raindrops on a mirror-calm ocean, we took five hours longer than intended to reach the island, but we arrived safely at high tide under a brilliant sunset, jumping into neck-high water littered with sharp coral. The captain carefully passed my backpack into my raised hands, but he wasn't so graceful with Sean's. When the boat swayed, he accidentally knocked Sean's glasses off his head, sending them to a watery grave.

"Okay, I come back three days," is all the captain said, and he turned around for home.

"Thanks, buddy," Sean muttered as he sailed away. "How in the fuck am I going to see anything now?"

But the good-luck gods must've watched his glasses disappear into the dark water. An English backpacker we met in the morning happened to have a spare set of contact lenses with Sean's exact prescription... 20/20 again. Later the next evening, as a giant, orange full moon crested over the ocean's rolling horizon, Sean looked at me with that glint in his eye.

"Let's put a night mission on the menu for dessert," he said, cracking open the tail of a fresh, boiled-over-the-fire lobster. "We can walk to the other side of the island and see what we find!"

In the middle of the night, as we tiptoed through a small village, taking great care not to awaken any of its sleeping inhabitants, out of a hut emerged a giant of a man. He must've been seven feet tall and was built like a baobab tree. Ninja-like, Sean and I immediately lowered ourselves to the ground, praying that the giant wouldn't notice. He started peeing and kept going for what seemed like ten minutes. As he was finishing, I noticed, to my absolute horror, that we were lying right next to a sleeping woman. *Why is she sleeping outside, in the dirt, with not even a sheet covering her?!* How did we not even *see* her? Mortified that we'd wake her and have the giant come after us, we lay in complete silence, too scared to even breathe, until he was back inside. We then crept on our elbows, arm over arm, military style, to relative safety on the other side of their bare-earth compound. The woman didn't move an inch.

After bushwhacking through marshland and palm forest, we emerged into a magical land made of sand and stars, with massive white dunes that dropped steeply into a sparkling sheet of moonlit water. Running down the dunes felt like stepping off the edge of the earth. At one point we gathered a few random sticks and made a small fire that flickered in the cool ocean breeze. Maybe it was there that a mosquito's microscopic needle delivered the fatal dose? There had been a few mosquitoes pestering us. I had the Mexi-blanket to cover me, but Sean didn't even have long sleeves.

We both dozed off periodically and at sunrise stumbled across a middle-aged couple beside a tiny, dilapidated grass hut. They seemed so clearly destitute I had a hard time emotionally processing their plight. Outside the hut, a single blackened pot hung from a rusty nail and a pair of flip-flops were tangled in a fishing net, with not a stitch of food or fresh water in sight. We couldn't tell if this was home for them or just a temporary squat, but it clearly reeked of abject poverty. The woman, sitting cross-legged in the sand next to a smouldering fire, was staring at Sean so intently I was certain she'd never seen a white man before. Sean offered some water, and then four little squares of chocolate, which was all the food we had left in our pack. They shared the water first, then the man accepted the chocolate gingerly, fumbling it in his hands for a few seconds before shooting me a blank stare like he didn't understand what it was.

"You can eat it," Sean said, cupping his fingers to his mouth. The man looked at his wife, studying the chocolate much like anyone would holding a foreign object, then took a nervous bite. As soon as it started to melt in his mouth, he panicked and spat it out. His spontaneous reaction made his wife crack a shy smile. He shot us a frightened look then held his two fingers together against his lips to say, "Do you have a cigarette?" Sean flipped the lid open on his pack, picked out two cigarettes and lit them both at the same time. Bizarrely, the woman took the cigarette and plopped the red-hot cherry end into her mouth. We pleaded with her to stop, waving our hands to say "No, no!" but she just held the stick in her lips, motionless. *In her entire life, had she never seen someone smoking a cigarette?* Finally her husband grabbed it from her lips, turned it around and poked it back into her mouth. She took a giant pull and coughed violently, spitting into the sand. The man cracked a sheepish grin and looked away, embarrassed, chuffing at his cigarette like he had an endless supply. I remember walking away from those people feeling utterly helpless and saddened by what life had dealt them. They seemed so lonely and afraid, and all we could offer were two foreign things of no value. For a long time afterwards I couldn't get them off my mind.

The other place Sean may have been infected was in Maputo, Mozambique's capital city. I remember both of us getting bitten while having a beer at a rooftop bar during our only night there. Sean stayed up until the wee hours with a crew of backpackers, but I wasn't into it. *Maybe the Anopheles tracked him down that night?*

Just four days before Sean's hospitalization, we found ourselves in Sabie, a beautiful little mountain town 350 kilometres east of Johannesburg, charging through pine forests and mud puddles on logging roads high up in the hills. It felt like springtime back home in Canada. After nearly three months in the saddle, we were closing up a great swinging arc from Cape Town, through the Caprivi Strip into Namibia, Zambia and Zimbabwe, and across the continent to Mozambique and the Indian Ocean. We were both overflowing with confidence and strength – transformed (well, I was, anyway) by the wildly spontaneous world of adventure motorcycle travel. In Sabie, we stayed with Kenny – a stocky wing nut of a man with bold features laid out in a ruggedly handsome way, like a boxer or a bulldog. I met him eight months ago, during my solo time in South Africa, and he owns a small bar on Main Street called the Spotted Dog.

"You're staying with us!" Kenny roared, half-pissed, when Sean and I arrived in front of the pub. "Bring your bikes over to the house. We'll unpack your things and have a *lekker* (great) *braai* tonight."

We were due to meet a man in Johannesburg named Zubair who was interested in buying our bikes. We also had to make travel arrangements to fly home before our visas expired. It was July 15, and our mother was getting remarried on August 28. The plan was to fly home a month early to take care of a few things in our respective towns, then meet up again for the wedding with Brad, whom neither of us had seen in three years.

·After three blissful days and a couple of rowdy nights, the time came to leave for the "City of Gold." Both Sean and Kenny's eldest boy, Tristan, had been feeling sick.

"Feels like the flu or something," Sean said.

They rested that day in bed but didn't complain of fever or chills, just muscle aches and a mild headache. Sean probably chalked it up to a mild hangover.

"Just be careful," said Kenny as we were set to leave. "You don't wanna fuck around. If it's cerebral malaria, you can die within days."

We looked at each other but didn't take it too seriously.

This stuff happens to other people, not us, right?

Nonetheless, we asked Kenny where we could find a doctor.

"Not today. It's Sunday. This town's too small and the doctors only come 'round if there's an emergency. But you can stay another night and see the doctor first thing in the morning."

"Think you're feeling strong enough to ride?" I asked Sean. "It'll be a long day, but we can see a doctor when we get to the city."

"Yeah, I'm actually feeling better than yesterday. I'll be fine, let's go."

After battling a relentless six-hour headwind, we rode into four lanes of bustling Friday night traffic in one of Africa's largest cities. Just like that, in a matter of hours our reality shifted, from days on end surrounded by rural African quiet to weaving our way through hundreds of speeding cars, trying to find Sean's friend Barry at the Randburg

Waterfront, a bright-lights, big-city cluster of shops and restaurants. We hadn't seen anything like it in months. By the time Zubair showed up the next day, almost three hours late, Sean was sprawled on the pavement in a parking lot, wracked with fever.

"Todd, I've never felt like this before. What should I do?"

A random stranger told us of a medical clinic nearby. After a quick test, the doctor diagnosed him with malaria and admitted him to the Helen Joseph Hospital, on the other side of town. I had no choice but to put him in a taxi and deal with getting the bikes someplace safe. On top of being late, Zubair and his big gold chains had seriously low-balled us, so I'd told him to get lost. When I went to see Sean early the next morning, he looked better but still felt weak and sick. My tough-love mentality brushed off the seriousness of our predicament, which I blamed on an innate stubbornness likely passed on by our grandparents. *His veins are coursing with a 24-hour intravenous drip of quinine, he'll be fine.* I stayed with him for a while but had to meet someone else that evening who wanted to buy the bikes.

Fucking Zubair! I shouted to myself, needing to place the blame on someone instead of myself. *What an asshole. Had he shown up on time, maybe Sean wouldn't be in the hospital right now.*

I returned to Helen Joseph early the next morning, but Sean was gone. He'd been transferred to another hospital in the middle of the night. In a state of panic, I raced to Baragwanath Hospital in Soweto to find him in deteriorating condition inside the ICU. When he saw me, a look of fear washed over his face, and he seemed unaware of what was happening. That was enough to finally convince me of the severity of the situation. Now *I* was scared. I imagined Sean wanting to rip the tubes out of his body to sprint down the hall and escape out the front doors, riding with me out of the city and into the wilds beyond...

The ringing pay phone snaps me from the daydream and back to my nightmare. I'm surrounded by concrete steps and concrete walls. Mozambique and our previous three months of no-holds-barred adventure seem like a distant, alternate reality.

"Todd, come quick bruh, Dr. Debbie wants you upstairs!" yells my barefoot friend Bryan Allott from the stairwell above.

I race up the stairs to see a blur of nurses and doctors in their green-and-white scrubs crowded around my brother's bedside. Holding his limbs in unison, they gently roll him onto his stomach in a last-ditch effort to save his life, hoping a dialysis machine will pump his blood for him. His breathing pattern is so faint I can barely see his body heaving. I keep my distance but want to stay close. The volume of beeping starts to gain momentum, and the doctors are talking in tones of medical immediacy. I can't make out what they are saying, but from the concerned looks swirling around the room, I know it's not good. The intensity consumes me. I feel neither here nor there, weightless, gripped with fear and panic so strong that it seems to pick me up off the white-tiled floor.

The dialysis machine doesn't do what it's supposed to. His heart stops beating. They flip him onto his back, and a nurse lifts a pair of white-corded paddles into the air.

"Clear!"

I see Sean's body thump into the air.

"Clear!"

"Noooo! Sean... I'm here... please stay alive!" I scream so violently that someone comes over to restrain me.

"Clear!"

His body jumps into the air again. Through the commotion, I strain to see his face. I need to see his face... It looks empty. Vacant. The Sean I hope to see, the brother I've just spent the best eight months of my life with, is not there. In desperation, I lurch for his body, screaming into the pile of green and white.

The doctors and staff pull me from my brother and try and calm me down, but I don't even know where I am. I can hear Dr. Debbie's voice but can't process what she's saying. It feels like I'm trapped in the Twilight Zone. As I'm being carried away from the room, I desperately manage one last glance in Sean's direction but see only a pale green sheet being pulled over his head.

"Noooooooooooo!"

All I can think of is escape. I swing open the doors and bound down the four flights of stairs in giant leaping strides. Once outside, I kick my bike over in anger, screaming so loud it feels like I'm going to rip a hole right through the African sky.

At the airport, I run up the escalator and see Mom for the first time in more than two years. She's in better condition than I expect, given the fact that her first-born son died 18 hours ago while she was on a plane over the Atlantic and she didn't get to say a final goodbye. To my great relief, she seems at peace instead of torn to pieces. Dr. Debbie called three days ago, telling my mom what I didn't have the courage to do – that her son was going to die. Emergency passports and plane tickets were taken care of within 24 hours by her fiancé Pat's three daughters, Denise, Leeane and Sheilagh, but it was simply too late.

"Oh, my dear son. I can only imagine what you've been through," she says, embracing me in a deep hug. I can't see her face but can hear the tears starting to form. "My heart aches with pain, Todd, but I am so grateful that you were with Sean the whole time. He was not alone, and that means the world to me, you don't even know. I didn't want him to suffer alone."

"He didn't suffer, Mom. He was scared, but the doctors were really so incredible. He didn't experience much pain." In fact, I really have no idea, but it seems to lessen the blow.

Dr. Debbie's parents, Lorraine and Peter, have graciously offered their guest house for Mom and Pat to stay in and get grounded. It's an absolute godsend. I didn't want them staying at a random hotel devoid of life and character.

"It won't feel real for a long, long time," says Lorraine, holding my mother's hand on the front porch of the cabin. "We've also lost a son. The pain will always stay, but you have to find that one thing to hold on to, something that will make you smile and remember the good times with Sean."

Father Patrick has arranged a special memorial service in two days' time, but first I need to deal with the hardest part: taking Mom and Pat to see Sean at the hospital mortuary. Given Sean's history with authority as a teenager, the irony that Mom is going to marry a cop in five weeks serves to lighten the mood a bit. However, Pat has spent 25 years in the RCMP, so it's second nature for him to serve and protect: without him, Mom would not be in such a calm state.

"I didn't care what it cost me when you guys called collect from wherever in the world," she says during the drive. "I just wanted to hear your voices. One day Sean called from Thailand. It would have been fall 1997, and he said, 'Mom, your voice sounds so happy.' I told him about Pat, and he said, 'Mom I'm so happy for you, but why a fuckin' cop?!'"

Laughter fills the car, and I glance at Mom in the rear-view mirror. She's smiling back at me. The brief glimpse of motherly love takes a huge weight off my guilt-ridden shoulders. Mom and Pat are gawking out the windows, and I'm glad that South African culture shock seems to be doing its thing – keeping her mind off reality. Life in JoBurg is a long, long way from life in small-town Alberta. Inside the hospital, Mom finally breaks down. Her son is lying in a temporary wooden casket, lifeless but still alive in her eyes. It's the first time Pat has ever met Sean.

"I'm so sorry I didn't make it here on time, my son," she says, leaning over his body, sobbing and shaking. "But look what you did, Sean. You got me to come to Africa, and that is something special. I know you lived an incredible life, and I am so, so very proud of you for choosing your own path. I love you, my son. You will never be forgotten."

The next day, a small gathering of new friends are seated at the Holy Trinity Catholic Church for Sean's homily, a spiritual edification delivered by Dr. Alan Peter, the pulmonologist who was with Sean until the very end. He approaches the pulpit and begins.

When Sean was struck down in the prime of his life, our minds are torn by the question: "Why so soon?" So many opportunities seem lost. We may console ourselves in thinking that Sean was able to pack into 29 years what most people struggle to pack into a lifetime. He gave himself to the grandeur of nature with a passion, he gave his life to be outdoors. So it was that the

outdoors claimed Sean's life for its own. His was a spirit that
refused to be chained to the treadmill of a nine-to-five job. He
preferred the company of eagles, mountains, snow, people on
the move. The thirst within Sean to continually look for the ultimate is a thirst rooted in all of us. What he was looking for lay
not in status, esteem and wealth... it lay in ultimate freedom.
Sean, your family will grieve and remember you all the days of
their lives. You too will remember them and be with them until
one day we meet in the joy of the Resurrection.

All is grace, God love you.

The sombre mood is soon livened by 30 of the most incredible voices
I've ever heard: the Soweto Gospel Choir, sending Sean's spirit into
the heavens on the wings of angels. It's a special treat organized by
the ICU doctors. As the voices swell and drape us all in beauty, I think
how our grandmother would be happy to know we're having a proper Christian memorial for her grandson; she can probably feel them
singing right now. Mom is crying with her head on Pat's shoulder,
and we're swaying back and forth to the powerful music. Bryan Allott
and his sister Gillian are here. Dr. Debbie and her family are here, Dr.
Roz Rabie is here, and Samantha is by my side, having flown out from
Cape Town to be here with me. And the Barbertons, an elderly Afrikaans couple who picked us up at the gates of Etosha National Park
two months ago, are also here. It's an intimate gathering of the human
spirit, and it means so much to my family. Faith is a powerful friend
to me right now.

It would be foolish to come to Africa and not go on safari (Swahili
for "to journey"), so Sam and I save the best for last as a parting gift
for Mom and Pat. I want her to see the real Africa, not the inside of a
hospital or a church. The Sabi Sands Game Reserve lies on the border
with Kruger National Park and is home to hundreds of species of wild
animals, including the "Big Five" – lion, leopard, elephant, rhinoceros
and Cape buffalo. But after three hours of roaming around in the car,
we haven't seen any big game yet. *Well, that would suck if they came all*

this way and didn't even see an elephant. While I search through binoculars for something to appear, a park ranger approaches our vehicle.

"Time to go, my friends, the gates will be closing in 30 minutes."

"Please, sir, my parents have come all the way from Canada. I want to show them one of the Big Five. Can we have a few more minutes?"

"Follow me," he says with a wink. "Let's take the long way home."

Within minutes, a tower of giraffes slowly saunter out of the bush. Stunned, my mom sits in silence, staring out the window like she wants this moment to be etched in her memory for eternity. Then Sam spots a herd of elephants walking towards us. I can see happy tears forming in Mom's eyes and closure sweeping over her face.

"Oh my god, there he is. That is Sean, that big one right there," she says excitedly, pointing to the biggest elephant of the bunch. She knows that Sean is now free and roaming wild. This is her goodbye to him.

"I can picture him laughing at me, in a nice way," she says. "To think that he got me to the furthest part of the world. I would have never come to Africa if it wasn't for you, my son. This is magical. Thank you, Sean."

Sitting next to a picturesque little stream near Bryan's house, I'm trying to come to grips with my sudden new reality. On top of the world a week ago, in a dark bottomless pit the next. Denial is ever-present, but the guilt is much worse. *Because you didn't take this seriously enough, Sean is dead. You fucking idiot, Todd. And he's not just your brother. He was a son. He was a friend. He was an inspiration.* I lie down and breathe, releasing the clumps of hair clenched between my angry fingers. Emotions I don't know I possess are creeping up the back of my throat. It feels like I'm going to puke. I close my eyes and think, *Sean, please give me a sign. Something to let me know you're still with me.* I open my eyes, and the first thing that pops into my vision are two small birds chasing each other at high speed through the trees. A glimpse of happiness enters my being. It's the first time in a week that I've smiled, and I take notice of how truly amazing that actually is. Just to smile. Sean *is* nature, he's all around me, I just have to look and see. Like Lorraine said, that's my thing to hold on to.

My final stop at the hospital is to collect Sean's remains and say goodbye to the doctors who went over and above to save his life. *How will I ever be able to thank them enough?* At the mortuary, a clerk hands me a blue cardboard box of Sean's ashes, and I know immediately that I want something else to take him home in. *He was as out-of-the-box as they come. I'm not bringing him back INSIDE a goddamn box.* On my way back to Bryan's place, a ramshackle cluster of roadside shops selling carved wooden elephants catches my eye. I pull over to get a closer look, and another emotional wave crashes over my head. I try to hide behind a wall, slowly sinking to the ground, sobbing quietly, when a man comes over and puts his arm around me.

"My man everytin' going to be ahlright. My name Lolongo, " he says, patting his heart with an open palm. "I am here for you, my bruddah. Who is the one causing your sorrow?"

I love his accent, his smile and his genuine warmth. He's wearing a green-and-white baseball cap with the words *BIG UP* in red script, and he has a wide gap between his two front teeth. I tell him about Sean while looking over his selection of elephants, each of them strong and stout, about a foot tall.

"I want to put his ashes inside this one," I say, picking up the one that reminds me most of "Big Red," our elephant from Namibia, "to take home to my mom."

"You can take him home!" he says excitedly. "Take a piece of Africa with him. Elephants, they never forget, my friend. They remember family forever, until the end of time. And your brother will never forget you. Carry him with you forever, my boy. I am proud to make this for you. This one here is very strong elephant, like you" he says. "Come back tomorrow, when you wish. I will have it ready for you."

I return eagerly the next day with money in hand, but Lolongo refuses payment.

"I cannot take money from a man in such grief. It is paining me to see you are in sorrow, so I am wanting to help. Malaria takes many. We don't need to talk about money now, that is not important, son. What is important is your family now. You go back home and you tell them about South Africa, my country. Your brother will be by your side now, forever. Like the elephants, he will not forget. And Africa will not forget him."

He presents me with the finished product. Inside the belly of the elephant, he has carved a cylindrical hole from the top, complete with a wooden cork, "so the ashes will never fall out." I clutch it in my hands and hug it like a trophy. Lolongo wraps his hands around mine and looks me square in the eyes.

"His spirit is now in Africa, and he is there," he says, swirling his hands above his head. "He will now move with you. He will be the one to show you the way."

The wooden elephant is proudly tucked under my arm as I board the plane home. Two young men sit next to me. They're on their way to visit their families in Khayelitsha, Cape Town's answer to Soweto. Settling in, they turn their attention towards me, with Sean's elephant now tucked between my thighs.

"What is your name?" asks the one sitting next to me in the middle seat.

"Todd, from Canada. What is your name?"

"My name is Sean."

"My brother's name is Sean!" I reply loudly. "He's inside this elephant now!"

Neither of them know quite how to react to my statement, shooting a confused look at one another and nodding politely at me.

"And what's your name?" I say to Sean's friend.

"Lawson."

"Your name is Lawson?!"

"Yes sir."

Too floored to answer, I just close my eyes and say thank you.

In my mind, Sean has come by to let me know he is coming back with me, like I am being escorted home by the manifestation of my desire to see a sign that he's "out there," somewhere around me. It seems too far-fetched to be real – Sean and Lawson, sitting next to me in the flesh.

"My last name is Lawson! And my brother's name is Sean Lawson."

Clearly delighted by my excitement, but still somewhat confused, they both high-five me, and I launch into the story of how my brother came to be inside this wooden craving between my legs. They are remarkably genuine, supportive and friendly.

"You are taking him home now like this," says Lawson, pointing with two open palms at the elephant. "The elephant for me is good luck, you know. Because they are always remembering. I think this is nice. Your mother will be too happy."

PART TWO

LIME-LACED,
HOT-SAUCED FREEDOM

MEXICO • November 2004–January 2005

From the outskirts, San Luis Río Colorado looks like a busy little city, but as we approach the border, I see no government buildings or signs, and no border cops with rifles slung over their shoulders. Half of me wants to just keep riding into the country Wild West–style, shouting, "*Vamonos, muchachos!*" through my helmet.

"Let's just go," I say to Christina. "If they ask where our entry stamp is when we *leave* the country, we'll just tell them nobody was there when we *entered*."

She shakes her head at my dumb logic. This will be her very first moment on Mexican soil, and she wants us to enter with good karma. My haste is fuelled by restlessness; I want to leave the US behind and enter the lawlessness of *Meh-hee-co* as soon as possible. Nevertheless, I agree to wait in the shade on a hard cement porch, hoping that whoever shows up doesn't ask about our expired insurance or lack of licence plates.

Thirty minutes later, a dapper gentleman with slicked-back hair and gold-rimmed shades steps out of a dune buggy across the street. He looks like he's going to a casino on the beach, but we're nowhere near the ocean.

"They are not here right now. It is siesta time," he says in excellent English, whispering the *siesta* part to Christina. "Maybe in one hour they will come back. Do you need an entry stamp?"

"*Sí, señor.*"

"If you wait, they will come."

He returns from a small shop next door with two bottles of Tecate and a bag of spicy potato chips.

"A welcome gift," he says. "Good luck, my amigos from Canada. I hope you will fall in love with my country."

Soon after, a jovial man in his 50s comes around the corner, whistling and flicking a coin into the air. He slows down to take stock of us and ever so politely raises the back of his hand about a foot in front of his face, nodding his head slightly. The respectful gesture, commonly used throughout Mexico, puts me at ease and a smile on Christina's face. He looks at us again, then our bikes, with a nod of admiration, as if to say, *You guys look like you're going to have the time of your lives.*

Credentials strung around the man's neck indicate our wait is over, and he leads us into a corner building about a block from the main road, sits behind a dark wooden desk and rambles off a few quick questions that neither of us understands. Finally, he drops his black glasses onto his nose and draws out the simple question, slowly and deliberately. *"D-ó-n-d-e v-a-n?"*

"Ohhhh... where are we going?" I respond, recalling my rudimentary Spanish from a four-month trip to Mexico and Central America years ago. "We don't know. But we have a map."

Señor Juan stamps some ink into our passports, officially punching our ticket for the next 90 days of Mexican *libertad*.

We battled wind and rain down the western coast of the US for the past week on our trusted bikes, which we've christened Lucky & Lucinda, and the landscape has now changed vastly. It's amazing how an imaginary line between two countries can bring about such immense differences. Gone are the freeways, strip malls and hip vibe of California. Instead, the warm orange glow of a pending sunset bangs home a stereotypical Mexican scene: tumbleweeds rolling through a scrubby desert filled with giant cartoonish cacti standing proud against a backdrop of jagged purplish mountains. I half expect Speedy Gonzales to race up beside me screaming, *"Ándale, ándale, arriba, arriba!"*

Our first night is spent on a small agave farmstead a day's reach from the Pacific coastline. The proprietors, a sun-beaten couple well into their 80s, seem ecstatic to be hosting strangers for a night and set us up on handmade cots built from strips of stretched cowhide. Within an hour, more family members arrive, one smiling lady clutching two fresh-caught iguanas destined to be slowly roasted for the *asado*, a celebratory barbecue at which we are the guests of honour. It's the first time on this journey that Christina and I are invited with open arms to stay with locals. I imagine there will be hundreds of nights like this to come, a night charged with beauty, adventure and that same intangible magic I felt 18 months ago, on the night Christina and I first met, when the snow fell in fat, juicy flakes as I pulled into a pitch-black parking lot at Wayside Park in Whistler, BC, on March 3, 2003.

Unknown to me at the time, a series of wonderfully serendipitous events had culminated in an event that would soon change my life. First, wanting to reinvent myself and inspired by Sean's love of photography, I retired from the golf industry and enrolled in an intensive, year-long photojournalism course in Victoria, BC. A creative spark was lit within me, and I took a job offer as an on-mountain photographer on Whistler Blackcomb. I'd only been in town a couple of months, and while I was having après-work pitchers of beer with my new photographer colleagues one night, my friend Alain Denis turned to me and said excitedly, "Holy shit, man, have you met Jimmy Martinello yet? He travelled with your brother in Asia. He's on his way. I told him you were here."

THAT Jimmy?! The one from Cambodia? Until then I'd only seen pictures and heard stories from Sean of their time together. When we met, I knew instantly we'd be best friends. Holding me by the shoulders with his eyes locked on mine, he said to me: "Your brother, man... he showed me how to *really* travel, you know. I'm serious. Not just fucking around following the herd. We spent quite a bit of time riding all through Cambodia. He taught me to let go 100 per cent and how to see the world in so many new, magical ways. He changed my life, Todd, honestly."

A month later, Jimmy invited me and a few others to a potluck slide-show gathering at the "Lake House," a character-filled home set in a quiet bay on the southern shores of Alta Lake. I'd heard tales of this place as a home base that Sean had frequented in years previous. Also accompanying Jimmy that night was his yoga instructor, a friendly ball of energy named Christina. He introduced us in the dark, and we shook hands politely before splintering into two groups down a snow-banked path to the house.

When the lights flicked on inside the house, I came face to face with the friendly voice I'd just met outside in the snowy night a few minutes ago. Our gaze lingered for a moment, enough to make me randomly, and somewhat oddly, ask if Christina would mind giving me a hair-cut. While the rest of the small crew settled into the couches in the living room, I sat in a chair in the kitchen while she looked for a pair of scissors from the junk drawer, and Jimmy made a couple of surprise vodka cocktails with frozen cranberries floating on top. Next to us, a crackling fire burned inside a vintage wood-burning stove.

"I left home in Winnipeg when I was 17 and took the train out west," Christina said, snipping off the first chunk of my hair. "I stayed here for a season and snowboarded every day, then I went back to Ottawa to study art. What brought *you* to Whistler?"

"I just graduated from photography school and got offered a job shooting on the mountain. I used to be a golf pro, and I've been skiing since I was a kid, but I've fallen in love with photography now."

"I love photography too, and golf! I got hooked a couple of years ago and play all the time." As the pile of hair on the floor grew bigger, the conversation kept rolling along with effortless flow.

"I suppose you like to travel too," I said sarcastically.

"It's probably my favourite thing in the whole world. Living here in the bubble is cool and all... definitely a lot of interesting people in the valley, but travelling makes me feel alive."

"It sure does," I said. "I can't wait for my next trip."

"When was the last one?"

"I was in Thailand and Cambodia in 2000, but I've been studying ever since. I need to go on another trip soon, though."

"Hey, how's that?" she said, running her fingers through my hair. "Let me know if this is a good length. I'll see if I can find a mirror so you can have a look."

When she left the kitchen, the butterflies fluttered deep in my belly. I couldn't deny the fact that I was definitely digging her vibe. I only hoped it was mutual.

"Here, have a look," she said, holding up the mirror.

"Perfect," I said, although I didn't want the haircut to end. Twenty uninterrupted minutes alone with this beautiful woman. *Keep going.* I was attracted to her energy as much as her looks. She had a fun smile, a curvaceous body and plump cheeks that were still rosy from the cold walk. It felt like a blind date, without the awkward date part. We settled in on the couch together and let the electricity flow, watching Jimmy's slideshow on a small screen in the living room. He sensed what was happening between us as the night progressed.

"Hey, Todd, it's snowing pretty hard out there right now, man, you probably don't want to drive to Pemberton tonight. Maybe you guys should just crash here? You can sleep on the pullout couch."

Christina accepted his offer with a mischievous grin that sent shockwaves buzzing through my heart.

I could hardly believe my luck. The great web of human connection throughout the world had worked its magic and brought us all together in mysterious ways. It can take years to find a crew of close friends in a new town, and yet people I had read about in Sean's journals – like Jimmy and T-Mac – were suddenly in front of me, in the flesh. Two new brothers-in-spirit who had both had intense travel experiences with my actual blood brother. I had discovered part of Sean's Whistler/ Squamish tribe, and now they were *my* tribe, with serendipity placing a beautiful woman into the mix as well. We all spent the summer hiking and camping and paddling and exploring my new Sea-to-Sky backyard in the Coast Mountains.

I convinced Brad to finally leave Houston and move back to Canada. He found work as a bartender in Whistler in no time. Meanwhile, the energy between Christina and me kept building. Six months later, I got down on one knee and popped the question: "Will you ride a motorcycle down to South America with me to keep my brother's dream alive?"

After realizing my proposal wasn't *that* kind of proposal, Christina laughed and said, "But I've never ridden a motorcycle before."

"I'll teach you. We'll go to a nice open area with nobody around. It doesn't take that long to learn, actually. You'll get the hang of it in a day."

"Yeah, right. What about getting my licence?"

"Well, I need to get mine also, so we can do it together."

"Okay," she said with a bright smile and a shrug of her shoulders. "I'm in."

I wasn't expecting her to give me an answer within the first two minutes, but there it was, straightforward and full of enthusiasm, just like her personality. I kissed her on the spot, long and passionately. The deal was done.

"When are we going, by the way?" she asked.

"I was thinking of October 1, next year. It's my mom's birthday, so that'll be a good omen."

"That's only a year away."

"I know. We better start saving."

She threw herself into the endeavour with more passion than I, almost like it was her duty to fulfill the grand task of keeping Sean's legacy alive. We pushed each other hard with finances and saving, buying only the bare necessities. Every paycheque and paper note went into a big glass jar that we called the "TF," our travel fund. We had four jobs each and saved every nickel and dime that passed through our hands.

And on October 1, 2004, we rode away from Whistler on the first day of what would come to be known simply as "the Journey," with no planned route, no guidebook, no cellphones, no GPS, no schedule, no timetable and no responsibilities. We made one final stop at Mom and Pat's on Vancouver Island to say our goodbyes. Before we rolled out of her driveway, Mom opened the cork of Sean's wooden elephant and handed me an empty film canister to fill. I wrapped her in Sean's Mexi-blanket to immortalize the moment with a picture before stashing the blanket into my saddlebag. Mom's tearful but proud eyes were the last thing I saw as we waved goodbye. It was heart-wrenching to leave her, but from that last glance, I could tell she accepted our fate.

A huge part of me still wishes I could've kidnapped her and plunked her in the seat behind me so she could feel this incredible freedom as we snake our way towards the Pacific coast of Sonora along a white ribbon of gravel road. She went to Acapulco on her honeymoon in 1967 and loved Mexico; we even had a taxidermied swordfish, caught by my grandmother Mary Lawson, hung on the wall of the outdoor deck at our house in Stony Plain. Passing hundreds of massive cacti, I can picture Mom's smiling face in my mirror. She probably would've tried the barbecued iguana too.

Of course, freedom isn't always free, and that white strip of perfect gravel soon turns into ankle-deep sand – an exhausting nightmare even for experienced adventure riders. It's Christina's first glimpse of what a hundred kilometres of deep sand with a fully loaded bike can do to one's psyche. She's the youngest of four siblings, stubborn and strong-willed, perfectly suited for what is yet to come. The yoga side of her mellows out her wild side, the yin and yang of a prairie girl who lives in the mountains and has a love affair with the world. This I love about her. It reeled me in and I let it. After we drop our bikes under a blazing desert sun for the tenth time in an hour, maintaining even a hint of positivity becomes a sweltering chore. Christina curses but soldiers on, drawing from a reservoir of strength and calm that impresses the hell out of me.

When we finally arrive in San Carlos Nuevo Guaymas, the light of a bonfire leads us to a beach party and a dozen people dancing barefoot next to a modified roofless school bus decked out with a sound system big enough for a wedding. Nobody seems to care about the two gringos who've just crashed their party, so we gingerly step inside for a closer look and meet Sveen, or Ben, as he pronounces it.

"*Hola,*" he says loudly with a big, bright smile plastered across his cherubic face. "*Bienvenidos.* Welcome my home, Guaymaaaaas!"

"This is *your* bus?" asks Christina, complimenting him with an incredulous voice. "This is amazing!"

"Thank you. Yes, is my bus. My baby. We make in my chop last year... cut the roof with, how you say, cheensaw? We always come to beach for party. Is nice to have you here, my friends. Where are you from?"

"We are both Canadians, travelling by motorcycle," Christina says. "We want to go all the way to Argentina."

"Whaaat! I love motorbikes! I am also mechanic, I have a chop. You will need to learn Spanish first," he says with a wink. "I can teach you. But tomorrow I want you go hike with me. We go Tetakawi."

We accept the invitation, and the fiesta rolls on, but even the party animal in me doesn't care. After all the sun and sand today, we need to sleep, which we do soundly inside the fifth-wheel trailer we're calling home tonight. It's owned by our Canadian friends Carlos and Shirley Mierlo, who spend their winters here like many other Canadian "snowbirds," but haven't yet arrived.

The sentinels of San Carlos are two iconic rocky pinnacles known as Cerro Tetakawi, meaning "rocky mountain" in the native Yaqui language. After we scrape our way through the prickly underbrush, our new friend Sveen leads the way along a rocky trail that hugs the base of the copper-coloured mountain. Nobody else is on the mountain, and there's not a breath of wind, so when a big rock somehow comes loose and trundles down the hillside, we hear every smashing sound echoing off the bronze walls.

"Hey, Sveen, when was the last time you climbed this?" I ask.

"Never. This is my first time."

I can see a slice of bright light pouring in through the rocks to my left and squeeze my body into a small cave to take a photograph of the coastline. Once my eyes adjust to the light, I notice a giant tarantula, easily the size of my entire hand, mere inches from my outstretched arm. I freeze, believing that if I make any sudden movements he'll jump on my face, and that will be the end of me. Thank god, he doesn't move. I manage to fire off a couple of quick frames with his hairy body silhouetted against the Pacific Ocean.

At the summit, Sveen is beaming with pride that his two new gringo friends are standing arm in arm on top of his new world. It's a wonderful moment atop another of nature's fine stages. Quietly, I hold out the film canister of Sean's ashes, and each of us puts a pinch in the palm of our hands, blowing him into a peaceful blue sky.

Christina and I have read about a pair of motorcyclists who meticulously planned their route from Alaska to Argentina along the Pan-American Highway with a *spreadsheet*. They calculated the exact distance to ride each day, which hotels to sleep in and how long the journey would take riding non-stop, with no smelling of the roses. That could not be us. That *would* not be us. *Where is the magic in that?* If I learned anything from Sean, it was that spontaneity rules the roost. Just let the trip happen, don't try and make it happen. To experience the true essence of our journey, Christina and I agreed to get off the bikes once in a while and explore the country on foot, or horseback, or bicycle or, in this case, along the rails of Mexico's greatest train journey, into the 35,000-square-mile Sierra Tarahumara wilderness, home of the famous Barranca del Cobre – the Copper Canyon.

We were hoping to score a berth on the super-cheap second-class train, with wooden seats and goats and pigs, but we missed that by a couple of years and instead take a comfy ride with heat-scorched scenery rushing by at 60 kilometres an hour. We're in the land of the legendary Tarahumara now, an Indigenous People who routinely baffle physical-conditioning experts by covering superhuman distances wearing *huarache* sandals made from old tires and leather straps, barely breaking a sweat in the process. The Tarahumara call themselves Rarámuri, "runners on foot" or "those who run fast." Because they live in sporadic settlements throughout the massive Copper Canyon, the Tarahumara developed a tradition of long-distance running for inter-village communication, trading and hunting. Even today, the world's best ultra-marathoners are awed by the long-distance feats of the Tarahumara who show up to hundred-plus-mile races in the US, smoking cigarettes at the start line.

Our train stops at the small village of Posada Barrancas, where we set up camp in the backyard of a kind man named Miguel, his wife, Luisa, and their eight children. Telltale signs of abject poverty are everywhere – dilapidated shacks with scraps of garbage and piles of old tires littering the yards. Miguel humbly asks us for a few pesos *"para mi familia,"* which we oblige. He also gets one of my T-shirts that doesn't fit me, which he puts on immediately and struts around the small adobe house like a rooster while his children laugh uncontrollably at his antics, slapping the thighs of each other in a genuine moment of pure joy. Over a breakfast of fried eggs, refried beans and homemade tortillas, we ask Miguel how to find the nearby trailhead that will lead us to the bottom of Urique Canyon, the deepest canyon in North America, 6,165 feet below his smoky kitchen.

"Follow these train tracks for a while, and you will see a sign that says *Cañon Urique*. It should take you three or four hours to reach the bottom."

"Is there a path marking the way?"

"Yes, the whole way down." He smiles. "Be careful on the trail, there are a lot of assaults."

He fails to mention anything about taking a guide.

The steep descent jams our toes into our boots as we switchback down natural rock staircases into the dark shadows of the canyon. After six hours of hot, steady travel, we follow the roar of running water to an oasis of banana palms and orange trees, where a warm waterfall eases us into two beautiful days of solitude and relaxation near the river's edge. Just before the long hike back up, a lone figure comes ambling through the bush without so much as a twig snapping. He approaches us silently, looking curiously at our stuff scattered about.

"Buenas días!" he exclaims, with three of his remaining teeth, crooked and yellow, poking out behind his lips to form a friendly smile. Judging by his wraparound skirt and bright red shirt, we assume he's Tarahumara. His name is Alejandro, and he's accompanied by an old weathered

donkey named Blanco. He says nothing else, only points in the direction we should be headed – straight back up the walls of the canyon.

We push on. Five hours pass. Six. Seven. Exhausted and sipping on the last of our smoke-flavoured water, we keep trudging along in the late-afternoon heat. The trail becomes steeper, with false summit after false summit giving us hope only to strip it away moments later. Nine hours. Ten. Eleven. We now can't find *any* path.

"Oww!" I hear Christina shout loudly below me. "Son of a bitch!"

I quickly scramble down to find her writhing in pain, laid out on her back like an overturned turtle.

"What happened? Are you okay?"

"One of these rocks came loose and I fell off that shelf and tweaked my knee I think."

"Shit, babe, you're bleeding too. You sure you're okay?"

"Just let me lie here for a while. The blood is probably just from hitting the rock… it's *inside* my knee that hurts. Hopefully I didn't tear anything."

Dusk sinks in, and darkness soon envelops the scene. We're alone on an exposed ridgeline, and all I can see are mammoth boulders and cliff faces but no signs of civilization. Not looking forward to spending an injured night in the cold with no food or water, I do the only thing I can think of. *"Ayuda!* HELP!" I yell at the top of my lungs.

We hear the echo for what seems like minutes, then we sit and wait. A few moments later, a figure materializes like an apparition from the trees 50 yards away. Christina limps in his direction while I grab both packs, relieved that we've just been rescued by a nameless, speechless man. After a short, quiet stroll over a soft path of pine needles, we drop to our knees and kiss the shining silver steel of the railroad tracks glimmering in the moonlight, less than 200 metres from the rim of the canyon.

Safely back at Miguel's little home, we rise to a beautiful morning on Christina's 30th birthday. It's no easy task to sneak away and secretly organize a celebration for the loved one you're with 24/7, so I leave her in bed and go looking for a little cabin to rent along the shores of nearby Lago Arareco. Miguel says he knows a family that has a nice lakefront cabin for rent. The owners, Tony and José, show up three sheets to the wind and can't find the keys. After a long, mumbling discussion between them, Tony grabs a rock and smashes the window of the back door, slicing his hand open in the process. The cabin comes with a beautiful stone fireplace, plenty of firewood and a canoe on the dock.

After ripping past mile after mile of cacti-filled desert for the last month, I can barely believe we're paddling a canoe across a lake in the mountains: our happy place. The lake is rimmed with tea-coloured bedrock, hemmed in by thousands of long-bristled pine trees, as tranquil a place as any to float aimlessly and sip cheap red wine from the bottle. The last glow of the sun fades behind the peaks, and I suggest we go back and make dinner for the birthday girl. Thirty only comes around once in a lifetime. Pulling the canoe onto the dock, I lose my footing and slip over the edge, falling into the lake, headlamp and all. Clambering back onto the dock, soaked to the bone and freezing cold, I notice Christina laughing her face off at my unexpected gift of comedy. After dinner, just as I'm about to give Chris a romantic birthday present next to a crackling fire, we hear a rap on the back door.

"Who the fuck is that?" I say, scrambling to put some clothes on.

I peer through the little square windows and see Tony and José, glassy-eyed and wobbling back and forth. Tony's bloody hand is bandaged, but he's feeling no pain.

"Oye, Tomás, quieres tomar? (Hey Todd, you want a drink?)" he says, hoisting up a big brown bottle.

Tony and José reek like booze, but the offer is purely neighbourly, a long-standing tradition amongst the Tarahumara. Inside the bottle sloshes an alcoholic concoction known as *tesgüino* – fermented corn beer, the lifeblood of their people. Intoxication is worn as a badge of honour, not shame, amongst the locals in the Sierra, and it's estimated that the average man spends at least 100 days of every year in a *tesgüino* stupor. It smells horrific, but I take a couple of proud gulps. The bitter aftertaste sends a clump of vomit creeping up my throat, which elicits riotous wheezing laughter from the *amigos borrachos*, clearly overjoyed that their nasty homebrew has touched the lips of a gracious gringo who's rented their *cabina* for a couple of nights. I manage to stave off their repeated attempts at making me drink more and watch them stumble off in the darkness, clanking the big bottles together.

December 20, 2004. A day's ride north of the tourist town of Puerto Vallarta, an old farm road leads us to a massive, leafy tree which appears to be home for the night. After nine straight days of camping, we're desperate for a hot shower and a restaurant meal, but it won't happen tonight. Even a cockroachy one-star hotel won't pop out of the sugarcane fields that have lined the highway for the past six windy hours. The zone feels eerily cold and quiet, shrouded in a thick layer of dusky yellow haze. I imagine what the place would look like from above; we'd be insignificant specks in a sprawling maze of green.

Unpacking our bags, Christina calculates the day's mileage and proudly announces, "Two hundred eighty-two klicks today, and 7716 kilometres so far. Isn't that about the same length as Canada from coast to coast?"

"Yeah, pretty much," I say, too tired and windblown to keep the conversation going.

A few hours later, I'm rudely awoken by a sharp stinging sensation on my upper right thigh. I lay the blame on some cactus quill that must have stuck to my sleeping bag. Just as I doze off again, another sharp prick pokes me in my right leg. Then another...

"What the fuck?" I say, waking up Christina to see if she's feeling the same pinch. "Babe, are you sleeping okay?"

"What are you talking about?" she responds with a groggy whisper.

"I swear something is biting me in the leg."

"Can you see anything? What do you think it is?"

Peeling open the zipper, I shake out my sleeping bag in the cold, dark night, put on another layer of clothes and hope for more shut-eye. Just as I'm poking my head back into the tent, Christina gets jolted awake.

"Ow! What the fuck *is* that?"

"I don't know, but let me shake out your sleeping bag too. It's probably just some burrs from the other night, when we camped in that scrubby spot."

She joins me outside, and we shake them out vigorously. The last few days have been long, hot and hard. We need more sleep. Twenty minutes goes by, but the biting doesn't stop.

"What the fuck is going on?" she says. "It feels like we're getting electrocuted or something."

We clear out the contents of the tent, and I reach into my jacket pocket for a lighter to illuminate the scene. Its flickering flame reveals the horror – a thousand plump army ants chewing a thousand holes through the tent floor.

"Oh my fucking god," Christina says, astonished that these ants were hungry enough to rise from their abode deep within the cane soil, devour one layer of tent fabric, chew through our yoga mats and into our sleeping bags to sink their needle-sharp pincers into our flesh. All in a night's work. The sight stuns us into silence, and we listen intently, *hearing* them eat our only home.

"I am so creeped out right now it's not even funny," says Christina, visibly disgusted.

The faint light of dawn reveals the ravenous insects clamping their mandibles on the tent fabric, dangling down like droplets of black wax. We turn our sleeping bags inside out and another hundred are still enjoying a breakfast of goose feathers and ripstop nylon.

"Ahhh! They're still biting me, Todd, get them off!" Christina screams, jumping into the air like a cartoon character.

"Take off your clothes, babe, they're inside your clothes!"

In seconds, we're both stark naked, hopping around and swatting ants off of each other with our clothes, when I see a few men walking slowly down the road towards us in the distance. To them, it probably looks like we're practising some sort of interpretive dance. We duck into the cane field to put some fresh clothes and a brave face on.

"*Mira, mira...* take a look," I say anxiously, pointing at the tent, as they approach.

"*Sí, hormigas del ejército. Debes ser muy hambre* (Yes, army ants. They must've been very hungry)," says a man dressed in warm clothes and a wool toque. This elicits an uproar of laughter from the rest of the crew, and so, with the bottom of our beloved "Casa Verde" in tatters, we gift it to them. They accept graciously, still laughing and chattering amongst themselves before heading off for another day of farm labour. Four days later, we are still finding dead ants clutching our sleeping bags.

Palenque, Chiapas
Saturday, January 29, 2005

I thought of Sean on the road yesterday, of his final moments gripping onto the fragile strings of life and how he was taken from us so quickly. This journey with Christina has brought so much freedom, happiness and togetherness to our lives, and I can thank Sean (and Jimmy!) for that. She surprised me with a sprinkling of his ashes in the palm of my hand that I released into the air while driving today. Letting him go at high speed was a nice surprise. She seems to have a connection with Sean even though she never had the chance to meet him.

Sean would have struck me down with lightning had we not visited Chiapas and the ruins at Palenque, so here we are, and wow is it incredible. I wish everyone could see this place. Howler monkeys roared from the treetops of the thick jungle as we explored the intricate, lifelike characters carved into the rocks. Truly spectacular. Now I'm writing by candlelight, our new tent on the grass, safe, secure, taking in all the memories of this great country: sunrise at Monte Albán, street tacos, Christmas on the beach with Julien and his merry band of Alcoholics Anonymous amigos, making tortillas by hand. And the green, white and red of the Mexican flag in every single village, town and city. Cerveza and cilantro. Rice and refried beans. Hot sauce and carne asada.

Viva Mexico, we love you.

BACK-A-BUSH

CROOKED TREE, BELIZE • February 2005

The unrelenting Caribbean sun pulls us off the highway to rehydrate and consult our cherished map, crinkled and full of tape with a thick red line spindling its way from Canada down to the Pacific coast of Oaxaca, straight across Mexico to the Mayan ruins at Tulum and now poking over the border into Belize.

"Crooked Tree. The name sounds pretty cool," I say.

"Okay, let's go check it out."

Thirty washboard-gravel minutes later, the road turns into a dyke that slices through a big brown lagoon, the only road in or out of the village. A hand-painted sign reads:

Welcome to Crooked Tree
The Village of the Cashew
Established in the Early 1700's
Population 886

As we begin our campsite search, the smell of cow shit triggers a vivid childhood memory – us boys with our grandfather, milking cows in the barn. I stay with the memory for a while, thinking of the hay bales and summer bonfires and jumping off the rooftops into deep snow in the winter.

I like Crooked Tree instantly: clapboard houses built on stilts; spacious, grassy yards; and a pace so slow you can almost smell it. A dirt path along the shore of the lagoon leads us beneath two sprawling cashew trees and into the sights of two young children who spot us through a wall of cooking-fire smoke. I hardly have time to put my kickstand down when the youngest, a handsome boy maybe 5 years old, darts towards me with a face full of excitement framed by crooked bangs of jet-black hair. He looks like a little Indian cherub with big dimples, a mini version of Sveen from Guaymas. Plopping himself on my gas tank, he pretends to rev up the bike and makes the *vroom-vroom* noise.

"Bwai!" shouts his mother from a few yards away. "Wah you wahn do 'pahn de bike, bwai?"

His big sister follows, mounting Christina's bike like a horse, a mess of dark ringlets poking out the back of her pink ball cap.

"Oh my god, they're so adorable," Christina says. "I don't know what they're saying, but it's like love at first sight."

Their mom realizes we're receptive to her kids' precocious spontaneity and belts out a big, welcoming belly laugh. A man emerges from their weathered plywood dwelling, helping a bobbling baby walk like a marionette.

"Yah, mahn... dis be de bes' place," he says. "Me name Mitch. You can stay 'ere long as you wahn. Ain' no problem a'tall. You can camp ovadeh... you bring de tent?"

He's tall and slender, with big, bulging eyes; he could definitely pass as Snoop Dogg's Belizean brother.

"Thank you," Christina says, getting off her bike while the little girl stays on and grabs the handlebars. "Yes, we have a tent."

"Dat good. Dis me wife, Claudette," he says, lovingly putting his arm around her. "Dis one ere 'pon de bike, he Gabriel, we call him Gabo. Him looooove moto'bike. And she... dee wahn on you bike, dat Candylee. Over der playin' in the sandbox, dat Antonia... tree yeauhs old. And dis baby, he Abra*ham*."

"Dis de bes' place!" Christina says, mimicking Mitch's Creole accent. They're hard to understand, but it's nice to hear some English after three months of *español*. Claudette introduces herself and tells the kids to go fetch some water. She tones down her Creole and speaks in clear English with a gentle voice.

"Welcome to Crooked Tree," she says, now bouncing the little baby off her hip. "Tonight we gonna bubble up some beans... you will eat wid us."

Gabo and Candylee help us set up the tent underneath the cashew trees then take us wandering around the property barefoot, drinking water out of ceramic cups while dinner is prepared.

"Auntie... Uncle... ?" says Gabo in a sharp, inquisitive voice behind a steaming plate of red beans and rice.

Christina and I look at each other, melting in adoration for this little kid and his accent. We've known him for a few hours and already he thinks we're family.

"Yes, Gabo?" Christina answers.

"Mahro we gwahn go for ride de moto'cycle go backabush? True? Auntie... Uncle."

"Ummm... what did he just say?" Christina asks, laughing at Gabo's quick-fire Creole.

"He say tomorrow he wants to go for a ride on the motorcycle, back up in de bush. Like back up there," Claudette says slowly, pointing with her arm past the big trees. "Back-a-bush!"

Mitch is up early the next morning making "fry jacks" (a deep-fried dough) and instant coffee on the fire hearth. Candylee walks out of the house, smoothing her hand over a clean blue-and-white school skirt, trying to iron out the wrinkles. She doesn't see us yet and sits down on the picnic table, nesting her head into her arms.

"Move up, gyal!" Mitch shouts with authority. "Move up!"

He places a few coins in her hand and sends her off, a stern look creasing his forehead. I glance over at Mitch, who shakes his head as he lights up a cigarette. We're far enough away from the house that he doesn't notice us brushing our teeth beside our bikes when Candylee comes back minutes later, holding a plastic bag. Mitch takes one look at it and smacks the side of her head, hard. Recoiling and cupping her right ear, she drops the bag. A puff of white escapes when it hits the ground.

"You bring flour instead of shugah?! What wrong wit' you, gyal?! You wahn drink flour in de coffee? I axe you for shugah! G'wan back and bring me shugah!"

He hits her hard enough that I don't know if I should confront him or let it be. These are his kids after all, not mine. Candylee skulks away down the path, sobbing. Meanwhile, Claudette is pounding the laundry with a large pipe in a drum barrel, with baby Abraham fast asleep in a sling across her back. Little Antonia is playing in the sand-box again.

"Claudette, can we talk to you about something?" Christina asks later, having waited until Mitch is nowhere to be seen.

"Yes love, anyting."

"Earlier this morning, we saw Mitch smack Candylee pretty hard across her head. Todd was going to say something to Mitch right then, but we thought we should talk to you first. Maybe it's none of our business, but it seemed like a pretty harsh punishment for bringing home flour instead of sugar."

"Well, dat Mitch for you. He don't treat the kids good. Hit 'em up all the time. I already had to leave Mitch once cuz he did this to me," she says, grabbing her blouse and pulling it down to reveal a long white scar across her shoulder.

"Oh my god!" Chris gasps. "Mitch did that to you? How?"

"He cut me with a machete."

"He did what?"

"He lash at me with a machete."

"Wow, that's a pretty serious scar."

"Oh, guys, I remember that sad day when Mitch hit me," she says, continuing to pound laundry in the sloshing water. "It was a blessed morning, and I ask him to please help me wash the dishes. He told me I am too lazy, but at this time it was me bringing our food on the table, so I told him, 'It is you who are lazy, Mitch. It is you always sitting there doing nothing!' I was getting tired of doing all of the chores for the whole family, and when I mention that, he explode. He told me he tired of punishing me so softly, so he grab the machete and lash me with all his strength. All I get from Mitch is abuse. No help with the kids, no food on the table. Just drunken abuse. I am a living testimony to abuse, Christina, I tell you."

She speaks with such dignified confidence that our respect for her increases tenfold.

"And what about now, Claudette?" asks Christina, enveloping her in a hug. "What are your feelings now for Mitch? Is he still abusing you physically?"

"Well, now it not bad, actually. At least he got a job for two days each week, so he bringin' *some* money to the table. Now the kids can go to sleep with belly full-up. He a good cook too, and funny, so the kids like 'im."

Later that evening, we accompany Claudette and the kids across the village to attend church. The pastor begins his lively sermon by personally welcoming his two new guests to what seems like the entire village, everyone turning to watch the only white faces in the crowd turn an embarrassed shade of red. Claudette walks on stage to lend her voice to the power of the gospel, joining a trio of smiling women who belt out each song loud and proud, sending all the churchgoers into an arm-waving, hand-clapping frenzy.

Why wasn't church this lively when I was a kid?

As a youngster, church did not sit well with me; the bulk of my quasi-Catholic upbringing centred around attendance, at the behest of my grandmother, of midnight mass in St. Paul every Christmas Eve. Kneeling in front of church pews before shuffling laterally into a wooden seat next to a morose stranger didn't inspire me to further the religious agenda. Even worse was trying to pay attention (or stay awake) as the pastor delivered his service in a dark pulpit gown. That sorrowful experience was the polar opposite of these ladies on stage, belting their hearts out to Jesus Christ. Not since Sean's funeral service have I felt the rapture of a Black church choir. Hearing the Soweto Gospel Choir sing that day had me wholeheartedly believing that Sean was being carried to the heavens on golden wings.

A couple of days in Crooked Tree soon rolls into seven. Without the need to get up and ride every day, we're slowly adapting to the rural pace of village life, which is even more relaxing on the days when

Mitch is not around. We've been back-a-bush once or twice to hunt for iguanas, a Sunday lunch special. We haven't even thought about our next destination until Mitch brings it up at the dinner table one evening. Thankfully he's not drunk. Around the campfire, Gabo and Candylee express their desire to sleep in the tent with us. We tuck them in, read a book and watch them fall asleep, their limbs spread out like starfish. Our bond with the Mejia clan is growing stronger each day, but we know we can't stay forever. In the morning, we reluctantly tell Claudette we must leave.

"I know already," she says, unnerved. "The day you came, I prayed to God that someone would come that day. Night before, we had to put the kids to bed without dinner. That's how much I believe. I have faith, Todd, you know. We don't have nuttin' but we got God. And we have each other. That's all I need."

Mitch overhears us and walks away down the path, not bothering to take the kids to school. Gabo won't let go of me. He's crying so hard it wrenches my heart out of my body. Candylee is doing the same to Christina. Cleverly, Claudette tells them we can take them to school "'pon de bike" as long as they stop crying. They stop immediately and hop on. I know we'll cause a scene at school, so we say our good-byes outside of the school grounds and watch our two new little best friends wipe the streaming tears from their faces while looking back at us every two seconds.

"Oh my god, that was so hard, Todd. I love them so much. I really hope we can come back here one day."

We return to pack up our bikes and have some final moments with Claudette – our brave warrior friend, with whom we have a bond that we know will last for life. Never once did she show us she was ashamed to be poor or abused. Her faith is her power, and she believes the universe will provide everything she needs.

"You know, Todd and Christina, one thing I learn from you is dat love de strongest thing. I think I can finally leave Mitch now. I love my kids and they love me, and that's all I need. You show my kids what real love can be, and Mitch, he feel real jealous right now, I know dat true. *Real* jealous."

"Claudette," says Christina, clutching her arm with both of her hands. "We will try and help you any way we can. We want to stay, but we have to keep moving. I hope you understand that we're not abandoning you. Please stay strong."

"My child, I know everyting gonna be alright. The kids are gonna be very sad for a few days once they come back and you're not here. I don't think they felt love like dat yet from anyone 'cept me. Me, I love 'em with all my heart but I'm they momma, they know I love 'em... but this is different. I felt safe with you both here, but now I got to be real strong and face up wit Mitch. I gwahn tell him to go."

"I think it's better if we're gone when he comes back," I say.

"Okay, guys, be safe and keep spreading your love, guys. I'll never forget you. Not ever. God bless."

After squishy, lingering hugs, we kiss Antonia and Abraham good-bye and ride off slowly through the village, sobbing hard under our helmets. Then I notice my gloves aren't on my hands. *I can't leave those gloves behind, they're the only ones I have.* Wheeling back to the house, we find them, but the timing couldn't be worse: Mitch is wobbling back up the path towards the house, a cigarette in one hand and a bottle of almost-finished cashew wine in the other.

"You think you can show love to my kids like dat and then just get up and leave!" he shouts at me in a drunken stupor. "Why you do dat?! You come into they lives and you smother 'em wid all dis love and now you gwahn jus up and leave? How me gwahn tell me kids dat?! Huh? How me gwahn tell 'em?!"

"Why don't you love these kids like you should, Mitch?!" I shout back. "We've seen you hit them and talk down to them every day. Why can't you love them like a man! Look at Claudette. That woman right there is the best thing that's ever happened to you, and you treat her like shit too."

Mitch is now inches from my face, with his big googly eyes popping out of his head, mumbling incoherently.

"Here dey come 'pon de path," he shouts. "Why you not tell 'em straight up? You tell 'em you leave now."

I look over to see Gabo and Candylee running towards us.

Oh, no, not now. I don't want them to see this.

I glance over at Christina, who's now moved closer to Claudette and the kids. Everyone is in tears, even Mitch.

"Mitch, we are truly sorry if this is hurting you," I say in a calm voice. "Yes, we love your family very much, and yes this is a very hard goodbye, but we have to keep travelling. We'll remember you all, but we can't stay here forever. Mitch, I hope you do change and see the good in your kids and your wife and love them like I know you can."

He slumps to the ground, still clutching the bottle in his right hand. We never meant to hurt Mitch like this, but it's hard to accept his abuse of his family. I look to Claudette and the kids to gauge their reaction. Gabo is angry and Candylee looks ashamed of her father. Claudette says it like it is, even if it means she'll face his wrath later.

"Todd, just leave him right there on the ground," she says, making sure her voice is loud enough for Mitch to hear. "He so drunk he probably forget everyting tomorrow. He not gonna do anyting now. He just sit there, *drunk.*"

We have no other choice but to go. I try peeling Christina away from a teary embrace with Claudette and the kids.

"Promise me you'll be okay," she pleads to Claudette.

"We'll be fine. Everyting be alright, my love. God will protect us."

– 10 –

DECAPITATION, REALLY?

ALDEA SANTA MARIA, GUATEMALA • February 2005

"No! No pasen. Aqui no!" shouts a local peasant farmer, waving a scold-
ing finger as we approach his rolling, fenced-in farmland. *"No gringo.
No gringo!"* he says loudly, flicking his hands as if to shoo us off his
property. We're high in the forested Central Highlands of Guatemala,
searching in the waning light for a place to rest our road-weary bodies
after five hours of riding a dusty spiderweb of roads that don't seem to
lead anywhere. Through a mouthful of crooked teeth, he continues.
"No confianza. Vas a cortar mi cabeza, y vender en mercado negro."

Our Spanish isn't good enough to pick up the gist of his rant, but
his vivid, and repeated, neck-slicing mime act adds more tension to
an already hostile encounter. We don't know what to do or what he's
saying, but he keeps shouting the words *cabeza, mercado* and *gringo.*
Head. Market. Gringo. *What the fuck is he talking about? Does he think
we're going to kill him?!*

When he comes closer I catch a whiff of booze. I tuck Chris behind
me, and a tinge of fear heightens my senses as the man draws closer,
a sheathless machete hanging from a belt in his pants. Thankfully the
rest of his family gathers around to calm him down – two ruffled boys
dressed in tatters, three young schoolgirls still in their navy blue-and-
white uniforms, and the man's wife, draped in a bright shock of traditional Guatemalan colours. She carries both a quiet confidence and

a concerned, empathetic demeanour that brings a welcome sense of reassurance to the situation.

The eldest girl, maybe 16, walks up and says in Spanglish: "Ees okay. No problem. *Todo tranquilo aquí.* Here is no problem. My father only is scare from the war. He name Alejandro."

"What is he saying?" Christina asks her. "Why is he slicing his neck like that?"

"He say he no trust you. You will wait for us sleeping and cut off the *cabeza* for to sell in black market!"

"We can look for another place, no problem," Christina says slowly, explaining our situation. "We are not bad people. We come in peace. We only need somewhere to put our tent so we can sleep for the night. We are lost."

I glance back at my bike and notice the old man staring at the front fender. He's looking at our sticker of the Canadian flag. Or at least I hope he is. In Guatemala's brutal civil war, from 1960 to 1996, more than 200,000 people were killed, most of them Indigenous, and the United States was heavily involved in training and equipping the Guatemalan security forces responsible. It was a brutal, bloody time for the country; more than half a million were driven from their homes, with many more raped and tortured. But I still can't understand why he thinks we would want to chop off his head. And then *sell* it. *We don't even know where the black market is.* Finally, a young man walks forward, and in a smattering of more broken Spanglish attempts to explain the old man's side of the story.

"Him family die. *Todo.* Mother, father, brother, sister, cousin. All people is *muerte.* The town... is, is burn like big fire. Many fire. He run away. Only alive is he."

I look at Chris and slowly mouth the words *holy shit.*

We say nothing for a while, nobody does. Finally his daughters plead with him.

"*Tranquilo, Papá,*" they keep saying. "*Todo es tranquilo. Por favor, Papá, no pasa nada. Ellos son Canadienses.* (They are Canadian.)"

He reluctantly agrees, muttering a few unintelligible words to us before ducking inside his adobe-brick home. We explain to his children that we don't want to cause any problems, we'll just keep rolling along, but they insist, and show us a flat cement pad where we can set up our tent next to a hairy white pig chained to a post. We take turns filling pages of our journal with the day's wild events before a concert of cicadas, accompanied by the pig's grunting and snorting, lulls us to sleep. Wanting to shoot a few landscapes in the morning glow, I wake before the sun splits the horizon. The shadows are long and dark, spilling into fields of short green grass neatly hemmed in by rustic barbed-wire fences. The old man is also up, mulling about the compound and talking to himself. With my camera draped across my chest I reach for my tripod, but it accidentally falls out of its protective case. Alejandro leans back into a defensive stance and asks, *"Qué es eso?* (What is that?)"

Oh shit, he probably thinks it's a gun, I say to myself, shaking my head at my own stupidity. *Leave the tripod alone, man, you don't wanna trigger another wartime flashback of soldiers killing his family, for fuck's sake.* I make some small talk about how nice his land is while I shoot a hand-held frame of two cows lying in the grass, pressing the shutter button deliberately so as to disarm Alejandro's apprehensions. Instantly, the image appears like magic through the LCD screen on the back. I hope he sees it. I take another photograph and invite him to look through the viewfinder. Nervously, he peers through the little square of glass, bewildered at the device. I click the shutter again, and this time he sees it: a picture of his own cows, on his own land, appearing on a miniature one-inch television out of thin air. My attempt at diplomacy works; he's completely mesmerized. His eyes open wide and, for the first time, a thin sliver of a smile appears across his crinkled face. He walks me over to the two cows.

"Ellos son enfermos," he says. "They are sick."

Alejandro strokes the cows gently, and I'm tempted to shoot this beautifully lit moment of a fragile farmer with his fragile cows but decide against it and take a picture with my mind instead. He has my trust, and I'm not jeopardizing that now. Chris is inside making pancakes for the family when we return. They've never eaten pancakes before, nor have they tasted Aunt Jemima syrup. As I take a seat on a small bench, the first thing I notice is the unmistakable emptiness of poverty – no trappings of a modern household whatsoever; no cup-boards, no framed pictures, barely any plates or cutlery with which to eat. The earthen floors are smooth, and shafts of light pierce through tiny holes in the walls, a mixture of hard-packed earth and straw made into thick bricks. Displayed most prominently upon a wooden shelf is a delicately carved crucifix and the dripping remnants of spent can-dles. A tangled heap of dirty blankets spread over a layer of brown hay serves as one large bed for the family of six.

It's a hard sight to take, the kind of poverty that plucks at the strings of our Western conscience. The value of our motorcycles and all of our gear is likely greater than the wealth they'll see in their humble lifetimes. A subsistence farmer in these parts makes two or three dol-lars a day, and our budget is ten times that. I feel embarrassed by it, almost ashamed. We do our best to not flaunt this wealth-on-wheels, but there are times when I feel the eyes of envy staring a hole through my chest. But with Alejandro there is no resentment. He's not holding his hand out and asking for anything from us. When it's time to leave, the family gathers around our loaded bikes. Alejandro is standing on the cement pad, mumbling to himself with two fresh corn cobs in his hands. *"Que Dios te bendiga,"* he says, pointing proudly to the sky with a cob in his right hand. He repeats it again and again, almost uncom-fortably so, still pointing to the sky like a televangelist preacher. *"Que Dios te bendiga.* (God bless you.)" At least we'll leave them with a mem-ory, I think. I wonder if, in years to come, they'll remember this brief encounter as much as we will.

Of the 13,271 kilometres we've travelled thus far, no road has produced as much of a challenge as today's rough-and-tumble stretch from Barillas to Nuevo Edén, a small mountain village in the heart of the Guatemalan Highlands. Our bikes sputter in the snappy chill of high altitude, switchbacking up a rock-filled mountain pass 8,000 feet above sea level. Pine-scented forested ridgelines bathed in swirling clouds of fog pull our eyelines to the distance, but we must remain focused – the road is changing constantly from soft dirt to hard, from jarring ruts to tight corners to narrow bridges, our bikes continually dodging pigs, dogs, roosters, chickens, goats, cows, horses and the odd farmer eking out enough sustenance for his family. While waiting for our bikes to catch their breath in the thinning air ,we hear someone calling at us from above.

"Hello!" they shout in English. "Hello, you come!"

Between a stand of pine trees, we follow the voices up a narrow pathway and are greeted by a young boy playing marbles in the dirt next to a small wooden house. His grandmother appears, not at all surprised that two gringos have suddenly walked off the road and into her smoke-filled kitchen. She wipes tears from her eyes, and the sweat from her forehead with the bottom of her shirt, revealing two saggy breasts that hang down to her belly button.

"We have oranges now," she says, "and some onions growing. The rest we can get from the village up the road... my husband is not here..." And on and on she goes, not really caring if we listen or not. She ducks back into the kitchen to stir whatever she's cooking in the deep blackened pot with a wooden spoon, and comes out again, wiping her eyes and forehead just the same as before. By now the little boy is trying to tune in a small black radio with round silver dials.

"You like rock?!" he says in English, rolling the *r* with perfection. "Sometimes I can get rock."

The secluded village of Nuevo Edén is the only preplanned destination on our entire voyage to South America. We've been invited on behalf of the Squamish Rotary Club to volunteer with a brief hands-on stint in building Casa Colibri (Hummingbird House, named after the hundreds of bright red hummingbirds that call these hills home). The Casa is a medical clinic that will serve Nuevo Edén as well as 22 surrounding villages.

Hacked out of the jungle between 100-foot trees dripping with flowering lianas, Nuevo Edén is home to exactly 25 families and 138 residents. Here, necessary medical assistance is almost unattainable, and for a woman in labour, a complicated pregnancy can quickly turn into an epic ordeal that involves a bone-jarring, uterus-bouncing, four-hour trip in the back of a four-by-four to the nearest hospital, in Barillas. If an emergency Caesarean is required, it can cost as much as US$700 – almost a full year's worth of work. Women in this area earn money pitching into the Indigenous textile economy, hand-making the strikingly colourful clothing worn by the country's Mayan population.

Christina and I must look ridiculous covered in mud from head to toe, but nonetheless we arrive to a hero's welcome, greeted by the Rotary liaison Pablo Salvador Antonio and most of the townsfolk, many of whom we'll get to know on a first-name basis. Pablo sends a boy to fetch the keys that unlock our wood-planked cabin: a round, rustic dwelling with wooden beds, a smooth concrete floor and a small attached kitchen with a gas stove and pots and pans hanging from nails on the wall. The setting sun includes an orchestra of bellowing howler monkeys, high-pitched whistles of tropical birds and a hundred barking dogs. Only when the consistent roar of cicadas takes over does the day's exhaustion give way to sleep.

Building materials for Casa Colibri have not yet arrived, so we turn our attention to the 33 students inside the wooden walls of the one-room school, teaching them some basic English words like *healthy*, *happy* and *clean*. Sadly, it's evident that Nuevo Edén is falling victim to the single-use plastic "sachet" economy; mindlessly discarded wrappers litter the community and surrounding roads, as they do in most of Guatemala. With the help of their teacher, Mira, and two village elders, we hatch a plan for tomorrow's class, a clean-up effort we call *Proyecto Basura*, the Garbage Project.

"A clean village is a happy village," Mira says at the start of class. "Today we will all take part in a group project. Each student will take a bag with them at recess and fill it with garbage collected around the village. The winning team will each receive a new notebook, and we will all help to make our village a happier place."

Eyes alight, they all seem committed to pitching in – jumping up and down, hugging each other, smacking palms together.

"Listo?" says Mira. "Are you ready? One... two... three... GO!"

The first students race into the soccer pitch, madly scooping up bits of plastic and rubbish, working in a frantic scramble before dashing back to their teammates all lined up in a row, high-fiving for the tag. Midway through the challenge, Mira looks over at us with an eyebrow raised as if to say, *I'm impressed with this kind of engagement.*

With 20 stuffed bags piled in a heap, the impact is clearly visible. Other villagers come to the school for a closer look. Men with unfathomably large loads of firewood strapped to their foreheads with tumplines drop their burdens to stare at the pile. "A clean village is a happy village," Pablo says to them. "I will make a sign the next time I am in town."

Like most yogis, Christina loves sharing her knowledge with others, and I can tell she is missing her students back home. Mira says they have group meetings to promote women's literacy and sees no reason why Christina can't teach them afterwards.

From Christina's Journal:

February 17th, 2005

I want to connect with them in ways that don't really need words. My Spanish isn't good enough to teach a full class, so I'll just get a feel for what their perception might be, and go from there. If they take anything away from it, I hope it's just that simple connection with one's own body and breath. Even with a really simple practice I feel like I accomplished what I wanted to do, not knowing what they would or wouldn't understand and knowing how it reflected in them. They were all very present, draped in their layers of skirts. It wasn't about pure movement or asana. It was an incredibly uplifting experience to watch them figure it out, whatever it meant to them individually. "We feel peace in our hearts," someone told me after class. She said they found it medicinal and enriching. I almost melted. That made me realize that I am on the right path to becoming a teacher.

On the last afternoon of our five-day stay, a group of village school-girls lead us up a muddy hillside, tidying up the trail with slashing machetes to proudly reveal a hidden lagoon, unbelievably blue and untouched by litter – a respite for the children to play away from the peering eyes of the adults. I think about pressing a pinch of Sean's ashes into their palms before they dive in, but relent. *Is that taboo or not? Do they believe in cremation?* Most are God-fearing Christians in these parts; who knows if their parents would appreciate, or understand, a stranger offering up the dust of his dead brother so it can dissolve into their sapphire-blue lagoon.

Instead, I drop some into my palm and grab Christina's hand, and together we run off a rickety wooden dock, fully clothed, into the lagoon amidst a roar of exuberant laughter. *They're rich beyond dollars*, I think to myself, listening to their joy bounce off the water.

The next morning every soul in the village comes by to wish us *buen viaje*. We didn't have the opportunity to help build the new clinic but hope we helped in some way. They're keen to pose for the camera so I shoot a few frames, and we spend the next 30 minutes in a swarm of hugs and gratitude before strapping on our helmets. I give Christina the ready-to-go thumbs up and I hear Mira say: "Namaste, Christina. The ladies want to thank you. They said they are going to practise breathing today."

FROM MORRIS, WITH LOVE

JULY 2005

Before the Journey began, I was most afraid of an unexpected encounter with a Central American gang, especially the notorious MS-13, or Mara Salvatrucha. Horror stories of the viciously cruel, tattoo-faced gangsters have painted a grim picture in the minds of many travellers, precisely the reason we'll steer clear away from Guatemala City and San Pedro Sula in Honduras, two of Central America's most violent cities. We know we'll need to be alert at all times. Never ride at night. Always stay together. Spending as much time as possible roaming the farms and villages of the dusty countryside will, we hope, be the best way to avoid danger.

As the miles click by, our ingrained, "civilized" obsession with time has begun to distort. We no longer care about the math behind hitting the road at a certain hour in order to cover x amount of distance for the day. I wake every day at six a.m., put some coffee on and go hunting for first-light pictures while Christina sleeps for another hour or practises yoga. We watch our own shadows grow longer as the afternoon sun drops, signalling that we should look for somewhere to camp. This simple routine allows for a stress-free environment within our relationship, and adds another welcome element of freedom into our lives, much like riding our bikes gives us the freedom to roam at will.

March 19, 2005. Cruising along the salty, rugged coastline of El Salvador, an unmarked trail leads us to a patch of manicured grass – a dream spot to camp for the night. A friendly *cuidador* can't let us stay, he says, "but the owners are coming soon, you can ask them."

An hour later, six young adults, the oldest maybe 21, pull up in a Volkswagen bus and invite us to join their Friday night fiesta. Even though it's my 33rd birthday, we feel like saying no. Setting up camp alone on this lush grass near the ocean is exactly what we need right now after many consecutive days being surrounded by people at almost every hour of the day – whether shopping for groceries or getting gas or getting lost on roads that aren't on our map. No matter how hard we try to escape the tentacles of civilization for our own sanity, even for just one night, there always seems to be a swarm of curious villagers who come by to visit at sunset and sunrise. We realize we're a curiosity travelling throughout their homelands, but we are craving some solitude right now. Nonetheless, we follow our young new friends through a wrought-iron gate and into an eight-bedroom, seven-bathroom seaside mansion perched 60 feet above the Pacific Ocean, with an elegant swimming pool and curved staircase spilling down into a large saltwater pool built into the rocks. The kids have brought nothing with them except for two turntables, a crate of vinyl records, and a keg of beer.

We're only a few years older than most of them, but I envy their youthful exuberance. They remind me of myself when I was the same age. Sean too. I became known as a party animal and drank alcohol, often to escape my fear of being myself and the fear of being judged. I loathed judgement so much that I vowed never to put someone in a place where they had to defend themselves – not physically, but from verbal barbs and bullying. When I was on the drink, my inhibitions would disappear. I'd become happy, outgoing, keen to make friends with anyone I met, whether or not they belonged in any idiotic social circle. But because of the lasting power of labels, I was still a party animal in the eyes of those from whom I most wanted respect. I wanted to shed that reputation, and when I began to travel as a solo backpacker I *could* be myself – nobody could judge me, because nobody knew who I was. I felt as though I could lead a second, anonymous life in a foreign country and began to understand why expats wanted to be expats. By the time we pushed off on this Journey, I felt freed from the shackles of judgement and taught myself to let go.

And let go we all do tonight: dancing double-fisted to the thumping beats of remixed Latino cumbia, jumping in the pool with our clothes on, and devouring frozen cheese pizzas at two a.m. while being serenaded by the "Happy Birthday" song, with a lit joint serving as the only candle in my "cake." We wake up hungover, but the kids leave abruptly, inviting us to enjoy the house "for as long as you want." This generosity comes amidst a cascade of other offers to stay in different parts of the country at their wealthy parents' vacation homes: a summer cottage on the shores of Lago de Coatepeque, where we kayak and jet ski and lounge in the sun, drinking cold beer from buckets; then further north amongst the pine forests in a small log cabin on a coffee plantation; and finally in the heart of San Salvador, where we arrive before dusk at the home of Eduardo Kriete, whose family owns Taca Airlines, the flagship carrier of El Salvador. When Vera, one of the beach-house kids, introduces us to her father, Eduardo, he's casually playing with six fully grown lions in his backyard. Eduardo was once a trophy hunter who suddenly changed his "barbaric ways" after seeing the dead carcass of a lion lying next to him, shot by one of his other trophy-hunting friends at a game park in Kenya.

"I have rescued them from an inhumane circus in Honduras," he says before even shaking our hands or looking at us, his eyes fixated on every movement of the felines prowling around the property. "We plan to open a 600-acre wildlife sanctuary soon, so they can roam free. For now, this is the only place we can keep them safe."

The curious lions come in for a closer look and start licking Christina's face from behind the chain link fence. I know it will be quite some time, if ever, before my feet touch African soil again, so I'll savour this moment for now.

Central America's dusty roads take us from one coast to the next – into the lives of welcoming people no matter rich or poor, and into the hands of one incredible experience after the next: scuba diving on the Caribbean island of Utila in Honduras, climbing volcanoes in Nicaragua, and learning to surf along Costa Rica's stunning beaches. After eight months on the road, we're due for a pause in the action to give Lucky and Lucinda a rest and to meet up with family – a surprise encounter with Uncle Ed, Auntie Cathy and our cousin Lee (they didn't know we were coming, so we tracked them down) – that results in two spoiled nights at an all-inclusive resort, getting pampered with fine dining and bottles of wine, capping it off with US$300 in winnings on the blackjack tables. It feels both luxurious and alien to suddenly live this lifestyle, but after losing Sean, I will never turn down a chance to connect with family. And $300 will last us at least a week on the road. We pull away from the resort refreshed and reinvigorated to get back to the Journey.

In the shacks-on-stilts town of Almirante, in Panama, we consult with the local fire chief, who agrees to look after our bikes while we explore the sleepy islands of Bocas del Toro. After haggling in the bay with a stubborn teenaged water-taxi captain, we're dropped off an hour south of town at a place called Polo Beach – a pocket of pristine Caribbean paradise on nearby Isla Bastimentos. Once on shore, we meet the beach's namesake owner, Mr. Polo, a tousled old local as salty and foul-mouthed as a pirate. He's wearing ripped board shorts and speaks loudly with a thick Creole/Garifuna accent, peppering select Spanish words here and there for emphasis. Local legend has it that Polo left the spoils of civilization and settled on this secluded stretch of sand in 1968. He started planting fruit seeds and herbs, living off the land and sea and bartering with locals while driving himself self-avowedly mad from a hazardous tropical concoction of rainy-season solitude, bouts of binge drinking and run-ins with the law. Our boatman said Polo could feed us, and we politely ask him about lunch.

"*Teléfono llegó*," he shouts loudly to no one in particular.

The phone has arrived?

He repeats it again, pointing to a fly buzzing around his ear.

"You see dat?" he says excitedly. "Dat me *teléfono*. When dee fly come 'round, dem come 'round. We got *pollo* comin', we got tahtle comin!"

Less than ten minutes later, a few locals arrive in a fibreglass boat and unload everything Polo mentioned: ganja, beer, cigarettes, six or seven fresh fish, four dead chickens, a bag of salt, a few onions and one live turtle. Polo does a funny little booty-shuffle and lets out a gracious belly laugh.

"Me tole you we got everyting comin'! Hah-hah-hah-hah!"

Polo and his buddies line up the beers and knock them down – all day long. Exhausted from day-drinking and enduring Polo's drunken howling, we retreat to our tent to pass out after sunset. In the morning, we can clearly see that Polo is operating with two distinct personalities. One minute he's Mr. Happy Rasta-Man with music flowing through his heart and beer through his veins, a living legend in the eyes of those around him. The next, he's a racist blowhard, stomping around his kitchen, negativity and antagonism boiling through his veins.

"*El hombre negro es un* fokkin' *perro*," he says, over and over again while trying to start the morning breakfast fire. "The Black man is a fucking dog, I say! I savage Ras man. I savage Ras man. Me no wahn dem fokkin' *perro* come up 'ere."

Two hours later, he's all smiles and laughter again, half-pissed and hunched over a plastic tub of mashed coconut, making a batch of oil. He lends us two masks and snorkels for the underwater dream world in front of us, and we escape to the water, gliding over shallow reefs teeming with barracudas, stingrays, starfish and a giant schools of silver minnows sparkling like a thousand shining swords drawn from their scabbards at once. Polo invites us into his compound for dinner, laying on the charm as thick as his delicious fish stew.

"Me like dem Canadians. Dem good people. And beautiful like she," he says with a wink in Christina's direction.

It's hard not to like Polo. I can tell we'll remember him for a long time. "Happiest man in the world, me am. Beer and ganja all day long.

Dis *my* place, dis *my* beach. Nobody gwahn fuck wit me 'ere." And no one does, aside from the occasional (and implausibly reliable) telephone-fly.

Back on the mainland, we hit Panama City in search of new tires and a few random parts. At Moto World we not only find good rubber, we also discover Morris, an Indigenous Guna man who stands at four and a half feet on his tiptoes and is possibly the friendliest human in Panama. Once he catches wind that we're trying to skirt around the roadless Darién Gap to Colombia via the San Blas Islands, his eyes light up like a torch.

"Maybe you can visit my village?" he says through a translator. "My island is called Manitupo. I am from there."

He gives our bikes a thorough wash and shine, then draws a map inside a tattered school exercise book. "This is a map of the islands. You can take a *cayuco* to find my island, they will know how to reach it. And please, give this to my mother," he says, handing us a handwritten letter folded into a small square.

I take the letter but don't have the heart to tell him the chances of us finding his mother in a remote archipelago of 378 islands are slim to none. Secretly, though, I hope Morris's Hail Mary will be caught. *Wouldn't that be cool?*

The starting point on his map is Colón, a putrid port town that reeks of squalor and neglect. Trash spewn all over the streets makes for a city centre entirely devoid of colour and character, except for the rancid slurry of god-knows-what flowing like brown lava down rusted cement gutters. The whole place seems spidered together with a tangled mess of overhead power lines. It is, undeniably, the darkest shitstain on our Central American map. Calling it the asshole of Panama would be a compliment. Coincidentally, we'd read a few days ago about a week-long ferry from Colón to Cartagena, and head to the docks under a downpour to ask around.

"Yes, there is a ferry, but you're about two years late," says a security guard on a bicycle, laughing amongst his circle of peers.

Someone else mentions a gringo-owned sailboat that takes motorcycle travellers along the same route, but we find out minutes later it's travelling in the opposite direction; we'll have to wait at least three weeks until the next sailing. Christina pulls out the map, and one of the guards points to Miramar, a town at the southern end of the road, half a day's ride away.

"They have many merchant boats going from island to island. Ask the locals. Maybe you can find a boat big enough for the bikes?"

It's our only hope. Later the next afternoon, we find ourselves nervously loading Lucky and Lucinda into an oversized canoe-like vessel, long enough for 20 passengers and deep enough for the bikes to lie snugly against the gunwales. At the captain's orders, I push off from the dock, leaving the mainland exactly nine months after saying goodbye to our life in Canada. Our fate now rests with our plan to hitchhike from island to island through the territory of the Guna Yala People of the San Blas archipelago. I hope Sean is with us now. Motoring slowly through the northern end of the archipelago, the captain snakes his way through palm-filled islets under the hot Caribbean sun. South America is only days away, a continent neither Christina nor I have ever set foot on. But our next ride isn't as tranquil. After a worrisome three days stranded on Isla Porvenir with almost no boat traffic, a dugout canoe, no more than 15 feet long, pulls up near a dock on the beach. It seems much too small, but with fingers crossed we beg and plead with the captain to take us further south. He seems dead set against the idea when he sees the size of the bikes and all our gear.

"*No puedo*," he says. "*Muy pesado. No puedo.*" I cannot. It's too heavy.

He finally gives in after three hours of expensive negotiations; diesel isn't cheap on the islands. Together, we muscle the motos in a V-shaped arrangement, hoping to obtain perfect balance, then his 5-year-old kid pushes us away from the rickety wooden dock with his bare feet. There are no life jackets on board, but I reason if he's bringing his kid with him, we'll be safe. The little *cayuco* vessel holds its own in the rolling swell until the wake of a passing boat throws us into a wobbling fit. To think, it could all be over in the blink of an eye. In this instant, I feel terrible for having negotiated so hard, for having put him and his son in jeopardy. *Would it have been so hard to wait another day for another, bigger boat?* While bailing the boat out with a cut-in-half plastic bottle, I find myself saying a quick prayer to Sean. I look back at the captain – his son wedged between his knees – who's as calm as a sunset, scanning the horizon without concern.

Our next hitched ride is aboard the *Ocean King*, a merchant boat captained by a beer-bellied, barefooted, tank-topped gentleman by the name of Bernilissio.

"You call me Bernie, amigo. I lived for ten years in Estados Unidos, so I learned English there, as a kid. But I want to know more about Panama, my country, and I don't go back for long time. Now my life is this," he says, fanning his arms out at the ocean in front of him.

The Guna People have a history of mercantilism, selling goods through family-owned boats and shops, and Bernie is doing his part, "for the last 41 years," to keep the tradition alive. His boat holds all manner of goods, from frozen chickens packed into a chest freezer to bars of soap, toothpaste, cases of beer and ice cream treats that are a hot-ticket item with the island kids. He charges us a modest fee for room and board, and we set up our tent on the fibreglass rooftop just in the nick of time. Within minutes, the sky cracks open with brilliant flashes of white lightning, unleashing a downpour of biblical proportions. We're shocked that after the 20-minute rainfall, our new $25 Walmart tent is bone-dry inside (bonus: no ants chewing through it). We show the map to Bernie, hoping that he'll recognize Morris's home island.

"We will not pass by," he says without hesitation.

Flashbacks of Sean in the hospital are with me all the time but intensify in the middle of July every year. Since he died, I've always reserved July 19 as a solo-mission day; a day to reconnect with my brother, to talk out loud into the open so he can hear my voice, to seek seclusion and complete immersion in nature with no signs of humanity – no power lines, no people, no roads, no buildings, no light pollution. This July 19, however, that is not possible. We're stuck on an island so small it can be circumnavigated on foot in less than 20 minutes. I manage to find some privacy in a nearby coconut grove where, alone and lying on my back on top of a fallen palm frond, I see Sean. Only this time he's a pelican, circling overhead against an azure sky before dive-bombing headfirst into the sea for his breakfast. Then another pelican joins in a graceful airshow. *Typical Sean, always looking for a girl to chase.* The thought brings a smile to my face, and I rustle myself up to join Christina for a late breakfast. This day, and this remaining grief, is never easy, but with her around it doesn't feel so hard. I couldn't imagine doing this with anyone else.

Two days later, dusk chases the last glow of sun into the sea when we arrive on yet another island. Bernie expertly moors the boat next to a long wooden pier. He pokes his head up top and announces that we're in Manitupo.

"Hey, check the map," I say to Christina. "Isn't this Morris's island?"

"Yes it is. Holy shit! Bernie, you said we weren't going to pass by here?"

"I wasn't, but I change my mind because big business here. But I cannot take you more far."

"Gracias, Bernie, esta bien," says Christina. "Is it okay if we stay on the boat tonight?"

"No, but you stay with my cousin."

As we're unloading the bikes, a pack of smiling kids swarms us like honeybees leaving a hive. I quickly pull out my camera to document the hysteria; some are touching our skin and hair, others groping at our bikes and helmets, while most of them are scrambling over one another, pushing each other's heads back to get as close to the camera as possible. Amongst the crowd, we spot the unmistakable faces of ten albino children. It's hard to peel our eyes away from them, markedly out of place with their pink skin and golden heads of hair, but we later learn they are pure Guna Yala, born and raised in these sun-drenched islands. Anthropologists report that the Guna may have the highest albino birth rate on Earth. In Guna mythology, albinos were once treated as a special race that would rescue people from disaster, especially during lunar eclipses, when they would climb to rooftops to frighten away a jaguar or dragon believed to be devouring the moon. This mythology gave rise to the term "children of the moon," and over the past few centuries, albinos have oscillated between esteemed social status and outright rejection.

The moon hasn't yet risen over the Manitupo dock, but most of the kids have left and the mayhem is settling down, so Bernie walks us over to his cousin's place, a rundown wooden house on stilts with a "long-drop" toilet situated directly above the ocean. Surprisingly, the water isn't shit-brown but is as clear as the shots of vodka that Bernie's cousin starts pouring the moment he meets us. A bottle of vodka isn't seen very often in these parts, but hosting travelling foreigners is a big deal. Soon, the music kicks in and the tiny house is packed with all ages and all eyes upon us, until the diesel in the generator runs out and the party dies as fast as it started.

In the morning, we hear whispers of Morris's name and the words *la ciudad*, a colloquial island term for anyone who has left the islands and is now living in Panama City. Before breakfast, we've probably shaken hands with 100 people, each of them extending a warm and grateful greeting along the narrow dirt paths of their village. Eventually we're taken to a cluster of grass huts where a small crowd of people is mulling about. A young albino girl, maybe 12, wearing a pink taffeta dress with a shiny white ribbon in her hair, grabs Christina's arm and gently guides her to a small wooden stool, next to an elderly Guna lady adorned head to toe in colourful beads, with her hands folded neatly in her lap.

"This is Morris mother, María Ángel," she says in English.

"What? We actually *found* her?" Christina says, her eyes and mouth agape in awe.

Tenderly, she passes Morris's letter to María Ángel, who accepts it timidly in her hands. It's clear she can't read Spanish, so the albino girl, whose name is Margarita, comically snatches the letter and starts reading, scanning over the inconsequential details before translating the last paragraph to Morris's frail mother, who's still clutching Christina's forearm.

"Hello, my dear mother. I had to leave Manitupo. I am living in the city. I am okay. I will try and return to my home one day before you die. I love you. Morris."

The shocking presence of two white foreigners delivering news of her long lost son's whereabouts via a handwritten letter by her son himself is almost too much to comprehend. And we're still in shock that we really did find Morris's mother. Tears roll down her cheeks, and she whispers something that neither of us can understand.

"She say no see her son in many years," Margarita says. "She is sad, but also happy because Morris not die."

We leave María Ángel to rest, and we return in the morning to say goodbye. Sobbing and holding on to Christina's arm, she rocks back and forth in her chair, staring into the sky.

"*Por favor dile a mi Morris que vuelva.* (Please tell my Morris to come back.)"

After two more days and two more boats, we're inching closer to Colombia, and the words *peligroso* and *drogas* start popping up as we ask around town for a final ride to Turbo, where we'll get stamped into our first South American country.

"The water is too rough and the bikes are too heavy," says the water-taxi captain on the shores of Panama's last isolated village. This *after* we laboriously loaded our bikes from the shore into his empty boat.

"It's only one hour," we plead. "You're going that way anyway. Please take us!"

Although not impressed, he agrees, shaking his head at the unwanted proposition. Under a dark grey sky, the water looks black and boiling, like a witch's poisonous potion. A huge rolling swell rocks the boat from side to side, and the ocean comes pouring in over the shallow gunwales. I bail water but see that Christina is quickly being overtaken by the nauseous whirl of seasickness. Then the rain comes pounding down. I bail faster. The wind smacks splashing water into our faces. I bail even harder. The captain doesn't even flinch, nor does he say a word, but I know he's nervous... and so are we. Finally, the gale subsides and we catch a glimpse of shining lights in Turbo's tiny harbour, as welcome a sight as one can imagine.

– 12 –

THE NATURE IS PRETTY
COOL HERE

AUGUST 1999

I'm seated on a wooden bench in my grade-school gymnasium, except I'm an adult, and it's my turn to take the stage at Sean's memorial. I'm the last one to speak, and all goes well until I realize I haven't brought anything to place in the casket. I dig, frantically, into my pockets while saying my final words. My fingers find a Canadian quarter shaped like a teardrop, so I lean in to place it inside the casket, my final goodbye.

Suddenly Sean blinks at me! His arms start twitching and moving as if he's about to awaken. "Look, look!" I'm crying hysterically. "Oh my god, he's alive!"

I turn to the crowd. My family, Sean's friends – they're crying too, but then, nonchalantly, everyone begins murmuring in unison, "Oh, it's just zombification." Like it's nothing, like it's normal. I turn back… Sean looks perfect; his face no longer swollen, his skin not that pallid yellow I remember from the hospital. He seems fit and strong and happy. The next thing I know, we're now alone, the gym is empty save for me and Sean's now-dead-again body, which is somehow now lying outside the coffin on the polished gym floor. "Somebody help!" I'm shouting. "I can't lift him back into the coffin all by myself!"

Pat comes in and helps, then leaves once my brother is back in his coffin. Suddenly Sean opens his eyes again, but this time he's awake, bewildered, and very much alive. He looks straight at me and says, "Thanks for the good run, Todd. Don't worry about me, man, the nature is pretty cool here."

Startled, I clutch his right hand. "Thank you so much for everything, Sean. Thank you for our time in Africa, thanks for being my brother. Did you see the slide show in Rossland? Were you atop KC with all your friends?"

The very next moment, Mom enters the gym and almost faints when she hears Sean speak. "Hi, Mom, everything is great," he says, so calmly. "I'm having a nice time."

Next, Brad walks in, then Grandma, and I rush them straight over to see Sean. He acknowledges their presence and says a few words. Grandma keeps repeating, "It's me, Sean, it's Grandma!"

"He knows it's you, Grandma, he knows."

"Can't you just hop out of there and come with us?" she asks, peering down at him, teary-eyed but joyous.

"No, I can't, but make sure they don't nail this thing shut!"

"Okay, man." I'm laughing and crying at the same time as I place the teardrop quarter in his hand. "Just use this to get yourself out."

Then I'm driving my mom home, and when we arrive, my Auntie Fran is walking up the driveway, which is surrounded by huge industrial-sized dump trucks in the neighbour's yard.

"How was the funeral?" Fran asks.

Mom doesn't answer, just turns to me and says, "We should get back to the coffin before they bury it."

When I woke up, it felt like the inside of my soul was set free. The guilt was finally gone. I tried hard to fall back asleep and re-enter the dream, but I couldn't. Instead I reached for the night table lamp and instantly wrote down every detail on a manila envelope that held a stack of Sean's postcards. Since that day by the creek when I spotted the two birds chasing each other, I had been searching for another sign – something, anything – to let me know he was okay. Since he died, I had wanted that moment of connection, even hoping I'd see his

The Marchuk Farm at Flat Lake, Alberta, 40 years in the making.
A true testament to the immigrant homesteader's unflinching
spirit to survive. Circa 1982.

Rita, Helen, Edmund, John and Wanda Marchuk, circa 1978.

Brad, Todd and Sean Lawson on the family farm. Spring 1980.

Michael and Rita Lawson, Edmonton, Alberta, 1969.

Me, launching off the infamous "washing-machine" ramp
in the Umbach Road cul-de-sac. May 1979.

Sean was a master in the art of immersive adventure travel.
Phnom Penh, 1995.

If there was some kind of adrenalin fix to be had, Sean would find it.
Rooftop bus surfing, Nepal, 1994.

Sean Lawson, Open Class Enduro Champion at the Mild Seven
Cambodia Motocross Championships. November 1998.

After ripping around the pine forests and mud puddles in Sabie,
South Africa, taken just a week before Sean went to ride with the angels.

On the rim of Namibia's spectacular Fish River Canyon, Africa's largest canyon.
April 1999. We spent three nights and four days hiking into the canyon,
and got completely lost trying to find our way back to the top,
only to be saved by some other hikers.

Sean in his absolute element. He lived and breathed for moments of unbridled
freedom like this. Somewhere along the coastline of Mozambique, July 1999.

Experimenting with double exposures on slide film.
Sabie, South Africa. July 1999.

It rained non-stop from our first night in Washington State
all the way down Highway 101 to southern California.

It was a challenge to get a good action photograph of both of us
riding at the same time. Thanks to our friend Roland "Rolifrijoli" Franze
for this one. Tikal, Guatemala. March 2005.

The stoic young boys of Nuevo Eden village.
Guatemalan Highlands. March 2005.

"Despite the language barrier, these K'iche'-speaking women were listening so intently to my imperfect Spanish that I knew some were really grasping the theory of yoga I was explaining to them from my heart." Nuevo Eden, Guatemala. February 2005.

Teaching English to the local students at Nuevo Eden, Guatemela Highlands.

We're still in touch with the Trejos family today.
One of many families that took care of us on our journey.
Isla Ometepe, Nicaragua. April 2005.

Claudette (with baby Abraham), Candylee, and Gabriel out for
a Sunday stroll. Crooked Tree Village, Belize. February 2005.

High-fives from schoolkids were a very common occurrence throughout rural Latin America. San Isidro, Nicaragua. April 2005.

"Me like dem Canadians. Dem good peeple. And beautiful like she."
Polo during one of his happy times. Bocas del Toro, Panama. March 2005.

Placing your trust in locals is critical to any overlander's survival. Panama's Darién Gap is a roadless, impenetrable jungle that we had to find a way around in order to get to Colombia. This was one of the scarier adventures of the entire

journey through the Americas, and the smallest boat we placed our trust
in to get us to the next island. The fact that this captain had his five-year-old
with him sealed the deal for us.

Our needle-in-a-haystack adventure to find Maria Angel (Morris's mom) was a success! Manitupo, Panama. March 2005.

Julito and his wife Isabela, proud stewards of the Arhuaco territory.
Nabusimake, Colombia. August 2005.

"Holding a steady gaze on top of the world. I felt like I was on the moon."
Christina. Mt. Roraima summit, Venezuela. September 2005.

"Every rustled leaf, snapped twig, and random jungle sound seems to us like
a hungry creature ready to climb into the tent and crawl on our faces.
Sleep is rarely deep." Somewhere in the Suriname. October 2005.

We were continually surprised by the abundance of diversity
the Amazon River kept delivering.

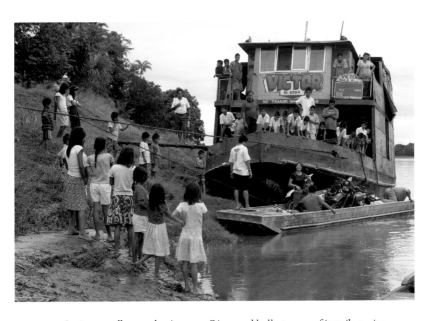

Saying goodbye to the Amazon River and hello to one of its tributaries,
the Rio Napo in Ecuador. Moving Lucky and Lucinda from boat to boat
happened ten times on our 35-day Amazon voyage.

Freezing cold and colourful — these two adjectives describe much
of our two months along the rural roads of the Andes.
Somewhere in Peru, December 2005.

Engulfed by the splendour of the Ecuadorian Andes.

Sometimes, spending all day every day with your partner is hard.
Sometimes it's easy. Salar de Uyuni, Bolivia. January 2006.

Undoubtedly one of the most incredible places in the world to ride a motorcycle.
It took two solid days to clean the caked salt off our bikes and clothes.
Salar de Uyuni, Bolivia. January 2006.

Our friend Herman in his element. Bora tribal territory,
Amazon River, Peru. November 2005.

Just one of the hundreds of "charcos" (mud puddles) we had to charge through
during one of the most physically demanding days in all of our travels.
We dropped the bikes a total of 13 times in just 70 kilometres.
General Garay, Paraguay. January 2006.

This was actually somewhat of a dry section en route to the Paraguayan border. El Chaco, Bolivia, January 2006.

Paraguayan mudbath. General Garay, Paraguay. January 2006.

Just reaching the start of Patagonia was a milestone in itself. You could spend
a lifetime here and never set foot in the same place twice. April 2006.

A proud moment for us. Our accomplishment called for a hand-painted sign.
Farellones, Chile. May 2006.

Christina running down the same dune that me and Sean did in 1999.
Retracing some of our steps and tire tracks from that first trip flooded me
with so many great memories. Sossusvlei, Namibia. April 2008.

Wild camping at its finest. Before darkness came we had our bikes perfectly
pointed towards the road in the distance in case we had to make a hasty escape
from any wild animals at night. Seems a bit silly, until you hear how loud
African animals are at night and how close they came to our tent.
Botswana, May 2008.

I'm grateful to have learned the art of photography, to remember people and moments like this. Zambia, April 2008.

A daily occurrence every time we stopped in Burundi. We were only granted
a three-day transit visa, so we didn't have much time to linger, but when
we did the crowds would swoop in and surround us. We loved it.
Kigoma, Burundi. September 2008.

Turkana tribeswomen. Beaded jewellery is highly valued and is believed to be a
symbol of wealth. These colourful necklaces are made up of thousands of beads,
and people never remove them other than when mourning or in an event
of ill health. Northern Kenya, September 2008.

Christina, stopped in her tracks and surrounded by a sea of extremely valuable one-humped dromedary camels. Northern Kenya, September 2008.

A rough, challenging day as we made our way through this sparse desert wasteland on the way to Ethiopia. Too many punctures, too much heat resulted in too many swear words. Marsabit, Kenya. September 2008.

"This encounter really did make me feel like a strange woman from
a faraway land, here in the middle of nowhere. This man did not expect the
person behind the helmet to be a woman. I could just tell by the way he held
my hand and shook it a little longer just to verify what he was witnessing."
Tanzania, August 2008.

I was so tired all I wanted to do was charge through this puddle,
but Msekwa and his passenger (pictured) convinced me otherwise.
"Is sometimes many deep holes," he said. Lake Eyasi, Tanzania. August 2008.

Dennis ("Mr. Each and Everything") and friends gather around to watch us make dinner over an open fire. They would stay until sundown and return at sunrise just to spend time with us and gawk at our camping gear. Kabale, Uganda. September 2008.

We hung out at the front of the barge to escape the noise of the engines at the stern, and to enjoy the breeze — a much-needed respite from the intense heat of Sudan. Nile River, Sudan. November 2008.

"I thank you for coming here, to our village," said Joseph, the white-haired elder. "We have been blessed by God. We cannot forget you. We shall all pray for your journey and we hope you will return one day."
Kabale, Uganda. September 2008.

The entire net distribution exercise in Northern Uganda was meticulously well organized. To say we were impressed would be a massive understatement.
Maracha-Terego District, Uganda. December 2008.

Bittersweet smiles on one of our very last days in Africa.
Proud and grateful to have helped in the malaria prevention efforts in Africa,
but sad to leave this continent and our life-changing experiences behind.
Arua, Uganda. December 2008.

ghost. Finally he had reached out through the vivid netherworld of a mind-blowing dream. Sean had come to tell me everything was okay.

Don't worry about me, man, the nature is pretty cool here.

After hearing those words, I felt like I could get my life back on track.

Less than a week later, I escorted my mom, clutching my arm, down a red-carpeted aisle so she could marry the new love of her life, Patrick William Maguire, who had also been widowed just two years previous. Finding each other allowed them the freedom to live a new life together. In Africa, they'd spoken of possibly cancelling the wedding, but Lorraine Ibbotson, Dr. Debbie's mom, convinced them otherwise. "No matter when you have the wedding, Sean won't be there. Sean will not be there whether you get married in three weeks or three years. And he would definitely not want you to postpone the wedding."

But the honeymoon would have to wait. We held Sean's memorial service two weeks after the wedding, in Edmonton. Knowing his story would be better told in pictures, I had prepared a slideshow of our African adventure, together with a collection of Sean's photographs from around the world – 29 countries, 29 years. I knew Sean wouldn't have wanted it to feel like a funeral, he'd want everyone to know who he *really* was and what he loved about the world. Many in the crowd couldn't believe the places he'd been to and the things he'd done. The outpouring of condolences felt good in the moment, but I soon found myself wallowing in a deep pool of self-pity. I knew they were simply trying to provide love and warmth, but I began to resent the sadness that people had placed on me, in spite of the relief that crazy dream had brought me.

After the ceremony, I flew to Houston, Texas, to see Brad, who was three days removed from an extensive surgical procedure that involved plates and screws to fuse his spine together. It made my heart hurt all over again to see him writhing in pain in a hospital bed. Not only had his oldest brother just died, he had been unable to travel for Sean's memorial service *or* Mom's wedding. It seemed such a cruel twist of fate, and I couldn't do anything to help his physical state. When he was released from hospital, I set up a screen in his bedroom and brought our African adventure to him, an old-school slide show projected against his bedroom wall. I placed Sean's Nyami Nyami (the

Zambezi river god known to protect people) around Brad's neck. Sean and I had each bought the small wooden carvings for one another in Zimbabwe after our epic day on the river, and I wanted Brad to have this piece of our adventure, and our bond. We reminisced about childhood memories of playing field hockey in the park behind our house in Stony Plain and climbing roofs on the farm.

"Todd, was he in pain when he died?" Brad asked.

"No, he was just scared. He was in really good hands, and he didn't suffer."

"Thanks for being there with him. I don't think Mom would've been able to deal with it had he died alone."

I stayed with Brad for ten days, enough time for me to share many of the memories of our adventure, to reminisce about our childhood, and to soak up the presence of the only brother I had left. When the time came for me to head back to reality, Brad was at least able to walk me to the airport gate. I didn't know when I'd see him again, but I knew our time together would help him heal in both body and mind.

– 13 –

INTO THE HEART
OF THE WORLD

NABUSIMAKE, COLOMBIA • August 2005

*"Maybe freedom really is nothing left to lose. You had it once
in childhood, when it was okay to climb a tree, to wipe out on your
bike, to get hurt. The spirit of risk gradually takes its leave.
It follows the wild cries of joy and pain down the wind, through
the hedgerow, growing even fainter. What was that sound?
That was life calling to us, the one that was vigorous
and undefended and curious."*

PETER HELLER, *HELL OR HIGH WATER*

Not knowing what to expect as the days unfold opens up a whole new world of spontaneity that whizzes past our helmeted heads. Surrendering to what's on the other side of the unknown delivers us our most cherished prize – unbound freedom, an intangible reward that fuels our drive to keep going.

We never have to catch a bus or hail a cab and can easily avoid the gringo trail, letting Lucky and Lucinda take us on a magic carpet ride to destinations full of wonder and surprise. We owe much to the engineers and road builders who've built the thousands of miles of road we travel upon, twisting lines on the landscape that open a new realm every single day: different people, strange new surroundings, new food and drink, new challenges. Without this tangled mass of roads, we would never be where we are, some 15,000 kilometres from home, having the time of our lives. Heads turn when we roll into a new town with our worn and dusty saddlebags draped over the sides of our tired bikes that have been battling the heat of the Americas for over ten months. But as the days march on, it feels like we need to find more balance between the Journey and reality, between being a couple and having our own personal freedoms. It's not all sunshine and roses, and we are both craving something up high in the mountains to escape this oppressive coastal heat that is, amongst other things, taking a toll on our relationship.

A gentle soul named Javier, a photocopy repair technician whom we meet at a Cartagena supermarket, invites us to use his place while we organize our affairs for the next leg of the Journey. His house is a modest two-bedroom cinder block home painted mint green, and he happens to have an extra bed for us to sleep on. I unfold our map in the bedroom with a rotating fan whizzing at full power three feet from our sweating heads while Christina reads *One River* by Canadian ethnobotanist/author Wade Davis.

"Just beyond the city to the southeast, however, lies a world apart," Davis writes. "The Sierra Nevada de Santa Marta, the highest coastal mountain range on earth. The peoples of the Sierra Nevada fled the onslaught of the Spanish conquistadors and settled into seclusion in the Sierra Nevada, where their ways have remained largely unchanged for 500 years. They consider their purpose in life to be the care and nurturing of the planet, and they regard themselves as the Heart of the World."

The Heart of the World? How could we *not* go?

We learn that the Sierra Nevada de Santa Marta isn't quite connected to the Andes range but is rather a somewhat miniature version of Earth, home to nearly every ecosystem on the planet: glaciers, tundra, alpine lakes, deserts, tropical rainforests, wetlands and coral reefs. The

crown jewel in the range is Pico Cristóbal Colón, a 5770-metre summit and the fifth-most prominent peak in the world. We can't afford
a guided expedition to the summit but are still keen to hike for a few
days throughout this mini-Earth. We ask around town for recommen-
dations with not much luck, until we meet Cesar, the owner of a cute
little red-and-white guest house called Posada Bello. He greets us with
a jovial smile and shoots a keen eye towards Lucky and Lucinda.

"My name is Cesar. Is okay take moto ride?" he asks, pointing at my
bike. He reminds me of Burt Reynolds, only much taller, with a big
gold belt buckle hiding under a beer gut and a friendly smile shining
through a set of silver-capped teeth – definitely *de rigueur* in this part
of the world.

"Sure, *cómo no?*" I say. I've only known him for 30 seconds. *What
could go wrong?*

He returns minutes later, his beaming grill fronting a head of
swept-back hair, and buys us a beer. His Spanish is so muddled we
spend the next hour nodding our heads and saying *no entiendo* over a
plate of empanadas and french fries. I'm not sure he understands that
we're looking for information on a hike into the mountains. His wife,
Margarita, emerges from the kitchen, sliding into translator mode.

"Tomorrow you can go up mountain," she says. "You take the four-
by-four to Pueblo Bello, and after is Nabusimake village. There you
will meet my friend Omar. He will take you. No problem. Many times
he climb."

"Can we ride our bikes to the village?"

"No. The road is rough. *Very* rough. And rainy season now, so even
more worse. It's much too dangerous for moto… the road is very
strong and many rain."

Do we take the advice with a grain of salt and go ourselves, or is it legit?
Sometimes it's hard to know what to do. If we'd followed the worrisome advice of everyone we'd met along the way, we wouldn't have
covered much ground. For many villagers and rural farmers, life beyond a 100-mile radius might as well be another planet. Uncertainty creates fear, and they pass that fear along to us. Our intuition, by
this point, is a finely sharpened tool. We did successfully evade some

dodgy Mexican bandits in Acapulco and were almost ripped off by a swift-handed money changer in Nicaragua, but both times we felt something was amiss and walked away before it was too late. This time we decide to trust the local knowledge.

At seven a.m. the next day, a feisty old lady swats a leg-tethered chicken clean off the bench seat of a four-by-four to make room for us in the back. The scraggly bird flaps his wings frantically, sending feathers flying into the crowded truck's cab. She grabs our heavy packs off our shoulders amid much laughter from the rest of the passengers, and flops them down next to a big black pig in the middle. I can't tell if she's half-drunk or just putting on a show, but we roll with it and sit down. A row of Indigenous ladies cloaked in thick white cotton dresses sit quietly on the opposite bench seat, each with at least 20 beaded necklaces dangling from her neck. They're staring at us intently, holding patterned bags on their laps, foreheads beading with sweat. The old lady breaks the awkward silence by slapping the pig on his arse, as if it's the signal for the driver to begin the journey. Next to me, an elderly Arhuaco man scrapes a stick against a small gourd, his *poporo*, like he's sharpening a knife. He dips the stick into the *poporo* – a small device that stores lime made from burnt and crushed shells – and when he pulls it out, the end of the stick looks like it's been dipped in chalk. He then slides it in his mouth and grabs a wad of coca leaves, ramming them into the side of his right cheek with a green-stained thumb.

It seems as though Cesar and his silver teeth were telling the truth. The red-earth road is pocked with massive slippery ruts that keep sucking the Jeep in every 20 minutes, creating an almost metronomic routine: unload everyone, push Jeep out of rut, keep going. When we arrive in Nabusimake, sacred territory of Los Arhuacos, Omar is waiting for us underneath a copse of giant eucalyptus trees, chatting on a flip-phone with a great wad of coca leaves bulging through his cheek. Aside from the driver, he's the only one dressed in Western clothes.

"*Lo siento,*" he says calmly, sliding the phone into the pocket of his beige slacks. "But you cannot climb the bigger mountains."

"Why not, *señor?*" I respond, feigning disappointment.

"Seventeen army soldiers were killed last night by FARC rebels in another village close to here, so it is prohibited to climb anywhere past this point. But here you are safe."

FARC (the Revolutionary Armed Forces of Colombia) is the country's largest guerrilla rebel group, funded by cocaine, kidnapping and extortion.

"Thank you, sir," I say. "Is it okay if we stay in the village?"

"Yes, but you must obtain permission from the Chief. I will take you to the home of your hosts now. We can walk."

The Chief finds us moments later at the home of our hosts, Pascacio and Serena, a humble, aging couple who have lived in the old-world village for more than 38 years, raising 15 children on these pastoral grounds. The Chief grants us entrance – five days only – and he has a few requests. We are not allowed to enter the village dwellings, but we are welcome to eat any ripe fruit growing in the area. No photos of him or his family, nor can we take photographs within the village square.

"Please enjoy Nabusimake and our people," says the Chief, draped in traditional hand-spun clothing and the conical hat unique to the Arhuaco People.

"The hats are worn in reverence, to resemble the snowy peaks of the Sierra," Omar later explains. Although he only wears his traditional dress for special occasions now (he works most of the time in Pueblo Bello), Omar is a well-respected voice in the village because he has travelled and lived "outside," in the Estados Unidos.

"Balance is the one central theme to the culture and life of the Arhuacos," he says, walking us slowly through Serena's garden, full of carrots, peas, beans, strawberries and sunflowers. "They believe that everything must be kept in order, and the laws of nature rule over everything else to maintain perfect balance. You will see as you walk around. Tomorrow we can go up the mountain, as far as we are allowed... but for now, please take a stroll to the village and just be."

Just be. How refreshing. It's been too long since we've been able to just *be*. The travel grind has taken its toll on us: border-crossing stress, complicated logistics, bike maintenance, laundry, groceries –

they all eventually snowball into heated arguments, of which there have been many. Without the opportunity to communicate through our helmets, it's easy for tempers to flare up, especially arriving in a crowded town when we're both hangry. "Why the fuck didn't you stop at that store on the corner when you know we're both starving?" *Bitch* and *asshole* are popular words on the hardest days, when nothing seems to go right between us and it's always the other person's fault. "Just be" sounds just right.

In the village, hardly anyone seems interested in our presence, and no one makes eye contact. Most of the locals seem busy eating some sort of yellowish stew or soup made from meat and boiled plantain. They're gathered in small groups at the entrances to their homes, sturdy, round dwellings made of smooth river rocks, thatched with thick blankets of spiky yellow rooftop grass. Other than a few murmuring whispers, everyone is completely silent. *Have we entered the rock-walled village at an indiscreet hour? Do they feel animosity towards us for invading their space, their culture, for peering into their lives?* I almost say it out loud: *Strangers in a strange land.*

The next morning, Pascacio sketches a rough map of a loop trail into the surrounding mountains. "I cannot go with you," he says, "But you will not be alone." Midway into the hike, along a technical section of the trail, we encounter a young Arhuaco man travelling with a wooden walking stick. His jet-black hair billows out the sides of his fez-style white hat like a burnt marshmallow. Julito is his name. Draped across his shoulders hangs a pair of knitted, satchel-sized bags. Steering me gently to one side, he places a knitted satchel full of coca leaves around my neck as if awarding me a medal on a podium. I can't tell what he wants me to do, or what it's for. Muttering something in a language I've never heard, he stuffs his left cheek full of leaves, waits for me to do the same and then motions for us to follow him uphill along a small track that snakes its way into the scrubby subalpine. Thirty minutes later, my lips feel tingly and slightly numb, and a bitter taste lingers in my mouth. In the distance, a thousand peaks stack atop one another underneath a cloudless sky. Christina opens her pendant, pours some of Sean's ashes into my hand to set his spirit free into the Sierra Madre. I know he'd want to be in Colombia once again.

From Sean's Journal:

June 17, 1995
Cali, Colombia

I read this quote somewhere and wrote it down instantly cuz it applies to me very well. "I gotta keep travelling – I'm addicted to the thrill of the unexpected."
For example, I don't really know anything about Peru or Chile or Bolivia or Paraguay even, and I have no guidebooks… but I will search for maps as I love them. It's like a game to figure out which route to take where, when and how. I really get into the freedom of it all, it keeps me alive. I always dream of exotic, far-away places and wanna go away soon – maybe volunteer at that project in either Guatemala or Costa Rica. I change my mind often and do things at the spur of the moment. I love the any-thing-goes atmosphere of the third world, it seems kinda like a drug to me. I seem to get along with the locals too… they're always yelling "Sean Sean! You no leave" and stuff like that. I could be lured somewhere else on the planet soon, who knows.

Julito asks about Canada and if we have Indigenous People like him. Using a stick in the sand, Christina sketches a picture of a tipi and tells them that many First Nations People in Canada have long black hair like he does, and describes the harvesting of wild berries and salmon for sustenance. Back at the homestead on our last morning, Serena wraps us both in a warm hug and hands Christina a Thermos full of coca-leaf tea and a new *mochila* (backpack). She senses the melancholy of saying goodbye and tells her young ones to embrace us in a group hug that brings a round of heartfelt laughter. Hand in hand like a big chain, they walk us down the canopied path under the huge eucalyptus trees, where Omar is waiting on the same grassy field where he left us days earlier, leaning against the same bashed-up four-by-four, chatting on his flip phone.

– 14 –

BLAZE OF GLORY

VENEZUELA • September 2005

Swarms of giant mosquitoes wreak havoc around our heads. I hate them all – the buzzing, the bites; it's barely tolerable. Worse, however, are the *niguas*. Known in English as sand fleas or chiggers, these tiny flea-like insects are slowly burying themselves into the flesh between the toes of our wet feet, gorging on our blood. The only way to stop them is to pluck them out with a needle and tweezers then burn them alive with a lighter – something we've been doing each night at camp as we work our way higher up the steep, misty chutes on the way to the summit of Mount Roraima.

In his book *The Mapmaker's Wife*, Robert Whitaker recounts the observations of Antonio de Ulloa and Jorge Juan y Santacilia, two young Spanish naval officers who were sent to South America in 1735 as part of a scientific expedition:

> … the two Spaniards dwelled at great length upon the nigua, a flea that would pester them for the rest of their days in Peru. The insect liked to bury itself in "the legs, the soles of the feet or toes" and make its nest there, depositing its eggs and eating the hosts flesh for sustenance, all of which caused a "fiery itching." Removing the insect and its nest often caused extreme

pain, because sometimes "they penetrate even to the bone, and the pain, even after the foot is cleared of them, lasts till the flesh has filled up the cavities they had made."

Our guide, Braulio, tells us of a common local saying in La Gran Sabana (Venezuela's "Great Savannah"): *comer como una nigua"* – to eat like a nigua. It's similar to how we'd say "to eat like a pig" back home. No bigger than the head of a pin, they slide out of our toes painfully, but there are too many to extract. Our feet ooze with droplets of blood. Tiny strips of flesh, like hangnails, surround each extraction wound. But it's a small price to pay for the breathtaking scenery and the joys of reaching a place like this. I guess sometimes we must bleed for what we love. Although Roraima is hailed as the most impressive table mountain in the world, it's dark and gloomy when we finally set foot on the summit – no sweeping vista to reward us for the arduous and bloody four-day ascent. Giant mushroom-headed rocks scattered between pools of black water provide a million different ecosystems atop what has often been described as El Mundo Perdido, "The Lost World," the same mountain that Sir Arthur Conan Doyle used as inspiration for his novel of the same name.

Wearing leather-strapped sandals and a baseball cap, Braulio leads us carefully across the rocks to a small overhanging cave that we would have never found in this foggy haze. In the silence, I think of how little the local guides need to survive these treks. Whereas we stuff a mountain of gear and food into a backpack for a week-long adventure, they're so minimalist it boggles the mind. I imagine Braulio looking at us thinking, *What do they do with all that shit in those heavy packs?* He's brought nothing on the six-night hike but a small pack with some extra clothes and a round loaf of cassava bread that resembles a giant, thick tortilla, which he occasionally breaks into chunks, washing it down with scoopfuls of stream water that cascades down from the rocks.

As we explore the flat summit, the sun eventually bakes its way through the layers of wisp to reveal a panoramic landscape of staggering beauty. Massive orange cliffsides poke through delicate cotton-candy clouds hovering above the mountain's lower flanks. A dozen thin waterfalls spill down into the lush jungle below. In the distance, a shaft of sunlight strikes the imposing walls of the nearby mountain known as Kukenán-tepui. Sean had often spoken about one day visiting and maybe even climbing nearby Angel Falls, the highest waterfall in the world. Now I see why. I could see him exploring these unique mountains for months on end. After a long summit stroll, Braulio takes us to the point where the borders of Venezuela, Brazil and Guyana all converge.

Hey, Sean, thanks for showing me how to truly live, I whisper inside my head, sending a pinch of Sean's ashes into the wet air 9,000 feet above the valley floor. The white puff whips up into the blue sky like a little tornado, carried away by a sudden gust of wind that arrives as if on cue. Watching the tiny flecks of white dust get swept further up by the thermals, I realize that spreading Sean's ashes has been the best way for me to let go. I'm not thinking of the hospital anymore. The nightmare that played over and over in my mind for a long time is occurring less and less as the Journey creates new memories and experiences for both Christina and me. The barefoot descent to Braulio's home on the sprawling Gran Sabana reminds me of the vast grasslands of Africa, and my mind travels back in time for a long while. Hiking is good for that.

Much inside of me has altered since Sean's death – my identity, my personality, my outlook on life. Some of it I didn't even like – but the people of Rossland changed that when I arrived in town for Sean's *real* wake, in September 1999, with Sam by my side. She had flown from Cape Town to Canada in time for Mom's wedding to be with me – a city girl adjusting to a rugged new Canadian life.

"You may have lost a brother, but you've gained a whole town," said Christy Anderson, a key member of Sean's Rossland posse. Instantly I felt the high regard in which his old tribe had held him, and my self-pity evolved into self-confidence as they quickly accepted me. I was their new adopted brother. Because of the circumstances of Sean's death, I felt that I had to become the link in a chain that held all the collective grieving together. It did make me uncomfortable. I was hardly the worldly crazy man with a flair for the offbeat. I was a golf pro. Personable as I was, or thought I was, I wasn't my brother. But they didn't expect me to be like him either. Many of them frequently visited Sam and me at the house we shared, to write quotes and memories in a special book I kept, which I shared with Mom when she came to visit with Pat.

He made the scariest thing funny – humour was part of his medicine to us. He was a gangly, laughing, curious troublemaker. He was a geek and also in touch with his inner geek.

—

I never witnessed him speaking ill of others, ever. It just wasn't in him to do so. He loved people. Lawson pulling back into town, totally interested in all our lives, dogs, loves, kids' lives, pictures, tales and possibilities. When he called you brother, he meant it.

—

In everything he did and all that he saw, he expressed it in such an honest way. I can honestly say he never spoke from his ego. He did his thing and he didn't care what anyone thought about him.

—

Fearless. His glasses were always hanging crooked on his face, but he was always into something good that challenged him.

—

He possessed the rare gift of being able to bring joy to each situation he entered. Laughter followed Sean like music.

—

We all saw and travelled to incredible, hard-to-reach amazing places on this planet vicariously through Sean. He was like a comical, tale-telling world atlas. Flip a page and hear the story.

On a beautiful September evening, the tribe gathered at a friend's house in lower Rossland for phase one of the wake – a typical Rossland potluck with too many salads, not enough meat and lots of beer. Sam and I arrived with a boxful of slide trays, Sean's Cambodian motocross trophy and the wooden elephant, Sean's earthly remains nestled safely in its core. Drinking and pot-smoking and much teary-eyed laughter ensued as I was introduced to a sea of friends who had sandwiched themselves between the walls, primed and ready to see Sean's slide show. After the last picture that Sean ever took flashed on the white wall – a high-action shot of me flying over the handlebars after a creek crossing gone wrong – 50 stammering people made their way at midnight to the summit of Kootenay Columbia (KC), Sean's favourite place in Rossland. On the ascent, we passed around the wooden elephant one by one, drunk, stoned and caw-cawing like ravens, cherishing the fact that we could hoist him in our hands and walk with him up the mountain. A brief image of Mr. Phil from Nyanga popped into my head. I wondered if he had been thinking of us at that exact same moment. *Maybe I should write and tell him the news?*

Sean's best friend, Dano Reid, wanted to launch Sean's ashes from the top of KC, but his homemade potato gun wasn't cooperating. Built from varying lengths and thicknesses of PVC pipe and tube, and fuelled with household supplies, the apparatus resembled a plastic rocket-launcher without the scope.

"Fuck it," Dano said after trying and failing too many times. "We'll bring it and see what happens. If Lawson is with us, he'll make it work."

By midnight, the rowdiness of the tribe had reached its crescendo. Fifty people sounded like 500. It was time. Dano placed the bazooka in my hands, rammed a potato into the barrel and filled the chamber with hairspray and lighter fluid. I panicked when I couldn't see the wooden elephant in sight, but Sean's friend Sparky suddenly appeared behind me and, with perfect comedic timing, trumpeted loudly in my ear like an elephant. He sprinkled a healthy pinch of ashes inside the barrel and passed the elephant around for others to do the same. Then the countdown began; "Five, four, three, two, one… " I slammed the palm of my hand on the igniter, and BOOM! A fireball shot from the gun with a loud, walloping thud. Dano's temperamental spud gun had fired off the best crack of its existence, sending Sean's spirit into the night sky with a fiery blaze of glory.

THERE'S NO MONEY
IN THE JUNGLE

GUYANA, SURINAME, FRENCH GUIANA • October 2005

We know nothing about the Guianas except that malaria is prevalent in their dense jungles. Christina and I have been diligent with our medications lately and prioritizing self-care – daily sun salutations, shoulder massages and cooking good meals even with our limited pantry. We've experienced so many ups and downs, but these days we're a well-oiled unit, united and happy. And we do make a good team, especially now, when it feels like it's us against the jungle, which seems eerily alive, eyeing us up as prey. At night, things get worse. Every rustled leaf, snapped twig or other random jungle sound seems to us like a hungry creature ready to climb into the tent and crawl on our faces. Sleep is rarely deep.

By day, I keep thinking it's an honest-to-god miracle that people managed to carve a road through this impenetrable forest. Just past the Guyanese border, our bikes cough on the last of the fumes left in their reserve tanks and roll to a stop. We have no money, no spare gas, a flat tire, no phone numbers or emails for anyone in Guyana, and no idea what to do aside from hauling our gear across the ditch to sleep in the woods for the night. But the Journey has put us in tough situations before, and we've come to trust the wonderful workings of serendipity, which, as if on cue, presents us with a gift. Her name is Eve, owner/operator of Georgetown's Channel 9 cable TV Station, and she stops abruptly on the shoulder of the national highway to say hello.

"Where have you come from, my friends?" she says, rolling down the window.

"We are from Canada, but just now we are travelling from Venezuela," Christina responds.

"Oh my, all the way from Canada... but... uh... really?!" she says incredulously. "Wow, amazing. Canada is very far, no, to ride a motorcycle?"

"Yes, only about 20,000 kilometres from here," I say, sarcastically.

Her friend, "Mr. Terry Fletcher!" as he enthusiastically announces, pokes his hand out the window to shake ours. Judging by the smile on his face, he's equally surprised to see two wayward travellers caked in red earth.

"We're headed out of town for the weekend to a friend's wedding," Eve says, "but you are welcome to stay at my guest house in the country. When we come back we can show you around Georgetown."

I look at Christina and her raised *holy shit!* eyebrows. "Wow, really? That's very kind of you. We would gladly accept, but we are in a bit of a predicament. We've just arrived from the jungle in the north, where there are no ATMs or banks in sight. We spent our last ten dollars on gasoline yesterday, and now that's all gone too."

After some whispering, they reach into their pockets and purses and hand us a fistful of cash, about $60 in total.

"This should get you to the house, it's only an hour from here. There is also some food there. On Monday, when we return, we can take you to the bank."

Mr. Fletcher then opens the trunk of the car and magically produces a 20-litre jerry can of gas, almost enough to fill both tanks. It feels like we're in Belize all over again: a tiny seaside country with a checkered history rooted in slavery; English-speaking Black people; dilapidated wooden houses on stilts; and beautiful human kindness around every corner. We make it to the guest house and, without the jungle anxiety pushing on our tent walls, get two incredible nights' sleep. When Eve and friends return from their sojourn, Terry Fletcher promptly invites us to the Georgetown Club, "the most prestigious members' club in Guyana," to discuss the merits of motorcycle travel with a few of his close friends. The club's main room is full of vintage maps and wooden tables, with lively games of dominoes being played amidst laughter and banter.

"Mr. Todd," Fletcher says. "You have been on a long journey now with your wife here, Ma'am Christina, all to honour your brother. On behalf of my colleagues, we are very sorry for your tragic loss in Africa. I think this is very respectable... what you are doing. And I know we have had many cases of malaria in this country. One day I hope there can be a cure."

Drinking their beloved El Dorado rum, the locals pepper us with questions from around the table:

"Do you feel powerful when riding your motorcycle for so long?"

"How have people received you in other countries?"

"Do you ever argue from being together all the time?"

"You came from Venezuela on the Kurukupari road," Terry tells us. "My friends, that is not an easy way to arrive in our country. I have been there once, many years ago, and it took many days. The jungle has a mysterious allure."

Their engaging dialogue makes us feel like distinguished travellers rather than dirtbags covered in dirt.

"Now my friends," says Terry. "You should be all set for the next leg of your journey. We have arranged for you to stay with Mr. Marcel Meyer in Paramaribo. He is an engineer, and also consulate general to the Kingdom of Norway. A very nice man, very well connected. You should be in good hands. Please travel well, and come see us again."

Soaked to the bone from an afternoon downpour, we call Mr. Meyer from a pay phone upon our arrival at a gas station on the outskirts of Paramaribo.

"Stay where you are, I'm coming to get you now."

He arrives 20 minutes later, unrolling the window of his silver BMW sedan to greet us. "Welcome to Suriname. Mr. Fletcher told me to expect your call. Follow me, and we'll get you out of those wet clothes."

A stout metal gate closes behind us as we roll into his rather stately home, what I would expect an international diplomat would live in. A young man, perhaps his butler, leads us to the guest bedroom.

"Please come to the kitchen for some tea once you have had a hot shower," he says. His English is perfect, tinged with a lilty Dutch accent.

"I hear you have travelled all the way from Canada. You must be very tired," Marcel says with a wink, handing me a Scotch on ice. "But in all seriousness, it is a very long way to travel, and now you are here in Suriname. Did you ever think you would be here in this tiny place? Well, we enjoy visitors here, so I hope you can stay with us for a few days. We will show you around and educate you in the history of Suriname, the smallest independent country in South America. Oh, and I apologize for rambling on... this is Steven. He is my personal assistant and helps my wife and I with affairs of house and home. If you need *anything* at *any time*, please ask him, and he will gladly be of assistance. Please excuse me, as I now must retire. I have important business to attend to tomorrow. After that we will have dinner together. Please make yourselves at home. Steven, please ensure the bikes are secured in the garage."

Since our first day in Mexico, we've been riding without licence plates and have somewhat miraculously managed to cross 11 different borders without them. I wonder if Steven can help us organize new ones.

"Just let me know the numbers and what you want on them," he says. "We will organize it for you. Mr. Marcel has also asked me to take you shopping. You will need some new clothes and perhaps some gifts for your family, *riiight*?" he finishes with a deliberate wink.

"That's very kind but we have everything we need," I say, tapping into the firm sense of self-sufficiency we've established on the road.

"Sorry, Mr. Todd, I'm afraid it isn't an option. Mr. Marcel insists."

Okay, if he insists... New headlamps, socket wrenches, screwdriver, electrical tape, postcards, curios for our families and, best of all, a few new books. Beaming like kids at Christmas, we are dropped off at home by Steven, who returns at day's end with two plastic number plates that say CANADA across the top in thick red letters, the numbers a perfect match to our registration papers. Finally we can stop relying on our "Sorry, sir, they were stolen" excuse when questioned by surly customs officials about our lack of plates.

"Yes, Suriname is quite an odd place," Marcel says later that evening over steaming plates of *nasi goreng* (Indonesian fried rice) at a cozy Indonesian cafe. "You've got traditional Natives that have lived here for centuries, then the African slaves and the mixed races from different countries… Netherlands, India, China and Indonesia," he says, unfolding the four fingers on his right hand one by one. "The food is very eclectic for such a small population, and the people are much the same. It is quite an interesting place, shall we say."

Marcel tells us he's flying to Holland in the morning. "But please feel free to stay. Steven is there, and has prepared the guest house so you can enjoy some privacy. And we also have a surprise for you."

He lets that hang for a moment and picks up the tab. We're itching to rise early and explore more of Suriname's countryside, but instead a small film crew from the national cable TV station shows up in the morning to deliver Marcel's surprise.

"This will appear tonight on the national news," says the host. "An adventurous Canadian couple tackles the Americas on two wheels. People will love it. There are not many Surinamese willing to take such a journey."

Steven is present, and gracious as ever, fussing about us until the end. "Be well, my friends. You will next visit Marcel's dear friend Françoise in Cayenne. Here is her number, she will be expecting you."

As we ride south along yet another red-earth road out of French Guiana and into Brazil, a rich orange glow bathes the road in shafts of light that pierce through dark shadows. A wave of gratitude swallows me whole. I think back on how serendipity worked its divine magic back on that steamy, hot jungle road in northern Guyana – how one flat tire led to us meeting Eve and Terry Fletcher and the whole Georgetown crew. Without that encounter, we would never have had the pleasure of being spoiled by Marcel Meyer and Steven, or eaten a fancy home-cooked meal with expensive French wine while the Atlantic Ocean lapped at our feet at Françoise's place in Cayenne. We're making it all up as we go and, much like nature, there is no order to this wonderful chaos on the road. The pattern is the people, and the people have been paving the way, opening windows and doors for us as we fleetingly pass through their lives. The Journey has become like some kind of anthropological time warp, a moving education in culture and humanity that started on the fateful day in Cape Town in 1999. Wrapped in equal parts adrenalin and discovery, part of me has felt like we were at times trapped inside an Indiana Jones movie, or tagging along with Wade Davis studying cultures and chaos in the wilds of the Amazon. And after one year on the road, we're still not even halfway there.

– 16 –

A LETTER TO GRACE

AMAZON RIVER, BRAZIL • November 2008

To accomplish our lone goal of riding through every country in mainland Latin America, we have two options on the table. Option one: circumnavigate South America in its entirety. Having travelled through Colombia, Venezuela and the Guianas, do we keep heading south along the Brazilian coastline to Uruguay and Argentina, with lengthy detours to landlocked Paraguay and Bolivia on our way back north? Or option two: dissect the entire continent from east to west via the Amazon River to Ecuador, then continue slicing south through Peru, Bolivia, Paraguay, Brazil, Uruguay, Argentina and, finally, Chile? The first option we know can be done, but a giant question mark looms over door number two.

In a small, crowded food stall in the port town of Macapá, we meet a kind woman named Grace, who sees us poring over our map and immediately invites us to stay with her family. Grace is a blessing – all 90 pounds of her. She and her 12-year-old daughter, Claudia, both speak passable English, a definite bonus since we speak zero Portuguese. We thought our conversational Spanish would be enough to get by, but I can't even order bread from the bakery. When we arrive at their clapboard home built on short stilts, her husband, "Big Paolo," is sitting on the wooden floor in front of an oscillating fan that has lost its protective front cover. At more than 350 pounds, shirtless and with his legs outstretched, he looks like a Latino sumo wrestler. Grace encourages us to lay our map on the floor and waits eagerly to translate any questions while the rest of the family (seven in total) gathers around intently. If we choose the circumnavigation route, we'll have more than 4000 kilometres of travel through Brazil alone. With petrol prices high, our savings account slowly dwindling and a long, long way to go, we rule out that option. Paolo chimes in on option number two, the Amazon voyage.

"The Amazon is just like a highway, but with boats on water instead of cars on a road," he says, translated slowly by Claudia. "We know some captains of the river boats. Tomorrow we can ask – Grace works on the docks sometimes."

The notion of travelling almost 7000 kilometres *upriver* to the Andes mountains on the other side of the continent seems outrageously absurd.

"Is it even possible?" Christina asks. "How long will it take?"

"There are many riverboats that are moving people from here to Manaus every day," Paolo says. "Is big business. I think it can take maybe ten days or one week. Big boats. But after Manaus, I do not know."

Paolo struggles to stand up, and the floor creaks as he waddles his way past plastic chairs, headless dolls and soccer balls to the family's tiny kitchen. The eldest son, Junior, has brought home a few small fish and a bag of rice, and Paolo is eager to cook for his new guests. He seems content sitting in his chair by the sink, scraping scales off the fish and laughing as he speaks. Thirty minutes later, he presents a fish-and-rice masterpiece, sending us to bed with a belly full of home-cooked cuisine.

Early the next morning, two brakeless bicycles carry us down to the busy docks for our first glimpse of the mighty Amazon. It looks like a muddy ocean, so vast we can't even see the other side. We quickly find Grace, who's carrying a list of boat captain names in hopes one might be able to help us. She left the house at five a.m. to wrangle up customers in need of a pedicure before their voyage to any one of the umpteen riverside villages to the west. Manaus, the most famous of all the Amazonian outposts, is a vast, isolated city built during the rubber boom of the 18th century. It lies a distant 1000 kilometres upstream, and we know we can get that far for sure. After that...

"I need to make money for our family," Grace says to us on the dock. "Paolo is not like this before. He is too fat now and no work. He only sit on the floor and eating every day. Is very hard on me. Only me is making money. I still love very much him, he has good heart and he love our children very much. But I am worried he going to die because of weight. It is destroy our marriage."

She scurries off to tend to a customer while we wait patiently, dangling our feet off the wooden docks. "I have good news," she says an hour later. "There is boat leaving tomorrow for Manaus. Is my friend Antonio the captain. He say that after Manaus you can take more boat, but not sure about arrival in Ecuador. Peru will be first, he say."

Grace helps us procure tonight's dinner ingredients from a grumpy fishmonger who thinks we should be paying more because we're "foreigners." She sets him straight by threatening to take her business down the street. Over dinner, Grace apologizes for burdening us with her personal problems. "I will remember you two. We only know you for three days, but you are in my life now. Please send me a letter when you arrive to Ecuador. Will you write to us, please?"

Christina promises, and in the morning, with the help of a few ragged "dock rats" (as Grace calls them), we load the bikes onto the bottom deck of the MV *San Francisco*, next to what seems like a million onions in huge pink netted sacks. The rats want money, of course, but Capitão Antônio shouts something in Portuguese and they shuffle away. We find a place on the boat's second floor to sling our hammocks amongst 50 others all lined up neatly in a row. Naively, we had envisioned more of an up close and personal adventure on the Amazon, perhaps on a smaller boat at our own pace, but apparently there are no small vessels capable of the long journey. And a few hours into our voyage, we see why – a strong afternoon wind has the river dancing with whitecaps bigger than us. Our bikes would have been at the bottom of the river by now.

Later that evening, we catch a drunk man (a "captain," so he claims) red-handed in the act of stealing our toiletries bag. The cops take him away in handcuffs at the next port, in Santarém. It's our first experience with thievery since the shores of Lago de Atitlán in Guatemala, nearly six months ago. Arriving in Manaus gives us a chance to restock our food supplies and look for another boat for the next leg of the voyage. Antônio, ever the gentleman, helps us find passage on *Fitzcarraldo* (named after Werner Herzog's film of the same name), departing in 24 hours. Although our entire lives are contained within a few saddlebags, we trust Antonio enough to leave them onboard to venture into the chaos of the city, where the *brasileiros* celebrate with carefree abandon: spontaneous dancing on the sidewalks, boisterous laughter and the ubiquitous thumbs-up.

The day ends with an exclamation mark when we meet Nir, an Israeli backpacker, at a small streetside bar. I ask him if he knows somewhere we can buy a map. A month ago, in Venezuela, our beloved South American map rattled its way loose from the exterior pocket of my camera bag, and I was distraught for two days afterwards. I've loved maps since I was a kid, and losing our own treasured map broke my heart. Nir reaches into his daypack and pulls out the *exact* same one. "Would this help?" he says.

I hug him instantly, and he gives us the map without hesitation. We celebrate with two big bottles of Brahma beer, then head back to the boat to excitedly retrace our route with a red felt pen, aided by cross-checking our memory with daily details in our journals.

Fitzcarraldo carries us along slowly, chugging across the water as we gaze upon the brilliant flickering light that illuminates the clouded horizon. The days linger on, the river passes by slowly, and there is absolutely nowhere to go to have sex or a even few minutes of privacy. Sometimes our river reality gets punctuated with gruesome sights, like the skinned, bloated dog that floats past us one day, his lower jaw protruding, maggots squirming around his wide-open eyes. Other days, boat life is the pitter-patter of sandals on the floor; the shrieking laughter of children playing; brushing our teeth while covering our noses to mask the stench inside the bathrooms. Boxes, bags and luggage sit piled underneath a sea of sweat-stained hammocks blowing in the tropical heat. Rusted-out holes in the ceiling are filled with chunks of white soap to stop leaks when it rains, and the boat crew heaves full bags of trash overboard. And then there is the odd segregation of men and women at mealtimes, herded like cattle to eat the same food three times a day: plain white rice, spaghetti with no sauce (both cold) with either chicken, beef or *farinha,* a polenta-like side dish. Sometimes we eat fish called *mota* – with undeveloped eyes and foot-long whiskers sticking out of their bottom lip. It tastes much better than it looks.

Friday, October 28, 2005
Tabatinga, Peruvian Amazon

I think back to the night we first met in Whistler. I can remember the lingering look in her eyes, very brief, but long enough to say "Yes, I also felt that electricity in your handshake."

The electricity was ignited by a spark, a simple but unique conversation where we didn't try to impress one another in any way, we were just being who we were, letting the desire build up into a bonfire of affection. And here we are today, floating down the mighty Amazon River. Day in and day out we are together and we are free, two souls swimming together like fish in this river. This is our dream and we're living it. May we always look into each other and keep this dream of freedom alive.

Only books and photography have kept us from being sucked too far down the monotonous black hole of boredom that fills our Amazon river travel routine: wake up in our hammocks, eat, read, write, shower, read more, work on our notes, sleep, shoot photographs. Sitting on deck, watching nothing happen at all, I imagine 20 years from now looking back at all of these pictures and remembering the faces of these incredible people who have opened their lives to us. We will know wholeheartedly that the world is full of nice people.

On their 1735 scientific expedition, Antonio de Ulloa and Jorge Juan y Santacilia, quoted here again by Robert Whitaker in *The Mapmaker's*

Wife, noted that aside from snakes, poisonous vipers, scorpions and rats invading their small huts on the banks of the river, the mosquitoes were the true worst menace:

> The tortures we received on the river from the moschitos were beyond imagination. We had provided ourselves with moschito cloths, but to very little purpose. The whole day we were in continual motion to keep them off, but at night our torments were excessive. Our gloves were indeed some defense to our hands, but our faces were entirely exposed, nor were our clothes a sufficient defense for the rest of our bodies, for their stings, penetrating through the cloth, caused a very painful and fiery itching… At daybreak, we could not without concern look upon each other. Our faces were swelled, and our hands covered with painful tumours, which sufficiently indicated the condition of the other parts of our bodies exposed to the attacks of those insects.

Thankfully, a steady breeze on the river keeps most of the mosquitoes clinging to the shoreline. Ironically, it seems like the perfect time to let Sean go for a swim. Instead of a customary pinch (supply is running low), we dip a wet finger into the film canister and submerge his spirit into the greatest river in the world. He spoke often about wanting to explore the Amazon, so it makes me happy that he is now swimming in it.

After the *Fitzcarraldo* comes the *Itapuranga III,* our seventh riverboat to date; within its rusted hull, we meet interesting folks like Betty Rodríguez, a Peruvian who has lived in the Amazonian city of Iquitos for all 55 years of her life. She reminds me of Mom, gregarious and full of warmth.

"We have no trains or roads, but it is a nice place to live," she says, spreading her arms wide at both distant shores. "Very hot, but nice. We always travel by the river in the Amazon. This is our highway."

Betty becomes Aunt Betty to Christina and I. A true *amiga,* she treats us to the odd sunset cocktail and teaches us lots of Spanish. And when the *Itapuranga* finally drops us on the muddy shores at the Iquitos port, she takes us under her wing and into her house, a two-storey cinder-block rectangle that she shares with her extended family of eight.

Getting this far upriver seems like a miracle, but after almost one solid month of continual movement *on* the Amazon, with nowhere to roam but the decks of the boats, it hasn't really felt like we've been *in* the Amazon. We want to experience what it feels like to interact with the people who call the river's edge their home, people I've read about for years in tattered copies of *National Geographic* – the real Amazonians, with weird haircuts and face paint and fish on the end of spears. But I don't want to be just another goddamn tourist looking for a photo op, Betty assures us that her friend knows of an Indigenous tribe a day away.

"You will have authentic experience," she says. "No *turismo* there."

Eight ass-crunching hours later, we're delivered by dugout canoe to a steep, grassy embankment with a tiny wooden dock jutting three feet into the water. We're met by Herman, Chief of the local Bora tribe. His name suits neither the surrounding environment nor his chiselled face, and within a few minutes it's evident that Betty's authenticity claim doesn't quite ring true. Teenagers in ripped jeans and Nike shoes mill about, a couple of women smoke Marlboro cigarettes under a huge leafy tree, and one of the homes has a small grey satellite dish poking up from its thatched roof. Herman's people all live in a rustic, government-planned community that runs on the roar of generators after dark – the man-made noise barely drowning out the raucous concert of evening cicadas reverberating throughout the jungle.

Within 20 minutes, a dozen people in traditional Bora attire – woven skirts, beads, face paint and fancy headdresses made from the blue and red feathers of the scarlet macaw – are waiting for their cue to start dancing. Like actors in a play, the men begin by pounding a long stick into the ground and chanting along to a low, slow drumbeat, completely focused on the dance, eyes and mouths flashed open wide. It makes for some compelling photographs. Then Christina gets nudged into the middle by a group of women, and the men go wild, ramping up the energy of the dance until everyone is dripping with sweat. At this moment, I have no cares about being a tourist (because that's what we are) and instead relish in the fact that an Amazonian tribe is dancing for us with every shred of authenticity beaming from their proud faces. It feels pure, and that's all that matters to me. And because they don't ask for money, it feels real.

Afterwards, along a jungle path in the pouring rain, Herman cuts off some giant elephant-ear leaves to serve as umbrellas on the way to his home. We've been invited for dinner, and while we're fumbling with the language barrier, his daughters bring plates of fried river fish and boiled yucca to a wooden table. Smiling wildly, Herman offers the eyeballs of the fish to everyone present. We politely decline, and he eats the fish eyes expertly one by one, digging them out carefully with a long nail on his pinky finger – the perfect tool for the job. With brilliant flashes of lightning flickering the sky with an electric-orange glow, we attempt an awkward sleep together in one hammock on the front porch. Huddled together, we remark how Grace and Paolo's place seems like a lifetime ago, but it's actually only been a month since we left that small house in Macapá, not knowing if we'd even be able to take the bikes the full distance. The whole voyage was a giant leap of faith, and here we are still leaping along up the river.

Staying with people we've met along the road has been a key ingredient to our monetary survival – budget vigilance is a big part of the daily grind. We're determined to be as independent as possible but happy to accept a free roof over our heads for a night or three, always careful not to overstay our welcome. Back in Iquitos, Aunt Betty takes us to the filthy Mercado Belén to stock up on supplies for the next leg, upriver into Ecuador on the Rio Napo. Anything and everything is for sale at the market: caiman legs and tails, giant grasshoppers, foul-smelling fruits, live monkeys, sacks of spices and rices, and more produce than we've seen in a month. It's hard to believe some people spend their entire adult lives as market vendors, breathing in the stench of rotting meat and vegetables, wild game, dried fish, mountains of garbage and body odour from the thousands of people who wind their way through the maze every day. I can't imagine the look on my mom's face if she ever set foot in a place like this. As a parting gift to Betty, we present her with a small electric fan to use outside while she passes the time in her wooden rocking chair on the front porch. Tears start rolling down her cheeks. Christina is so choked up she can't even speak. These goodbyes aren't getting any easier.

Late the next day we passed, to our left, the mouth of the Napo River. A Spaniard, Francisco de Orellana, sailed down the Napo from Ecuador in 1542 on what would become the first recorded navigation of the Amazon from the Andes to the Atlantic. His looting and killing set the tone for the subsequent conquest of the basin, and his scrivener, Friar Carvajal, inadvertently named the great river through his fanciful account of a conflict with women warriors who sounded suspiciously like the Amazons of Greek myth. They were "very white and tall, and have very long hair braided and wound about the head, and they are very robust and go about naked, but with their privy parts covered, with their bows are arrows in their hands, doing as much fighting as ten Indian men."

—Joe Kane, *Running the Amazon*

Four hundred fifty years later, there's no looting or killing or women warriors, just a 75-foot long *canoa* with twin 75-horsepower Yamaha outboard engines. That's where we're sleeping tonight. It's the last boat we'll have to take, on the last river of the voyage, and we don't want to risk missing the five a.m. departure. At full throttle, the sleek wooden boat eats up the river miles as endless impenetrable jungle slips past on either side. We pass the time looking for tropical birds in the trees.

"Two more hours to freedom!" I whoop loudly over the roar of the engines, when suddenly the boat comes to an abrupt stop, sending the passengers heaving towards the bow. We're stuck in ankle-deep water – I'm surprised the captain didn't anticipate the shallowness.

These guys have river water coursing through their veins, don't they?

Luckily, four of us manage to dislodge the boat and push her into deeper water. An hour later, after more than 35 days on the main artery of the continent, the bow of the boat touches the public dock in Coca, Ecuador. The end of the river, the beginning of the road. Three burly men help us unload the bikes and bring them up the steep cement steps. They don't ask for money. Smiling on the inside, I think of Grace and the dock rats.

Dear Grace,

We made it! We carried our bikes on to ten different boats during our long voyage and we finally touched down in Ecuador. Your Amazon River is incredible. I hope you and the family are doing well. Please send our love to everyone, and tell Paolo we miss his fried fish. Thank you so much for helping us. You have a very kind heart full of love. We will write again when we're back home in Canada.

Muito obrigado,
Tomas & Christina
xoxoxo

MOONSHINE AND MIRACLES

PERUVIAN ANDES • November–December 2005

Finally, the Andes. Countless layers of backlit ridgelines stretch into the purple evening haze, standing proud like silent warriors protecting a vast kingdom. In Colombia, amongst the Arhuacos, we sampled our first bite of mountain life above 13,000 feet, and it left a flavourful aftertaste. Now, the howling winds and alpine air of Ecuador carve into our faces crusty red cheeks and dry, burnt lips. Just a two-day ride from the Amazon's heavy heat, outside of Cuenca, we're stopped by four colourful *cholitas*. The cheery women are wrapped in colourful pleated skirts and wool sweaters, their long black braids flowing out of distinctive bowler hats. They've placed a knotted rope on the road and pull it from both ends when they see us approaching. With Christmas less than a month away, it's a clever means to stop traffic and ask for some money. They're much too charismatic to ignore, and their beautifully round faces have us shilling out a few one-dollar notes to help their cause.

When we arrive in Cuenca, Lucky and Lucinda are sputtering badly, but help is never far away. A gas station attendant calls his cousin, who happens to be Felipe Merchán, one of Ecuador's enduro moto champions. Felipe has his mechanics undergo a high-elevation carburetor adjustment at his shop and gives me a new riding jacket – a much-appreciated gift after a mishap in Venezuela, where I fishtailed off the pavement at full speed as my jacket was eaten by my rear sprocket. With freshly tuned motos, the simple act of riding makes the days flow fast and smooth; we feel like migratory birds, with no interruptions or interference. After the monotony of the river, this windy freedom is fuel for our souls.

We fly through the country in just ten days, earmarked by a completely out-of-the-blue encounter with two friends from Nelson, BC, Luke and Jake, whom we agree to meet up with in Bolivia for Christmas.

November 27, 2005

Fitful sleep, dogs barking, donkeys braying, roosters squawking. Peeing in the sand. Lumpy straw mattress. Boiled roots for breakfast. Crazy wind. Straight line. Nothing but sand. Small trees fade into pure desert. Dunes along the roadside. Thick gloves. More layers. Nobody anywhere. Nothing. Empty. Lonely. Another flat tire. Cafe "pasado." Dust. Brown bricks and yellow taxis. Ugly. No character. No color. Cement floor. Cement walls. Cement everywhere. Cafe con leche. Bucket shower. Crazy driving. Yamaha shop. Fix leak. Buy new tire. Drop off shoes. Run out of gas. Street lights. Third world chaos. Poverty. Driving in the dark. Spinach and soya sauce. Instant noodles. The comfort of a bed. Picking out a movie. Reading books. A friendly face greets us at the door – Jack, from the *Jimeiza*! Great family. A safe place to stay. Conversation. The energy of the day. Fatigue of the night. Ocean today in Chiclayo. Mountains tomorrow. Sleep. Dreams. Snuggling. A day in the life.

We met Jack a few weeks ago on the *Jimeiza*. He'd spent the last 14 months away from his family and was finally making the month-long voyage to his home on the Peruvian coast, some 4000 kilometres away. An IT expert, he had spent long days trying to install internet systems at various government outposts along the shores of the Amazon.

"Come see me in my town," Jack had told us. "You will see on the map it is on your route, maybe." He'd written his name and address in our journal, so when we arrive in Chiclayo it's surprisingly easy to track down his brown-brick house on the outskirts of town.

"*Hola, mis amigos,*" he says, welcoming us into a house full of close family. "I knew you would come. Everybody... this is Tomas & Cristina. All the way from Canada. I meet them in Brazil on the boats."

It's a Sunday afternoon, and most of the family are still in their pressed-for-church outfits, heaping piles of homemade food onto paper plates. He introduces us to his mom, who possesses some uncanny similarities to my own mother – they share the same name, are both short, outgoing and impeccable hosts. They've also both been widowed. Three days with Jack's family feels like ten, with conversations flowing as deep as our language barrier will allow. But today is Sean's 36th birthday, and no matter how much we'd like to stay and eat more of Rita's famous *pescado sudado* (sweating fish), it's time to celebrate.

Just outside of town a series of sand-mountains appears like a desert mirage in the salty-hazed distance. With our tires purposely deflated for added traction, like snowshoes for the sand, we scream around on the dunes until our bodies are drenched with sweat from dropping and digging out our bikes under the hot morning sun. Six hours and 12,000 feet of elevation gain later, we're bundled in full winter gear to protect us from the bitter bite of cold weather at altitude. Lucky is suffering from a dysfunctional gear shifter – it's been slipping off its "teeth" all day long, forcing me to change gears by kicking the shifter with the inside of my boot, to varying degrees of success. Over a long day and countless steep, rocky switchbacks, this repetitive kick-fix action starts to take a toll. My body wants to shut down. Tired and worn, we pitch camp high on a treeless plateau just a few feet from the road, the sky a medley of purple, orange and pink, and the first star has just appeared in the sky. I'm on dinner duty, making soup and pasta over a cow-dung fire while Chris sets up our bed. Just after four a.m., I awake to a strange moaning noise. It sounds like a cow outside the tent, but I realize it's actually Christina in the throes of a horrible nightmare.

"Are you okay, babe?" I say, shaking her awake.

"Water. Water. I need water," she says faintly.

She takes a long pull and tells me she feels "weird." I check for a fever. Nothing. "I have a headache, though, and it feels hard to breathe. I need more water."

We're unaware of our exact elevation, but I do know that gaining that much elevation in a single day without acclimatizing can be dangerous.

"Babe, I think we need to make our way down this mountain as soon as we can. You probably have altitude sickness. Will you be okay to start riding again after I pack up?"

"I'm not sure, babe. I just feel so weak and tired. Let me try and sleep some more. Then we can try."

The extra rest doesn't help, and I awake feeling light-headed and uneasy. We're struggling to strike camp, barely able to cram our sleeping bags into their stuff sacks. Our hearts feel sore inside of our chests. An attempt at another cow-dung fire to stay warm is abandoned quickly; blowing on the embers is making me even more dizzy. Everything takes more time and energy than it should. Another motorcyclist approaches, covered in so many layers he looks like a stuffed animal behind the handlebars. He's coming from Huaraz and tells us that we're only 20 minutes from the top of the pass. From there, it's 40 downhill kilometres to Caraz.

"You can fix your bike there," he says enthusiastically. "There are many shops, it will be no problem."

His upbeat attitude is exactly what we need. Huffing, puffing and shivering, we eventually push the bikes, unloaded, up to the road and return for our packs and saddlebags. It's not even 50 metres, but we're already spent. Strapping everything down takes another 30 minutes. My bike starts in neutral but won't kick into first gear, and a steep hill is staring us in the face. I know we need to descend to a lower elevation very soon, but I can't get my bike into gear.

"Let's attach the two bikes with our rope," says Christina, still in rough shape, pacing slowly to her bike. "I can try pulling you to the top of the pass, then you can coast downhill in neutral from there."

Lucinda sputters and chokes in the thin alpine air. She doesn't have enough power to pull Lucky and myself behind. *Fuck. What do we do now?* Walking my bike 20 kilometres uphill isn't going to happen. I say a prayer and give the shifter a solid Hail Mary kick with my left heel. It works! Christina straps my helmet on my head (I can't let go of the clutch, or we would be back at square one), and I make my way in first gear to the top of the pass.

Soon the incredible splendour of the Cordillera Blanca is shining off the peaks in front of us as we descend into Caraz and out of the altitude-sickness danger zone. These are the tallest mountains we've ever laid eyes upon. The loose gravel road, carved from the steep hillsides by brave men in big machines, falls away sharply into the valleys below. Many blind corners leave no room for mistakes, and my mind begins to go numb from concentrating so hard. Honking the horn is a must here, the standard way of warning others that we're about to approach. As I shiver beneath a mountain of clothing, the high-mountain chill saps my focus, and I narrowly avoid a fall amongst the sharp rocks and ruts. My fingers clunky and numb inside my winter gloves, this is the first time I catch myself wishing we had a car – heat on, drinking hot coffee, listening to tunes. That dream shatters when suddenly, out of the corner of my eye, I see a barrel-chested donkey dart across the road from a rocky embankment on the right. With no time to squeeze my brakes, I brace for immediate impact and T-bone the animal square in the ribs at 50 km/hour, a gut-punch that connects solid and sharp. I land hard on my right side, my helmet thudding the road. Writhing on the ground with the wind knocked out of me, I see Christina, sideways, turning back to come help. The donkey is about 20 feet away, unnerved, looking right at me. *I probably didn't even knock the wind out of that son of a bitch,* I mutter to myself, still lying on the dusty road. I've never seen a donkey move that fast before.

A few days later, we're alone at a forked road that's definitely not on our map. The distant hills and mountain peaks lie hidden in a swirling sheet of fog. There are no trees, no power lines, no people, no barking dogs. Flecks of dry snow pelt into our clothing, which is layered six deep to keep the bitter cold of the *altiplano* from chewing through our bodies. Frozen fingers, wind-battered faces, cold cheeks. Thank god for our small Thermos of hot tea. I see no signs of civilization except for the road we're now lost on.

Left or right? It's a difficult decision, especially at this altitude. Our bikes only have so much range (250 kilometres), and to run out of fuel and have to walk out of this mist is not something we're keen on. Dismounting from Lucky and Lucinda to warm our frozen bodies with a quick set of jumping jacks, we can hear our own hearts beating but nothing else. And then, out of the silence, we hear a faint rumble, and a bus emerges from the cold haze. The driver pulls over, a huge smile flung across his weathered face. From the predicament we're in, his enthusiasm seems wildly out of place. Inside the bus people are opening windows and jockeying around for a better look. *What in the fuck are these two gringos doing way up here?* I imagine them thinking.

An odd memory flashes into my frozen head, and a scene from Zimbabwe, of all places, snaps into sharp focus. I recall the day Sean first planted the seed for his dream ride. His face appears in my mind and I hear him speak:

"Hey man, we can do this in Canada!" he said, his infectious enthusiasm shining through his dirty face. "We can buy dirt bikes and ride them all the way down to South America. "Colombia is amazing... and Bolivia... and Peru... "

The driver's eager voice jolts me back to reality. *"Hola, dondé vas?"* he asks with a curious look pinned between his rosy cheeks. "Where are you going?"

"Santa Ines," responds Christina. "Do you know the altitude here?"

"5069 metres above sea level, exactly... the highest point on the road. It's that way to Santa Ines," he says, pointing over his left shoulder.

"No wonder why it's so fucking cold here," says Christina. An eruption of laughter pours out of the bus. I'm sure not many of them speak English, but they've obviously heard the word *fuck* before.

"Would you like a shot?" asks a smiling lady in Spanish. "It will help warm your body."

She pours two small glasses of *cañita*, a potent, pink-coloured moonshine, and hands them to her daughter, who straight-arms the potion out the window into our gloved hands. *"Salud!"* they shout simultaneously. The booze rips through our bodies like fire through a dry forest, and the bus roars with another eruption of laughter. We wipe the water from our eyes and the remnants from our quivering lips. As the bus pulls away, the woman's daughter, waving a long red scarf, squishes her body through the back window, looks straight at us and yells *"Buen Viaje!"* with such sincerity and compassion it has us both choked up in tears. As her smiling face fades back into the fog, we recognize the moment as a good time to spread some Sean, throwing his ashes into the swirling wind. The light is so flat we barely see him go.

The day Sean died, I made a promise to him. That I would keep his dream alive and, one day, ride to South America. Now, magically guided by the hands of fate, here I am in the thick of true adventure with the woman I love, living the dream he dreamed. For possibly the first time in my life I understand what it feels like to be blessed. With our insides still warm from the *cañita*, we kick-start the bikes, relieved to now be on the right path. The road narrows to a barely four-feet-wide strip littered with hundreds of muddy-water potholes. Every corner and curve produces its own magic, from rolling mountainsides carved smooth by the touch of ancient glaciers, to beautiful herds of llamas and alpacas that roam the hillsides and glance up in our direction with little red pompoms attached to their ears. We've only been riding for four hours, but I can scarcely remember where we began this morning. Some days are infinitely more intense than others.

For tourists seeking to experience Machu Picchu, there are only two ways to go. Either from Cusco, on board a train that snakes along the Urubamba River in the Sacred Valley, or by hiking the very popular (and very crowded) Inca Trail. But to set foot on that fabled Andean footpath requires first wrangling your way through a two-or-three-month waiting list. We have neither budget nor time for either, but a few locals at a roadside coca-leaf tea shop disclose some insider information about the *camino viejo*, the old route to the ruins. One particularly empathetic gentleman outlines a rudimentary map on a paper bag, and off we go, our fate resting in the accuracy of his scribbled line. En route, as the miles crunch beneath our knobby tires, I can't help but think about the incredible resilience of the people who live and survive at this altitude. Their cheeks and lips are cracked and their dirty clothes are torn to pieces, but this kind of high-mountain poverty seems strangely less harsh than the filthy squalor of a city slum. Maybe the sheer grandeur of these massive white peaks softens the blow? Outside of their tiny rock-walled abodes, the locals have space to roam, livestock to tend and each other to lean on as family. It's a hardscrabble life, yet they manage to smile through it every day, fostering an uncomplaining, stoic attitude that Christina and I try to adopt. Similar, I presume, to how my grandparents were forced to eke out an existence on the frozen Alberta prairies.

Hitting an unseen bump with my front tire, I rein in the horses of my imagination and focus hard on the road ahead, a minefield of rocks and ruts as hard as they come. Christina is ahead of me, leading like a champ. We're bitterly cold – my fingertips feel frozen to the handlebars – but no one, save ourselves, seems to care. As far as the Peruvians are concerned, this is what coca-leaf tea is for. Two days later, the *camino viejo* dead-ends at a police outpost. It's three p.m., our feet are soaked – even with plastic bags overtop our socks – and we're quite thrilled to have not gotten lost. It's amazing the lengths we will go to avoid tourists.

"Where are you going?" says one of two officers on the doorstep.

"We have ridden from Cusco and want to reach Machu Picchu," Christina explains. "We have been told to ask you for directions from here."

"You must first cross the river, and then you will follow the railroad tracks to Aguas Calientes. You must walk only. You can leave the motos here, and we will keep them safe."

I like his demeanour and know we can trust him, but leaving our steeds and most of our gear behind is always unsettling. *What could go wrong in this little stone-fenced compound?* Our bikes are locked together and our bags safely stashed. *Stop worrying and get on with it.* We set out on foot.

"Wake up early, stay up late." I hear the words pressing into my tired feet with each step. We've been walking on railroad tracks for almost six hours, an oddly difficult endeavour, seeing that railroad ties are not placed according to one's hiking stride. Walking atop the rails is just as difficult. As tired as we are, I know Sean's voice won't let me sleep in tomorrow morning. To be the first people to witness the sunrise as it crests over the sacred ruins will be like frosted sugar icing on the bucket-list cake, with sprinkles on top... and a cherry. At four a.m., we take our first steps up the steep pathway to Machu Picchu. When we approach the summit, the ruins are smothered in a thick white mist and a palpable mysticism. As the fog lifts, it unveils the terraced citadel amidst a backdrop of forested mountains. And we're still alone. Most impressive is the intricate stonework. The Inca were masters of a technique known as *ashlar,* a centuries-old method of stonemasonry in which large blocks of stone are cut to fit together tightly without mortar. As a symbolic gesture to Sean's solidarity in brotherhood and friendship, I place a dash of his remains in the crack between two massive rock slabs. Hordes of tourists begin to arrive, so we head to the summit of nearby Huayna Picchu, a steep, pyramid-shaped mountain that stands guard over the rest of the Incan site. Being surrounded by these ancient, beautiful ruins and mountains brings clarity to my mind and soul – gone is any travel stress, money stress or relationship friction. We are enveloped within these precious moments, like the mountains inside these clouds.

Back in Aguas Calientes, a friendly old lady making grilled corn on the street corner asks me: "Why do you travel?" I think about it for a good long while, taken aback that in all the thousands of questions we'd been asked, thus far I can't remember anyone asking us *why.* It's a simple question with no simple answer. I think of Christina and what she thought this epic journey of the Americas would be like before we even left. I think of all the people, the places, all the good feelings. Riding across the painted canvas of Latin America, our lives are changing as quickly as the passing landscape, layers upon layers of experience cloaking us in a cocoon of humanity. All throughout these unforgiving mountains, we have camped and cooked in the homes of strangers who opened their doors without hesitation. No matter what they have, they share – a common bond we've discovered in all of the Latin people throughout our odyssey, much like what Sean and I experienced in southern Africa. Slicing through their worlds for a brief moment or a few days, the bond of trust and friendship grows ever stronger. The Latinos have become our rock. But before I have time to respond, the woman is already asking us something else, as curious of our world as we are of hers. I smile and sit back quietly, enjoying her tasty cob of Inca corn.

THE PARAGUAYAN POLKA

JANUARY 2006

On the high pass from Piedra de Vaca, white-capped peaks shine brilliantly in our rear-view mirror as we say goodbye to our final day in Peru. After two slippery river crossings, the gravel switches to pavement so unbelievably smooth it feels like we're floating. In one silent instant, 60 days of struggling along the tortuous backroads of the Andes are over; now we're coasting through a wide valley full of yellow flowers and golden fields of wheat, spotted with distinctive old ladies in bright skirts and those ubiquitous bowler hats we'd like to buy. Lucky seems to have some water in the gas tank, but it clears itself and we push on, finally glimpsing the dark blue waters of Lago Titicaca. It's our biggest day ever, ten hours of non-stop riding to cover 533 kilometres. The sparkling lake pulls us off the road and onto the charming Isla del Sol for a well-deserved Christmas reunion/ recharge with Luke and Jake, as well as an old travel friend, Sylvain from Switzerland, whom I met in Byron Bay, Australia in 1996. After a few days of drinking, hiking and cruising around the lake on stunning reed boats of fascinating character and design, we glide into the new year amongst a sea of brown buildings and the steady pulse of urban mayhem known as La Paz, Bolivia, the world's highest capital city.

Going from rural ease to city chaos forces us to switch our riding mindset from free-flowing to completely on guard. City traffic can swallow us easily, and it's hard to follow one another, try as hard as we might. Normally we steer clear of big cities, but we need to take care of business: fix my camera body, get Lucinda's frame welded and buy new pairs of boots. The streets are packed with cars, buses and people, buyers and sellers filling the air with the sounds of continual bartering. You can buy a belt from a wrinkled old man for two dollars, then turn around and purchase a bag of popcorn from a 5-year-old with a baby slung around her back. *Such a crazy life, all this noise and all this movement. Do they ever have a quiet moment?* This is their station in life, I guess. Urban poverty. A street hawker for years upon years, vying for 20 square feet of sidewalk to make a few dollars. We're beyond grateful to just have the option to get up and go, but amongst this havoc I feel a tinge of guilt for even having that privilege. In the relative quiet of our hotel lobby, a long-distance call box provides an opportunity to check in with Mom and Brad.

"You were both missed at Christmas," Mom says, her voice as bubbly as ever. "Thanks for all the email updates and photos. It looks like you're having the time of your lives! Please stay safe and make sure you're taking good care of Christina. After all, she is a girl, you know… make sure you treat her well."

I should have listened to her. Three days later, my stubbornness to charge ahead into the sprawling expanse of Bolivia's immense Salar de Uyuni doesn't impress Christina. I don't stop to discuss our game plan, and instead I open up the throttle and tear into the blank mirage of the world's largest salt pan, leaving a rooster-tail of white water in my wake. Two kilometres later – when I finally realize she's not right behind me – I turn around and see her bike laid over on its side in eight inches of thick, salty muck.

"For fuck's sake, Todd, can't you just wait for me next time?! We don't even know where we're going, and there are no roads. It's pretty easy to get lost here… it's like a goddamn desert. Be fucking patient for once, and I'll have a much better time."

The only thing I can do is help right the bike and apologize. She's right; getting lost here with no compass could prove deadly; the Salar sprawls for more than 10,000 square kilometres, roughly the same size as Jamaica. A crew of workers shovelling salt into the back of a truck point us in the direction towards Isla Incahuasi, a rocky, cactus-filled outcrop of land 80 kilometres straight west into the setting sun, where a *refugio* exists for two-wheeled travellers. The monstrosity of the landscape swallows our imagination whole; it's easily the most unique place I've ever ridden anything. On a motorcycle, it's godlike – a mirage-making, mind-melting, salt crust to ride as fast and as far as you want in big, sweeping figure-eights, in any direction, with your eyes closed, your legs in the air and the wind in your face. If freedom were a place, it would be the Salar. It's hard for our minds to escape the fact that we're not riding over a frozen lake.

Incahuasi is only open to overnight visitors as a refuge for those who arrive on bicycle or motorcycle, so we're in luck. Victoria, the caretaker, lets us borrow two bicycles for a sunset cruise around the "island." After a sunrise photo shoot amongst giant cactuses, we aim the bikes towards a volcano in the distance, the only landmark we can see. When clouds roll in, even the horizon disappears under Uyuni's magical spell. As we ride atop what looks and feels like a perfectly thin slab of sparkling snow, a sudden side wind forces us to throttle hard to avoid getting stuck in the deepening layer of liquid salt. Losing our bearings and taking so many photos, it's hard to cover much distance; I realize we have no way of knowing how far it is back to town, or if we'll have enough gas to make it there. Our only choice is to trust our instincts and keep riding, hoping the horizon will eventually reveal some form of civilization. A few anxious hours later, as we wheel our way back into town, the salt is so thick on our exhaust headers it takes gallons of water to wash off. Our faces are crisp to the touch, jeans and boots and saddlebags caked in salt and hardened like armour – a small inconvenience for one of the most unique and memorable riding experiences of our lives.

Taped along the seams and stained with a squiggly red mark, our hand-me-down map of Central and South America has become our most prized possession; weaving so many lives into our own, through joy and pain, elation and boredom, across fields and mountains and into giant cities, to the shores of two different oceans and along mighty rivers, we've marked it with dots where Sean's ashes were set free to dance upon moments of fleeting bliss. I hope our grandchildren will see it one day. At the moment, however, it's laid out across two bar tables at the Joy Ride Café in Sucre, where we're trying to plan a route that will take us into landlocked Paraguay – but all we can find is a thin dotted line, which the map legend denotes as "a long, remote run out of Bolivia to the southeast."

"I haven't heard of anybody going that way, and I haven't been that way myself," says Gert, Joy Ride's Dutch owner. "The roads might be pretty slick right now, we've just had about three weeks of rain. I'm not sure I'd go, to be honest."

This kind of uncertainty might have changed our minds at the start of the Journey, when our inexperience might have led us to choose a more well-travelled route. But after all these months and miles, I find myself mulling over Gert's advice with an almost mischievous skepticism. As long as Christina is fine with it, I'm game for the challenge. Everything is firing on all cylinders for us right now: the bikes are in beautiful shape, our health is perfect, and it feels like we can will anything to go our way as we wish it to.

We head east across an alpine desert towards border number 20, peasant farmers waving as we ride past. Others glance at us with eyes of indignation as if to say: "Rich gringo on his motorcycle, fuck you! I have to carry this heavy load for miles draped across my shoulders." Children bolt up the hillsides and hide behind rock fences at first glance.

As we descend from the high plateau, the narrow, brown road splits the shrubbery like a snake in the grass, and the countryside morphs into a patchwork canvas of brilliant green. Thousands of butterflies emerge, all blue and orange and bright white, flouncing around us with surprising speed. The odd one flies into our faces, a piercing pain at full speed, forcing us to flip our visors down. The fluidity of riding the packed-earth road soon turns into a slip-sliding frenzy as we rooster-tail clumps of mud at each other for miles on end. In the late afternoon, the route gets even uglier, riddled with rocks and patches of thick sand; adventure riding at its finest, difficult *and* exciting. After a restless sleep through a pounding rainstorm, we wake up to a splattering mess of mud caked onto the sides of the tent, and strike camp just as another motorcyclist, wearing a lime-green helmet, arrives with a kind offer. We can follow him, if we like, to Padilla, a small town 60 kilometres ahead. He darts out in front quickly, unburdened by heavy gear, while we struggle to keep up. The road dives into a tight forest of tall, gangly growth, triggering memories of Central America's tropical denseness: vines twisted around branches, branches tangled around trees, trees wrapped around enormous dead trunks. We're navigating across rotten logs and basketball-sized rocks, all hidden below a mucky surface of knee-deep brown water.

"Aaaahh… this is awesome!" Christina screams under her helmet, laughing as she sends a mud-fountain spinning into the air while I run behind her. Her joie de vivre is one of the reasons I fell in love with her, and now in this desolate backwoods mud pit, that connection is growing stronger. Soaking wet and covered in mud, I wish I could throw her down in the grass and rip her clothes off, but we're too exhausted for any of that. I'll have to remain content with staring at her sexiness from afar. How did I find such a woman? *Lucky son of a bitch.*

After we struggle for hours in the dark, muddy forest, the road eventually empties us out into the open. We look ahead for our buddy in the green helmet but see only an electric sky hugging the horizon, charged with the energy of another impending storm. Hundreds of cattle stand like bored, fleshy boulders on and around the road, which is littered with steaming piles of cow dung. It all makes for a slippery affair, and we hit the ground more than a few times each, too many to count, sliding into cow shit and brown water time and time again. Drop the bike. Pick up the bike. Ride through more mud and drop the bikes again. My clothes are so soaked they're sagging. To keep our energy up, we stop to eat some peanut butter and jam sandwiches, but the late-afternoon lunch almost claims us. We know we need to push on before nightfall.

But when I attempt to pop the bike in gear, something feels wrong with the gear shifter again. "Fuuuck!" I yell.

Inspection by headlamp reveals the teeth that grip the internal gear-shift mechanism are stripped, the same thing that happened in the Cordillera Blanca. I pull out a wrench and begin to tighten the bolt, but a half turn too much shears it clean off. *Uh oh.* Christina sinks to the ground in frustration. With no spare lever and no spare bolts the same size, it's an entirely disagreeable situation, especially with the weight of dark clouds sagging closer to the earth, like water collecting in a tarp. Lightning cracks the black sky, briefly illuminating the emptiness of our surroundings – we've seen only one human being all day long, and no farms, no villages, not a single car. Seven hours and only 40 kilometres.

"Maybe we shouldn't have gone this way," Christina says, fuming. "Why don't we *ever* listen to these people, Todd? Why do we always have to take the roads we know nothing about? For fuck's sake, he even told us not to go! Fuck the crazy risk, I just wanna enjoy myself."

I look at her but say nothing. Silently agreeing that perhaps we should have heeded Gert's advice, I shut up and let her rant.

"We don't even know where we are, we're almost out of food and water, and in about 15 minutes it's going to be raining so hard we'll be even more drenched than we are now!"

"Hey, let me remind you you were just having the time of your life back there," I retort in the same angry voice. "I know this isn't looking so good right now but we'll be all right. If we can find a farm somewhere, we can probably fix my bike. Look, let's just set up camp, we'll make some food and get a good rest. Somebody's gotta drive past here sooner or later. I know we can't go any further right now... but at least we have each other. Sounds corny, but it's true."

"Whatever, it's all part of the Journey," she says, her nerves now calm. "Can't be sunshine and roses every day. But let's at least clean this goddamn mud out of our tires... it's so thick I can't even move my wheel. Sorry for yelling... I think I'm hangry."

Rumbles of thunder shake the ground around us, when suddenly a single headlight appears a couple of hundred yards from the direction in which we came. As it approaches us, the engine starts revving and the vehicle slips sideways into the ditch, coming to a full stop not far from our bikes. An older, grey-haired gentleman steps out from behind the steering wheel, introducing himself as Alejandro. His rusty red Land Cruiser is full of holes, there are no doors, and the inside is crammed with his family: his white-haired wife, a daughter, two grandsons, a healthy dog and a small black kitten.

"*Todo está bien?*" he says.

"Yes, thank you. We are fine but my bike is not."

"Our home is just seven kilometres from here. Maybe we can pull you to the house? Is the lady's bike running?"

"*Sí, señor. Muchas gracias.*"

Carlos, the eldest grandson, climbs to the top of the jeep and ties our packs onto a white metal rack before hopping down, eager to help with the next problem – the rear axle buried in the ditch. They have a winch, but no trees are within reach of the cable. Alejandro says something to the boys, who scurry off into the bush and return with a tree trunk about four feet in length and a foot in diameter. Digging a deep T-shaped trench about 20 feet straight in front of the jeep, Alejandro sets the tree trunk inside the trench, the winch cable wrapped around the middle of the log. The boys bury the tree and stomp up and down, packing the earth over top of it. *He's going to use this buried tree to winch the truck out of the mud?! Ingenious.* A make-do-with-what-you've got solution. It takes a Herculean effort from each of us to push, pull and crank the Land Cruiser out, but finally it comes unglued. Alejandro insists on pulling me to their house.

"I'll go slowly... no problem," he says, carefully hooking up the rope from my bike to the truck. "I have no brakes... but I'll go slow."

It's a riot. Everyone's laughing and cheering, the boys whooping loud from atop the roof rack, Christina yelling encouragement right beside me. Even Isabel, the half-blind grandmother, is shaking her fist out the passenger side. After ten solid hours of getting battered and beaten and thrown around, adrenalin is the only thing keeping us moving. But it's enough. They put us up in the barn, and we're both asleep in less time than I'd normally spend brushing my teeth. The gods have been kind to us and, miraculously, it hasn't rained overnight. Somehow, Alejandro finds the right bolt on the hay-strewn floor inside the barn to fix the shifter. It's not perfect, but it works. I can change gears again. The ladies gift us a loaf of homemade bread and a bunch of bananas to sustain ourselves through the slippery muck ahead. Paraguay is just 70 kilometres away.

Weaving through the spiky bushes running alongside the road is the only way to avoid the deep mud. The thorns scratch and scrape our exposed necks, but it's a price worth paying to gain some ground. We soon come upon the first of hundreds of *charcos*, massive mud puddles of unknown depth and length. We're faced with three options. First, we can dismount and walk the bikes through the wet stretches. This allows us to see how deep the water actually is, but it's much too slow and the ground is too slippery – we drop the bikes after our feet slip from under us. The second option involves finely tuned balance to ride the high ground in the middle of the road, but the rear tires easily slip into ruts on either side, sending us into the muck with ease.

"Sean must be watching us from above," Christina says. "These bikes have started every single time after they've gone down."

The third option is fastest and the most fun, but also the most dangerous: open up the throttle upon entry and plow through the puddles, our legs flung out to the sides for balance like outriggers on a canoe. When we arrive at what we think is the Paraguayan border, a rusted, bullet-riddled sign welcomes us into the country. Sitting on the veranda of a wooden shack, two army officials wearing stained white T-shirts, flip-flops and camo shorts rise slowly from their chairs to greet us. A crackling radio blares away, too loud to understand. There is no hint of a border inspection procedure, and they tell us to continue riding.

"You must arrive in Asunción, there you will find immigration. Have you brought anything for us?"

We give them each a slightly squished banana and our empty water bottles, which they kindly fill up with cold water from a clay pot.

"Is there anywhere we can find food or a place to stay?" I ask.

"There is a hotel not far from here, 16 kilometres, in General Garay. You will make it before dark I think. The road is good. Everything is there, even beer."

Beer? Is he serious? I would give my left nut for a cold beer right about now.

We steel ourselves for the final push, keeping a close eye on the odometer. Hunger pangs grip our bellies, but the puddles keep coming, hindering our speed. In some places, the water is too deep to power through, so we help one another by awkwardly leaning the bikes against the high right side of the road, our arms outstretched above our heads as we try to keep the bikes from slipping in this "ice-mud," as we've dubbed it. The grease-slick conditions make us wish our bikes had training wheels with spikes, and despite Herculean efforts we still drop the motos nine or ten times in the 26 kilometres after the border – and still have yet to see a hotel of any kind.

Darkness has engulfed us when I hear a jubilant "whoop, whoop!" from Christina ahead of me. She slows to a stop, ripping her helmet off anxiously.

"Check it out!" she says, pointing to a colonial-style building set back against a gunmetal sky. "Do you think this is the place they were talking about?"

Even if there is nobody here, at least it's *something*. A long hug is in order, a moment of pride and celebration for enduring the most physically gruelling, emotionally demanding stretch of road in all our travels. We're soaked to the bone, hungry and totally spent, but the accomplishment outshines the rest. We can hardly believe we actually made it. That road could have easily broken our bikes, bodies or minds. The last two months of physical punishment in the Andes, plus these last demonic days of riding through one of the most sparsely inhabited areas in South America, have undoubtedly transformed us. Our Journey has reached a new zenith. Accomplishing what we've done so far, this definitive act of travelling from one place to another, together, has become the greatest gift we could ever imagine.

A rustling in the bushes startles us. *"Hola,"* says a voice from the darkness, and out steps a man zipping up his fly. We hear more voices coming from near the building, and a crew of men soon appear.

"You have come from Bolivia?" one of them says in perfect English.

The others simultaneously reply in a hushed, incredulous chorus. *"Noooo!"*

"Yes, it has taken us five days on this road."

"*Ahhh, la ruta de los pesadillas.*" He senses that we don't know the word, and translates it for us. "The route of nightmares."

Brimming with excitement, the men invite us around to the back and, without asking, shove two of the coldest beers I've ever felt into our hands. There are 12 men in all, ranging in age from 15 to 55, and they've come to El Chaco on a week-long hunting trip, the fruits of their labour boiling in a big black pot over a bed of coals: delicious deer-and-rabbit stew. I'm sure most of them have never heard the word *vegetarian* before, but eventually someone produces a plate of rice, beans and stewed carrots for Christina. Our presence as unexpected guests elevates the atmosphere and out come the guitars, spoons and anything else they can bang on. Before long a smiling, semi-bald guy named Dario asks Christina to dance. He twirls her around between the picnic tables, do-si-do, to and fro, the Paraguayan polka in full swing, which elicits a riotous reception from the guys. We all jump in, every one of us shouting to the music, linking arms, taking me back to memories of Mom and Pat's wedding. *Holy shit, this is cool.* Never in our wildest dreams did we expect today to end like this.

Waking the next morning, we're sad to hear they're heading back home to Asunción, the capital. Christina and I are hungover and amazed that nobody else is – all we want to do is sleep all day.

"You must come with us. We can travel together," says Dario, who expresses his interest in riding Christina's bike because he loves the name, "*Luceenda.*"

We hastily pack our bags, throwing them in the back of an already overloaded pickup truck for the 12-hour journey. Christina, willing (and wanting) to take a break from sand-riding, passes Dario her helmet. He squishes his face in and gets his wish, darting out ahead of the trucks while I follow close behind. Thick sand throws him around like a dead fish, and he goes down exactly one kilometre into the day. Picking up *Luceenda*, he takes off the helmet that is two sizes too small. Beads of sweat the size of raindrops pour down his chubby face. He's as red as a tomato.

"No, Todd. I cannot do this. I can't continue, it is too hard. My god."

"Qué pasa, Dario?!" say his friends in the truck. "Hahaha... You need ride?!"

Dario's smile lights up the morning. He's gracious in defeat. "Aye aye aye, Christina, I can't believe it. You are strong on this machine. And all the way from Bolivia too. My god."

− 19 −

PATAGONIA WILD

ARGENTINA AND CHILE • April–May 2006

The nothingness of the pampas never ends. It's a gargantuan expanse of land teeming with prairie grasses and sparse habitation that seemingly belongs to no one but Father Time. There are no crops or cattle or humans in sight, yet the terrain is entirely fenced in along the arrow-straight Highway 23. What an undertaking to dig holes four feet apart, bury and fortify the posts and then staple thousands of kilometres of barbed wire in three rows on each post. Incredible. It makes me think of my grandfather and the work of his life on that farm. When fleeing Poland in 1925, my great-grandfather Jacob Marchuk made two separate steamship voyages from Poland to Argentina to secure land and a better life for his growing family. For reasons unknown, he chose Canada, but I could easily have been raised on *this* spectacular expanse of Mother Earth, more similar to our home in British Columbia than any place on the Journey thus far. Would John Marchuk have been a gaucho – a skilled horseman reputed to be brave and unruly – raising cattle on a windswept farm with these sparkling rivers instead of enduring the long, hard, cold Canadian winters? Would Helen Marchuk have canned different vegetables or made the same pickled chicken feet? I would have played soccer instead of hockey as a kid. I'd be fluent in Spanish. Maybe us brothers would have never set foot on a ski hill. Strange to think how it could have all been so different.

In hindsight, my great-grandfather made a sound, and bold, decision to leave his homeland no matter where they emigrated. Germany invaded Poland on September 1, 1939, generally known as the start of World War II. In the Canadian prairies, his family was safe from the atrocities of war. Worrying about putting food on the table was far better than worrying about being killed by a bomb.

Fast-forward 80-plus years, and instead of riding horses, we're riding our own trusty steeds. I don't know why we gave our bikes the names Lucky and Lucinda, we just did. They've been pushed, pulled, kicked, dragged, smashed, stalled, run out of gas, welded a dozen times, broken and fixed and broken again. We've been religiously obsessive about our morning routine – brush teeth, tighten chain, check oil – every single day without fail. But today that didn't happen. Over the noise of the unrelenting Patagonian wind, I suddenly hear a dreaded knock coming from the engine. *Fuck. I hope that's not what I think it is. Did I just seize the engine?*

I resist the stupid temptation to kick-start the engine, hoping that by some miracle it'll start and we'll be on our merry way. Instead, we stick our thumbs out on the side of the road. Even after 18 months, we're still hopelessly naive when it comes to motorcycle mechanics. We can change a flat tire like a racing pit crew, but anything that involves cracking open the insides with wrenches is best left to an actual mechanic. The fate of my beloved Lucky now rests in the hands of time and money. *Where's the silver lining in this?*

His name is Oscar Knecht, a motorcycle aficionado who spends the next three days rebuilding Lucky's engine, which had perished due to oil starvation (a.k.a. my fault). Oscar also lets us camp in his backyard and refuses to take any money for either his time or the new piston he had shipped overnight from Yamaha Argentina in Buenos Aires.

"We will repay you one day, amigo, with more than this bottle of wine," I say.

"Put me in your book," he says, smiling. "That will be enough."

For many overlanders, the end of the road at Tierra del Fuego is a geographical milestone, but simply bearing witness to the sharp, craggy spires of this spectacular mountain range is a feat in itself. With winter arriving soon in the southern hemisphere and another 3000 kilometres to reach the "land of fire," the southernmost tip of Latin America, we opt to experience Patagonia on our own terms. After 17 months, reaching its famed borders is cause for celebration. We're riding high once again, in both elevation and state of mind. Our zealous desire for bandit camping has led us to the camper's jackpot tonight – a private, grassy (and free) space close to the river's edge. Reeking with a moto-traveller's perfume of campfire smoke, gasoline and body odour, we're grateful for our reward before bedtime of two cupped hands' worth of warm soapy water to wash the rigours of the day away.

In the morning, I pull a toque over my greasy hair, step into my dirty jeans, and clamber out of the tent to steal a few slices of time: photographs of the sea dancing over the footsteps of the land, long exposures blurring colour into movement, motion into landscape, immortalized on a magical square of film. Snowy peaks poke out above the green glow of the forest, illuminated by crisp dawn light that's almost too saturated for the slide film in my camera. A shallow river flows at my feet. Birds of prey swoop and swirl amongst the treetops. *The garbage is the problem of man, not the forest* reads a sign on a little shack. After witnessing so much litter strewn throughout every country thus far, it's nice to see respect for Pachamama, the earth-mother goddess revered by the Indigenous Peoples of the Andes.

Later on, I amble along the wobbly river rocks back to our camp on the river's edge and invite Christina for an evening stroll. With a Malbec in hand, we salute Mother Nature for providing the beauty that greets us every day, for setting the mountains alight in warm rays of sun, for the clear, cold lakes and rivers that give us life and a splash in the face to start our day. One place to another, each with its own beauty, its own gift to share; from the roots of willow trees to this strikingly big sky.

Writing by candlelight and learning about the world. A lesson in humanity. But are Christina and I simply wandering around? Seeing things, doing things, meeting people. Just connecting dots on a map? We've taken food, shelter and advice from so many along the way, but have we given enough back to help those who have helped us? How *can* you give that much back? The beauty we've seen, the people who've changed our hearts and opened their homes and lives to us; the abundance is hard to comprehend. For now, some solace rests in knowing that maybe we *have* inspired those we've met to live a life full of freedom – not necessarily through a haggard journey on two wheels, but by any means possible. Maybe a glimmer in some kid's eyes as we whiz past her dusty village en route to the next dusty village? She'll never see us again, but the fleeting image of *libertad* is planted in her mind. I do hope we're at least spreading the *idea* of travel. Like the definition says: *to make a journey, typically of some length or abroad.*

Our Patagonian days crack on: check the map, choose a route, make a plan, pick a lake, look for waterfalls, take a hike, search for firewood, hot showers in a wooden shack, potatoes on hot coals, chopping onions, back massages, thick steak on the grill, coffee with liqueur. The wind shakes our tent nightly, billowing it in and out like a lung. During the day it's even stronger, and at times it feels like the gusts will knock us over, whistling so loud it's impossible to hear the sound of our engines. Riding for hours on end becomes insular and meditative, the continual thrum of the bike lulling us into a moving standstill where the road rushes under our feet in a blur. If you stand on the pegs and lean your hips into the handlebars, the front fender disappears, ushering in the visceral feeling of floating atop the road on a magic carpet ride at 100 kilometres an hour. Our tires are lucky enough to grace freshly laid asphalt on La Ruta de los Siete Lagos in Argentina's pristine Lake District. One would be hard-pressed anywhere in the world to find a more exhilarating track of tarmac to ride a motorcycle on, and the Canadian-like scenery sets a wonderful tone for the day. We can communicate only with hand signals, so we're left with our peaceful reflections as the clouds roll on by.

Although pitching our tent is still a chore after the rough, cold and windy days, the once-tedious process of packing and unpacking our lives has become a simple pleasure, an ingrained, systematic part of the Journey. Chris sets up the tent, I cook dinner. She washes dishes, I write in the journal, and vice versa. After 18 months on the road, we've put in our 10,000-plus hours and now hold honorary degrees in wilderness camping, adventure motorcycling and human communication. But our days are numbered. We're memory-bank millionaires, but our real bank account is dwindling fast. The inevitable winding-down occupies a sad place in our hearts. *How can we go back to our normal lives after living this adventurous life for so long?* It all seems unfair, and I hate to think about it. The final destination lurks somewhere in the distance, but we're not at the end yet. Wherever that is, neither of us wants to talk about it.

We achieve our goal of riding through every country in mainland Latin America when our wheels crunch the gravel at the Chilean border town of Pucón. The border is a breeze, and we give one another a long, proud hug to celebrate country number 23. Sparkling rivers snake through the savannah-like landscape, and the sheer monstrosity of Volcán Lanín stands tall, sandwiched between two flat-topped peaks in the distance. Fly fishermen cast in shallow creeks, horses graze on golden grass and cirrus clouds float wispily across the blue sky as though smeared on by a painter's brush. Back on the bikes, Christina handles the rock and roll of choppy stones and pockets of sand with ease and great confidence, passing over roots and underneath branches full of red berries and tiny spikes scratching our helmets. Switchbacking through the landscape brings back memories of the Andes – the mountains aglow in a hundred hues of orange, backlit bugs flying into our faces, cold fingers on the handlebars. Days later, we finally reach the Pacific Ocean again for the first time since Peru. Too timid to dive into its frigid waters, we instead run barefoot across the shallow, low-tide waters, splashing each other like kids, dark grey sand squishing between our toes. It's our last day surrounded by pure remote nature and our final night camping, and fitting that there is nobody around but us.

Sunday, April 23rd, 2006
Concepción, CHILE

Dear Sean,

We're almost there. We dedicated this day of riding to you, to thank you for the inspiration and showing us the way, for watching over us. I took your ashes from my necklace and threw them into the sky at the mirador high above the ocean. As we looked up, there you were, soaring over us, wings spread, circling in a wide arc, saying hello; a tilt of the head for congratulations. You really were here with us, from the first day to the last. The bikes will soon be on a boat and we'll be on a plane. We always feel you with us, your spirit expands for miles and miles into our dreams, through our hearts and into the hearts of those we've met along the way. Todd is much better now. Thank you for things you don't even know. Or you actually probably do.

Love,
Christina
xoxo

Staring off into the ocean, my mind is bombarded by a million random thoughts. *Where will we sleep tomorrow? Do we have any peanut butter left? I wonder where Roland the Austrian and Taka from Japan are now, the only other riders we travelled with? I wish we could have spent more time in Uruguay. Those beaches and pine forests were such a refreshing change of scenery. How's Brad doing with his chronic back pain?*
Family has been on my mind more than ever lately. Christina's love and the open road have been the best therapists I could ask for, but I've also been besieged by bad memories of Sean's last few days. Too many sad, wish-you-were-here moments that opened small cracks for guilt to creep back in. *Why was it him and not me?* Sean should be on this ride too, this epic world of everyday unknown that he introduced me to. When Christina and I rode out of Mom and Pat's garage on that sunny October afternoon 19 months ago, I wasn't even sure what I was seeking, if anything. Was I running away from life itself, having not properly dealt with the trauma that happened inside that hospital room? The more I tried to avoid my deep feelings by filling my days with external distractions, the worse it became. I was happy on the outside, living my dream now instead of Sean's. On the inside it was a different story. Mom had asked me many times if I wanted professional

counselling, but I shunned the idea. *I can do this on my own*, I thought. *I'm all good.* Even Christina didn't know how much guilt I was grappling with every day. *Smile and press on, right?*

"Todd, have you ever actually forgiven *yourself?*" she asks me as we're snuggled together in our tent by the beach. I pause for a long while, although I know the answer. No. It has never even occurred to me. She makes me say it out loud, on the spot, to myself.

"Todd, I forgive you for not seeking out the doctor in Sabie," I say, blinking back tears. "I forgive you for not looking for a medical clinic before trying to sell the bikes. I forgive you for putting this guilt squarely on your shoulders."

Only then do I understand that forgiveness is the great liberator of the mind. I realize that the crime for which I convicted myself – for being alive when my brother wasn't – is a crime that has existed only in my own imagination. They call it survivor's guilt, and I've been dealing with it for far too long. My first two-wheeled adventure with Sean was a tiny tip of the massive iceberg underneath my feet; a mere introduction to a life I didn't know was possible, or even real. I knew I wanted to carry on Sean's legacy, to live his dream, but the Journey has given me so much more. I *am* all better now. After 47,003 kilometres, I've learned that not all journeys take place on the road; some of them wind through the peaks and valleys of the soul.

That night, as the wind whips our tent ferociously, I tell Christina I want to go back to Africa. We're both addicted to the freedom of travel on two wheels, and I wonder if she will be as receptive to riding amid Africa's more intense poverty and corruption as she has been in Latin America. It would be her first time in Africa, after all. Given everything my mother went through, I'm reluctant to keep the conversation going, but Africa's warm heart keeps beating in my chest. I know it's only a matter of time.

PART THREE

BACK TO AFRICA

FEBRUARY 2008

I wake up to shafts of bright sun flickering through the train's windows on the way to Johannesburg. Propping myself up from our fold-down berth, I'm greeted by a fleeting image of the most iconic of all African sights – a lone acacia tree, its sprawling branches hovering above the grassy yellow savannah. The scene immediately alleviates some of the anxiety inside my heart, for Mom was on my mind last night. When Christina and I told her of our plans to return to Africa, things escalated quickly between us. A full-volume fight turned into anger, tears and resentment in the kitchen of her home.

"Why? Why do you have to go back to fucking Africa?!" she cried. "I've already lost one son there, and I'm sure as hell not going to lose another. Why can't you two just settle down for a while?"

The settling-down thing had never sat well with me. It felt like getting older, growing stale, giving in to the system. I'd moved out of home when I was 19 and had never looked back. The way I saw it, a life of security and predictability was no life at all.

"I don't want to settle down!" I railed back. "To me, that's not living. What do you want me to do, sit on the goddamn couch for the rest of my life? I know you're scared, Mom, but please, I can't live my life knowing that there's so much out there. This is our passion, this is what makes us truly happy. We're going to go back to Africa, and we're going to help."

With Sean's ashes sitting just ten feet away from us, I felt even more compelled to force her to see my point. Life is short, who knows when you'll end up inside the belly of an elephant. I know I need to make every day count and live it out of love, not out of fear. Pat and Christina had never heard us argue like this. They sat back nervously, listening to both sides of the fight.

"You selfish prick!" Mom yelled at me. "What about me? Now I'm going to have to worry for another year, living in fear of getting another phone call."

"Mom, I can promise you right now that we're going to be extra careful this time. I know so much more about malaria prevention now, and we're going to take a special test kit so we'll know right away, without seeing a doctor. It's been almost ten years... there are much better malaria medications now."

I could feel myself trying my best to douse the fire with justification, all the while knowing she wasn't buying it. "Mom, I promise you. I know it's hard for you, but please try and understand. I want to help people this time too."

The truth was, I *did* feel like a selfish prick, and part of me didn't want to go back to Africa, because of my mother, but thoughts of returning had kept creeping into my brain almost as soon as I left. I could *feel* Africa itself pulling me back. I suppressed dark thoughts of Sean's last days in the hospital and tried hard to replace them with memories of us sailing in the dark off the coast of Mozambique, or looking for somewhere to camp amongst village huts in rural Zimbabwe. Upon returning from Chile and the end of the Journey, Christina and I were both surprised at how challenging it felt to deal with reverse culture shock in Canada, our home since birth. How could it suddenly feel so difficult relating to people? We even had trouble connecting with our best friends – most of their conversations flowed around buying houses and doing renovations, and we had nothing to contribute to the narrative. Being immersed in poverty had made us astoundingly more appreciative of things the Western world takes for granted. We no longer had to build a stick fire to make our morning coffee. We could simply turn a faucet and enjoy a hot shower. Public washrooms actually had toilet paper.

When Lucky and Lucinda arrived in Vancouver after the month-long cargo ship voyage from Santiago, our spirits lifted considerably. We could explore again and get lost in the euphoria of riding mountainous backroads and camping near lakes and rivers in our own backyard. Thoughts of Africa wouldn't go away, however, and almost without discussing it, we agreed to revert to our money-saving ways. We gave ourselves 18 months to get ready.

When the tension between Mom and me calmed down, I explained why, and how, we planned on helping. Through online research, I'd found out that major headway was being made into malaria prevention via the distribution of mosquito nets in Africa, most notably in remote areas, where access to nets is nearly impossible. The idea hit me on an otherwise regular day, just sitting at home, preparing lunch. Why don't *we* take nets to people who need them? Christina and I could embark on another grand adventure, but this time with a purpose – our expedition would focus on something other than ourselves. We'd buy two motorbikes in South Africa and ride through the continent with the goal of preventing malaria in children under the age of 5. I pitched our idea to the CEO of the Against Malaria Foundation, a UK-based charity that facilitates fundraising for the distribution of long-lasting insecticidal nets (LLINs) to populations at high risk of malaria.

July 2, 2007

Dear Rob Mather,

We'd like to know how we can help. Eight years ago, I lost my brother to cerebral malaria at the end of a motorcycle journey in southern Africa. In February of 2008 my partner Christina and I will be coming to Africa in hopes of riding across the entire continent with the intent of spreading malaria education to small rural villages that we will access via motorcycle.

Can we help you in this manner? We would also be keen
on the idea of personally delivering bed nets to small, remote,
hard-to-reach villages in any or all of the countries we plan to
visit. It is our dream to help others combat the deadly disease
and we would love to have a real and true goal for our Journey.
We'd be glad to work in partnership with you to further spread
the awareness of this disease.

Sincerely,
Todd & Christina

We were elated to get a response from Mr. Mather just one day later.

Hi Todd, Christina—

Great to hear from you. Very sorry to hear about the loss of
your brother, Todd. What a great initiative. Delivering nets
along the way?! Where there's a will there's a way. We must be
able to sort out something. Lots of ideas come to mind. The
message to all would be: 100% of funds received, buy nets (at
the world's lowest price) AND they will end up over heads and
beds. AND we will demonstrate how that has happened.
Get back to me on these first thoughts and let's see where we go
from here.

Best,
Rob

A year later, we're on a train, chugging along through the desert
scrubland of the Karoo as the flickering sun keeps me in a daydreamy
trance. We flew into Cape Town, the "Mother City," and embarked
on a 26-hour, US$50 Shosholoza Meyl long-distance train across the
country to reunite with Dr. Debbie Ibbotson and her family. The special bond I formed with the Ibbotsons has grown stronger and more
impactful over time, and I feel like an adopted son coming home. At

the Ibbotson family compound in an affluent suburb of Joburg called Bryanston, Debbie sets us up inside the cozy guest house, where Mom and Pat stayed nearly nine years ago. Memories start flooding in, both good and bad, triggered by long dinner conversations and the feeling of being in a familiar place. It doesn't take long for Dr. Debbie's caring nature to shine through. Coming home after a long shift at the hospital, she brings us a full year's dosage of doxycycline.

"You'll both need to take these tablets every day once you enter a malarial zone," she says, her voice as caring and sweet as I remember it. "Doxycycline doesn't have the harsh side effects that Lariam does, but remember it's not 100 per cent effective. The malaria parasite is always developing resistance towards any drugs, so you must be diligent *as well*. If you have any problems, just please call me immediately, Todd. Tomorrow after work, I'll show you how to use the malaria test kit. They're actually quite effective."

Debbie's husband, James, kindly drives us to Centurion Yamaha in Pretoria to meet the two most integral pieces of our lives for the next year – our new bikes. Together with Rob Mather, we settled on Motos Against Malaria as our fundraising name. Securing this partnership also gave us more credibility to seek sponsors to help with the expedition and, fortunately, my random email to Yamaha South Africa landed in the right inbox. Yamaha's area manager, a kind soul named Andy Robertson, believed in our humanitarian-adventure angle and offered to outfit us with new Yamahas, a model called the AG200.

"I want you on motos that can take a beating," Andy explains when we meet him. "They top out at 90 klicks an hour, but other than that they'll do just fine."

Produced only for the southern hemisphere, the AG200s are Yamaha's answer to a workhorse motorcycle – made for agriculture, military, humanitarian aid and other rural uses. Aside from their scrambler-esque look, they're outfitted with an impressive array of components aimed at utility and survivability, like dual kickstands with enlarged "feet" (no more sinking into soft ground), front and rear gear racks (no need to design and build our own), crash bars to prevent broken levers, engine and chain protector (saves money on lube), and a

comfortable saddle seat that will become the unsung hero of the entire
journey. All hail the grandmaster champion saviour of sore-ass syn-
drome. Oddly, I name mine Willy, after the rock-eating dog we used to
have back on the farm. Christina names hers Jessie, after Bryan Allott's
newborn baby daughter, whom we just met in Kaapstad. Bryan was
so fantastically comforting to me during the troubled hospital times
in Johannesburg, and this will be a way for us to carry on *his* legacy in
an adventurous way. I know he'll be sending out positive vibes daily.
Andy also introduces us to Glenn Foley, the Publisher of *Dirt & Quad
Magazine*, who generously offers to publish a paid monthly article of
our Motos Against Malaria adventures. Any income while on the road
will help relieve some financial stress. With Willy and Jessie ready to
roll, our goal is to ride from Pretoria, South Africa, to Tangier, Morocco, trying to go as remote as the logistics of our endeavour allow.
When we arrive safely back "home" in Johannesburg, Debbie's parents, Lorraine and Peter, are anxiously waiting for us in the backyard,
beating the hot afternoon sun with cold cocktails in hand.

"I still want to thank you for the advice you gave me," I say to Lorraine. "Remember when you told me to always look for a sign to know
that he's with me? Well, anytime I see Sean's favourite number, 47, and
every time I see an animal in nature, I think of him. It really helps."

Lorraine, of course, is worried for our safety. She seems to live in
fear and constantly talks about the crime and dire political situation
of her country. Not that her point of view is entirely unjustified
– they live in the still-dark shadows of apartheid, with daily armed
carjackings and home robberies a still a common occurrence in South
Africa. Debbie, on the other hand, is more open-minded, although she
has to deal with the aftershocks of Johannesburg's astronomical crime
rate every single day: shootings, stabbings, accidents and all manner
of emergencies.

"I'd love to do a trip through Africa," she says to Christina. "Maybe
not on these bikes, but what an awesome experience to travel through
the whole continent. You must enjoy it"

The Ibbotsons' generosity knows no bounds; they won't let us pay
for anything and also insist on taking us to their weekend cottage for

some water-skiing and relaxation. Our time with Dr. Debbie and family sets a nice, calming tone to the start of our next incredible leg of the Journey, which suddenly feels like more than just a dream flickering in the sun.

February 16, 2008. My fingers grip the throttle with tingling anticipation. It's the first official day of the African Odyssey, the start line. Ahead of me, Christina keeps a brisk pace, and the sweet smell of freedom triggers a memory of Sean in his black denim jacket, snapping the throttle and flinging his legs in the air on the day we left Cape Town. Back in 1999, it felt like we could have travelled forever, and now it just feels good to be back on the road, this time with the love of my life. Contentment floods my veins, and my heart swells with pride and happiness. We have each other, all the gear we need and another film canister full of Sean's ashes to spread in a part of the world Chris has never laid eyes upon. Smiling inside my helmet with happy tears streaming down my face, I wish that, for even the briefest moment, all of humanity could feel like I do right now.

As Christina and I know from our experience, riding a motorcycle can be extremely dangerous and demanding, both mentally and physically. Certainly it's also thrilling and delightful at times – that's why we do it – but those moments inevitably fade the further you cross through physical distances and personal limits. The trick, we have found, is to keep going until you reach a familiarity with things like pain and fear. That's when things really start to get interesting – like our epic trip through El Chaco in Bolivia/Paraguay. I also know that all good things come with a price; it's just a question of if you're willing to pay it. I paid the price once already, harshly, and have secretly been praying that the gods will deliver Christina and I safely through the continent without serious mishap. I know they will. I hope they will. They have to.

On our way to the Mahamba border crossing into Swaziland (since named Eswatini), we ride past a million rows of eucalyptus trees, their sweet aroma scenting the hot afternoon air. As we look for a place to camp, four small heads pop out of a circular home, puzzled but smiling. None of them speak English, and Christina mimics the sleep sign, with two palms together at the side of her leaning head.

"We have a tent," she says to a lady who appears at the door, elegantly wrapped in a green-and-white *emahiya*, the traditional female Swazi outfit.

"Okay. We bring for you carpet, can put the tent just there," she says, pointing to a concrete platform in her backyard. She introduces herself as Blessing. "My husband gone now, but it is fine."

Our friendly confidence at asking strangers for hospitality worked well for us during the long, satisfying months in Latin America, and the Africans are no different. Rural folk are kind folk, and they understand we mean no harm. Night falls fast. Blessing and her family have no electricity, but under the flicker of candlelight, Christina notices a big green grasshopper crawling on the edge of the kitchen table. Blessing's daughter, Thando, quickly snatches it in her hand, rips off its wings and tosses it into a bowl. Only when I shine my headlamp do we notice dozens of other plump, wingless grasshoppers clambering over each other, all destined for a hot frying pan.

"What do they taste like?" Christina asks.

"Like chicken," replies Thando.

I summon up some courage and reluctantly put one in my mouth.

"How is it?" Chris stares intently.

"Not that bad, buuuut… it ain't chicken."

Later the next day, we meet Thando's big sister Thula, the woman who coughed uncontrollably for two hours straight in her bedroom last night as we made dinner. Blessing shoots us a hopeless glance.

"My daughter have TB," she says, shaking her head solemnly. "TB not good. Many have in Swaziland. This," she says, fake-coughing, "is from lungs. Sometimes is blood coming up."

Not until I have some time to think do I realize that Thula's tuberculosis will weaken her immune system, allowing the AIDS virus to potentially flourish. It's our first introduction to the litany of hardships that face Africans every day: drought, famine, disease, poverty – all giving rise to the resiliency that Africans are known for. Malaria isn't the only life-threatening issue they have to deal with on a daily basis. In just a matter of weeks, Thando will be Blessing's only daughter.

A fresh blast of clean air fills our lungs as we climb higher up the legendary Sani Pass into Lesotho, "The Mountain Kingdom." Back in the day, the pass was a mule trail used by tough drovers bringing wool and mohair down the mountain on donkeys to be exchanged for blankets, clothing and maize meal – essentials for life in this impoverished, landlocked African country. Now we're the drovers, riding our motorized donkeys laden with 100-plus pounds of food and gear up the steep, rocky ascent, a bucket-list ride for keen adventure riders, and the first true test for the underdog AG200s. Our legs flail about to keep balance while the bikes pop up and down like the heads of hungry chickens. The agility required for this kind of steepness may come from the rider, but the spirit of the bike definitely determines the success of the day.

The top of the pass delivers us onto the front porch of the rustic Sani Mountain Lodge and the "Highest Pub in Africa," at 2874 metres. After an obligatory pint, we opt to take the aptly named Roof of Africa route to the north, as it boasts to be the highest road on the continent, peaking at 10,416 feet above sea level. It reminds me of riding through the Andes, only here the mountains don't pierce the sky with craggy peaks, they cover the land in great bands of rock, like chunky bracelets around a wrist. Atop Tlaeng Pass, we come upon a roadside sign flashing the words *AFRI-SKI* in big white letters. Unfortunately it's autumn, and the only white in sight is a thin ribbon of packed snow underneath a single T-bar. What a shame; skiing in Africa would've been a blast.

"Do you ski here in winter?" Christina asks a young man standing on the sign.

"No, not me," he says, beaming a big, toothy smile. "It is crazy, this sport. Only the white people are doing it. For me it is too much crazy... eeish."

"You should try it one day."

"Eyyh, this sport is not for me, ma'am. Is too much cold and too crazy. I don't like it, you know. But many people are coming here for the snow. They love it too much."

Further north in a vast field totally devoid of trees, a Basotho herdsman approaches on horseback, peering down at me from behind a scary woollen mask, patting the shiny mane of his white horse. Draped in a thick wool blanket with a long staff in his right hand, he cuts a striking resemblance to the Sand People from *Star Wars*.

"From where are you?" he asks politely after removing his balaclava, cracking a smile to reveal a large set of yellow teeth.

"We are from Canada," Christina says, handing him a small booklet of photographs that we keep in our tank bag for these exact encounters. Pictures don't need language to speak.

"Aaah, this is where you stay," he says in quite fine English, looking at a landscape covered in a blanket of winter white. "Canada. The cold country. I was born in Malealea. Many horses, big land. Now I have a small trucking company. I have two trucks."

"You have a very beautiful country here," I say.

"Yes, Lesotho is too nice. We are happy here. We are poor, but we are happy. This valley provides for all we need," he says, pointing with his eyes towards a steep valley in the distance.

He is regal in stature and poise, and emanates wise energy; I admire him instantly. But a tinge of inadequacy swirls around my head. It feels like we don't belong on these hallowed grounds. Our privileged middle-class lives have brought us here upon the wings of an airplane and into the seat of another saddle, all because of money, and I feel like nothing more than a tourist passing through this fenceless land. We haven't spent hard years at the rugged hands of this alpine existence without the comfort of electric heat. We haven't built a sturdy house from river rocks picked by hand and with a roof built of thatch cut with a scythe, all while raising a family of five, eight, ten children. He reminds me of what my grandparents must have been like, scraping a hard life out of the Alberta prairies with nothing to fall back on. *What a difference two generations makes.*

"It is a nice way to roam, on these bikes" he chimes in, breaking the silence.

"You want to trade?" I ask, pointing at his horse, laughing.

He exudes such an aura of tranquility and togetherness that I secretly hope he'll invite us to stay at his home somewhere in these hills, to meet his family and see how they live. This is a traveller's adrenaline rush, brushing up with such pure authenticity in the most serendipitous of ways; people and places you know you'll never forget. Coming back to Africa was a difficult personal decision, but already I know it's the right one. Just to be here standing in front of this man is a manifestation of my desire to once again ride through this continent to meet people just like him.

After a few serenely beautiful days along South Africa's famed Garden Route, my head buzzes with flashbacks as one of the world's most iconic sights smacks us square in the face: Table Mountain, a white vortex of cloud spilling over its broad cliffs (known fondly as the "tablecloth'), proudly standing guard over the famed city of Cape Town. I had some of the best times of my life in this city full of juxtaposition: metropolitan affluence vs. township poverty, big-city chaos vs. big-time nature, beaches and forests vs. nightclubs and football stadiums – and now I get to share it with Christina. The contrast is all at once bizarre and welcoming, moments that instantly bring me back to adventures I had here with Sean, warm connections jolted within by a random smell or a faded sign. At other times I feel on the verge of tears, like I'm carrying an empty bucket around, searching for a faucet that will never appear. In Cape Town, seeing Samantha again brings a sense of joy. We parted ways while she was still in Canada, but she's still a dear friend. She accepts Christina with warmth and grace, not jealousy as I had (foolishly) feared.

Our old roommates from Hog Hoggidy Hog are still together as a band, and Sean's refreshingly offbeat climbing partner Garrreth Bird takes us traipsing around the mountains, climbing routes and flinging Sean's ashes; it's all really a vacation from the "real" Africa soon to come. We're but a tiny little dot on the southwestern tip of Africa, with tens of thousands of kilometres in front of us. It's a daunting endeavour, but I imagine the gracious smile beaming from an African mother's face when we drape a mosquito net over her child's bed. We're still trying to figure out logistics, but in the end naivety is a great educator. We might find ourselves on the worst road in the heart of the rainy season in the most tropical, humid part of central Africa, unable to pass through, but somehow there is comfort knowing if that happens, we'll figure it out on the fly.

With a fresh set of rubber gripping the earth and a new bank of memories with friends old and new, we bid farewell to Cape Town and head north along the Western Cape's stunning coastline, retracing the route that Sean and I set out upon almost nine years ago. As soon as the crunch of gravel strikes my ears, the memories come flooding back: the smell of dust and salty sea fog, and the great fields of red earth dissected by long rows of low-lying scrub bush, planted to prevent the coastal winds from whipping the sheep-grazing scrubland into big dunes. We spend the first night camping amongst the beach boulders at Tietiesbaai (literally, Bay of Tits) where a kid we call Little Lizard Boy skillfully snares and kills a lizard to give to his dogs. I can't seem to remember the directions to the sprawling farm where Sean and I spent a memorable night drinking brandy by the fire with the Afrikaners Alby and Adele and the farmhands Gert and Jony, who helped fix our flat tire. It would be nice to take Christina there to meet them, but it's not necessary. This is our trip together, and I do have another major surprise lurking a few hundred kilometres north.

The gate at Sesriem campground looks much the same as it did nine years ago. The price, however, is anything but.

"Yes, sir, it is 600 Namibian dollars (US$60) for one night," says the gatekeeper, a bald man wearing a thick wool jacket and black sunglasses.

"Just to camp?"

"Yes, sir, we only have campsite here."

"Okay, thank you. We will head into the park and come back later to set up camp," I say, hiding my white lie behind a friendly smile. I know full well we won't be coming back.

"Thank you. The gate closes just after sunset, so you will have about three hours to return." He steps out of his little hut and saunters away into the campground.

"Obviously we're not spending two days of budget on a little gravel patch to pitch our tent," I say to Chris. "We'll camp inside the park. Sean and I did it last time, and I think I can remember how to find the same place. It's a little desert oasis. We had to ride through some thick sand to find it, but at least we'll be really close to the dunes."

The steely night comes faster than expected, and we don't find the oasis but settle for a roadside pull-out picnic spot with two trees perfectly spaced apart for our hammock. At 4:15 a.m., our eyes open to a billion blinking stars, but the cold keeps us squished together. We don't want to leave the cocoon of body heat, but the race to Dune 45 is on. The air is silent and soft. Climbing the same knife-edge ridge that Sean and I bounded up with freezing fingers, I remember the sight of his teeth and the comical *holy shit, where are we?* amazement beaming from his bulged-out eyes. Christina looks equally in awe.

"Wow, it feels like we're on another planet," she says, a sliver of sunlight glancing off her cheek. "It's so immense, babe. The scope and scale is really hard to comprehend."

"I have a surprise for you," I say, holding out two clenched fists. "Pick a hand."

"Left."

"Good choice."

She peers into my palm at a small square of paper.

"No way. Really? What's in the other hand?"

"Same thing."

"I can't remember the last time I dropped acid." She shrugs and smiles. "But this is for Sean."

Wispy waving grasses carpet the valley floor, a sign of rare rain in recent months. The dunes are impeccably defined, cutting an unmistakably sharp line in the flat white landscape at their feet, as though they have been shaped from clay with a giant's trowel. Twenty minutes pass, and 20 more, but nothing happens.

"I guess they're duds," I say. "Oh well, this place is trippy enough as is."

"It sure is! I've never seen anything like this in my life. Thank you for bringing me here to witness this, babe – I'm sure Sean was in his glory here."

The sun starts its rapid rise to a shadowless high noon, and we're still negotiating the sweeping ridgelines that connect all of the dunes in Sossusvlei. I never imagined myself returning to the same spot so soon, and not under these circumstances. Namibia is, after all, a long, long way from home. Christina wraps me in a warm hug. To be alone with her under this spellbinding display of nature, reliving one of the best days of my life, is a bit overwhelming. As I reach into my pocket for the film canister of Sean's ashes, tears start forming in my eyes. Christina lovingly wipes them away, and we both take a pinch, throwing Sean's powdered remains into the sky to land upon this landscape that produced arguably the most memorable experience of my entire life.

When we arrive back at the campground, a stern-faced gate guard greets our sunburnt faces with an intense staredown. "Why have you not returned before sunset last night?"

"After we spoke with the ranger, one of our bikes would not start," I say. "We wanted to get back here because we were scared of colliding with an animal at night, but the bike would not start."

"Why did you not come back with the park warden?"

"We were going to follow him, but he left quite quickly and that's when the bike would not fire up. We were riding in very thick sand so I think some sand has clogged up the carburetor. I had to take it apart this morning."

He mumbles a few words and buys our story. By morning, he's forgotten all about the episode. He opens the gate, and we press further on into Africa. As we head into Botswana, our map shows us surrounded by dark green swaths of land: national parks, game reserves, safari camps and wildlife management areas. We're slicing through it all on a badly potholed highway, riding north to a town called Pandamatenga. There's supposedly a gas station there, conveniently about as far as the bikes can carry us with their ten-litre tanks. We haven't seen a single vehicle, village, house or farm for at least a hundred kilometres, and the road is atrocious – a far cry from Namibia's dreamy gravel roads. It's paved, but potholes the size of small cars pockmark both lanes of the road like craters in a massive slice of Swiss cheese. It's taking a long time to cover a little distance. Christina, riding ahead and dodging the huge holes with good rhythm, comes to a sudden stop when an elephant crosses her path at the crest of a hill. It's her first encounter with an elephant in the wild, and instantly it reminds me of "Big Red." I let Christina have the euphoric moment to herself, filming her from a distance.

"Oh my god, did you see that?" she says, her mouth agape in wonder. "Holy shit... my heart is pumping. This is so powerful. Look at him, he's beautiful."

Dusk is sneaking up on us, and we still have a long way to go to reach any form of civilization – this part of Botswana is ruled by the animals. *Do we keep going and take our chances on the potholed highway in the dark, or take our chances camping here?* An accident is our imminent, unwanted host should we dare break the house rule of never riding at night, so we opt to set up camp alongside the animal paths, hoofprints, and heaping piles of elephant shit next to the muddy watering hole, or "dugout," as my grandpa used to call them on the farm.

We begin animal-proofing the site, setting up the tent inside a border of trees and deadfall, positioning the bikes directly facing the road – keys in the ignition – in case we need to escape in the middle of the night. I reckon we can jump out of the tent, still naked with the sweat of an African night clinging to our bodies, start the bikes and be back on the highway in less than ten seconds. I take it one step further and attach two empty beer cans to a long piece of fishing line and drape them from the bikes to the tent. If anything comes too close for comfort, it'll act as our burglar alarm. I think it's brilliant.

At three a.m., Chris wakes me, her eyes peeled open in fear. "Do you *hear* that?" she says.

I can only hear the rustling of my sleeping bag, but she shushes me with her eyes.

"*Listen.*"

I hear a pack of hyenas laughing in the distance, followed by the trumpeting of elephants and then a few low, loud grunting noises that make Christina's hand reach for the zipper. Lions, maybe? Wildebeest? The bush is alive tonight, playing itself out for us to hear. I place my hand on Christina's, assure her we'll be okay, and we go back to sleep. Or, at least, I do.

From Christina's Journal:

Sunday, May 4th, 2008
Victoria Falls, Zambia

Mosi-oa-Tunya – The Smoke that Thunders. Big juicy droplets of fresh Zambezi water soaked our bodies to the core as we explored this amazing natural wonder of the world. Exhilarating! Spectacular! Any adjective you want. Everyone who ventured across the slippery bridge to the "Knife Edge" had a huge smile plastered across their dripping wet faces. The whole feeling of the place emanated with positivity. Friends, couples, strangers even, held hands running across the bridge and along the rocky pathways together. I made friends with a group of girls and showed them how to slide holding the slippery railing of the bridge, like Todd and Sean did in their underwear... haha! The girls screeched and squealed, embracing the feeling of innocence. We all felt like children today.

Standing amongst the raw power of the falls, I feel fortunate to experience one of the world's most magical places, not once but twice. And for the first time since Sean died, I catch myself feeling grateful that he died. *Did I just think that?* I realize the absurdity of the thought, but however demented it seems, I know it's true. He always inspired me, but losing him hammered home the importance of living a free life. Had Sean not died, I wouldn't be here right now. I probably wouldn't have even met Christina, or Jimmy and T-Mac and all the others in Sean's merry band of dirtbag life-lovers that are now my dear friends. In 1999, Sean and I veered south from here into Zimbabwe and on to Phillip's home in Nyanga. This time, Christina and I must point our tires north into Zambia to get some nets in our hands. After Livingstone, the Africa ahead will be unknown to either of us. We've been hearing much about HIV and AIDS lately, and have also been seeing a few giant billboards promoting the use of mosquito nets. Back in the UK, Rob Mather has been working hard, but so far the logistics are not working in our favour. We must remain patient.

A flat tire forces us off the road and into a small village called Bomakavumbe, where an intense game of girls' netball is underway. As soon as they see us, bedlam breaks loose – 100 chanting voices and 200 dancing feet churning up little clouds of dust, welcoming us onto their land with a tribal song sung so loud it stuns us into silence.

With darkness looming, a herd of children follows us back to our camp to witness the *azungu* (plural for *mzungu*, white man) and all their stuff. They light a fire and watch with wonder as I prepare a simple spaghetti dinner while Christina reads *Dark Star Safari* by Paul Theroux to the kids squatting behind us on a slab of slanting black rock. A boisterous, semi-drunk humpback dwarf with a chest like a balloon keeps interrupting her, but his physical deformities don't seem to affect his outgoing personality. He's wearing a dusty blue blazer, kneeling in the dirt with a piece of straw poking out from his big smiley lips.

"You speaky too fast," he says to Christina. "No understand, but me likey you!"

He makes a cigarette from homegrown tobacco rolled loosely in newspaper, rips the end off with his teeth and asks me for "fire." I light his smoke with the same duct-tape-wrapped red Bic lighter I have miraculously kept for eight months straight. As I write in my notebook beside the flicker of a kerosene lantern, bugs flying into my eyes and nose, a girl tears apart a short stalk of sugarcane, spitting the spent fibres onto the ground by my feet. I ask for some, and the sweet juice swirls around my mouth for a few seconds, dense and heavy, like syrup. A young man named Gilbert appoints himself as our host, politely shooing away the drunken dwarf, who's causing no harm, and pleading with the rest of the kids to respect our personal space and belongings. His eyes belie a great admiration towards us, studying my every move when I take him into town at 5:30 a.m. to get help to fix the puncture. We return to a group of young girls surrounding Christina, trying to teach her how to sing a strange, slow-building chant/song they call "Dongola Dongola."

> Doh Doh
> Dongola Dongola
> Ayah kumayaji
> Khumba sesa
> Oh topa topa!
> Sweet banana
> Are you ready?
> Just... make... a fashion.

The instant they pronounce the word *fashion*, the girls click their tongues in unison and strike a pose, their hands framing their face or pointing into the sky for five full seconds. Christina is bent over, howling with laughter, shouting for an encore. It's the oddest mixed-language song I've ever heard in my life, and soon becomes a repetitive chant in our heads for days to come.

MALAWI WOWIE

MAY–JUNE 2008

Mosquito nets aren't due to arrive in Tanzania for another six weeks, so we're in no rush to make mileage – after seven months of continuous travel, we need to give our bikes and bodies a rest. Willy and Jessie have performed admirably thus far; we're proud of their 200cc underdog determination and in some ways I think they resemble us; stubborn, a bit feisty and ready for a good challenge.

"When you guys feel the need for a break, go to Lake Malawi and find a place called Usisya Beach Lodge," our Cape Town friend James Mader had advised back at the beginning of the trip. "It's not easy to reach, but it's well worth the drive. Remember to bring food, because they often run out."

The ride to Usisya is a scrappy one, climbing through forests, coffee plantations, and tall stands of eucalyptus trees before descending back down to the beach in a minefield of deep ruts, slippery mounds and chunky rocks that demand full attention. At one point the road becomes so narrow that the tall swaying grasses whip our faces as we roll past. Then the trail (calling it a road no longer seems fair) abruptly ends in a sandy field with no signage in sight. Luckily, a pack of kids push us through the final 300 metres in the dark, shouting "Go, go, go!" with great enthusiasm.

In the morning, we know paradise isn't lost anymore; we stumbled upon it in the pitch black of night. With the comfort of real pillows and a mattress to sleep on every night under the stars, we know instantly Usisya Beach will be our home for a while. No electricity, no cockroaches, no scorpions, no running water, no humidity to swamp our clothes into a sour tropical stench and no salt water to turn our skin into a crusty itch. Best of all, there are no rules.

"You can do anything you want here," says Tygo, the lodge manager, when I ask him if it's okay to smoke a morning spliff. "Is no problem for me. Please feel at home." He flashes a childlike smile, wearing a fancy kitchen apron over his clean jeans.

"When you run out, is no problem I buy *chamba* for you, Mr. Toddy and Miss Christina. Hahaha!"

"Where can we put our valuables?" Christina asks Jane, the lodge's maid and cook.

"In all, ten years here, and no problem, no taking. People respect the lodge. It bring money to the community. Your things will be fine. Nobody is taking."

James had also mentioned renting a kayak and exploring Lake Malawi, the world's fourth-largest freshwater lake by volume and ninth-largest by area. After two weeks of beach bliss, playing ping pong and working on our notes, an early-morning ferry takes us south to Nkhata Bay, the only place nearby that rents sea kayaks for multi-day trips. The plan is to hug a fraction of the undeveloped northwestern shoreline past Usisya and paddle further north to Ruarwe to check out the "spectacular waterfall that spills onto the beach," as a local guidebook says, before doubling back to Nkhata Bay – a 180-kilometre round-trip journey.

"Aye, it is too fah," says one of the workers at Monkey Business, the kayak rental shop. "To go there and back, you cannot. It is too windy. You can take the ferry back. It will take you many days, maybe ten or nine."

He's reluctant to let us rent a tandem kayak for a whole week without a guide and no knowledge of the conditions, but we manage to convince him that we have sufficient paddling experience to make a safe journey. As we push off, tall yellow grasses wave at us from the steep forested hills above as the last rays of sunshine dance upon the lake's glassy surface. Gangly shoreline trees bend their branches into the water for a drink. It's an inviting evening to be dipping a paddle into the water, a welcome respite from long days in the saddle. Although it looks nothing like Nabusimake in Colombia, my mind goes there anyway when I think of the village Chief and his sage advice to "just be."

Three days later, when we arrive back at the beach in Usisya, a day ahead of schedule, Tygo and Jane prepare a delicious fish dinner.

"How is the *mwera* wind?" Tygo says with a devious smile. "It is too strong on the lake, I think. We are worrying."

"Thank god we were paddling *with* the wind," Christina responds. "It's gonna be hellish if we have to paddle *up* these waves into the wind on the way back."

We point our kayaks south in the morning, and the gusting wind hisses and snaps like a cornered beast, whipping the water into an outrageous mess of whitecaps. Fighting to make any headway, for four exhausting hours we plunge our paddles into the lake's turbulence until finally we approach the shoreline, where shouts of "Sweetie Banana!" overtake the sound of lapping waves and draw us towards a group of giggling girls. We visited this same village, Thoto, on our second night and taught them the "Dongola Dongola" song from Zambia.

"Yes, you have no problem to stay here," says Derek, a muscular, bald-headed man who approaches us with a warm smile. It's odd to hear such a Western name in these parts.

"We are living peaceful here. Nobody will come to do bad things or to take things from you. *Dooon't* worry. You are always welcome here."

I admire his secluded existence, untouched by the sound of cars, trucks, buses or air pollution. Almost all of the men ply the waters nightly in a battalion of dugout canoes, fixed with paraffin "tirry lamps" that attract the fish to the surface. The fleet returns before sunrise with their boats full of squirming silver fish. What they don't eat, they dry and package for export.

"This is our food, *usipa*," Derek says. "If it's been a good day, there are some green vegetables to mix, or even a piece of meat with some sauce. Many times is hard, but is okay here. I like it too much."

The camaraderie is soon spoiled by a stammering drunkard clutching a milk carton full of thick sorghum *chibuku* beer in his giant hand. He spits out his words in my face and tries to wipe his slimy palm on my shirt. I react by telling him to fuck off, and the others agree, pushing him out of my way.

"Fuck you!" he yells at me from behind the crowd. It's the first instance of hostility we've encountered in Malawi, but as the words come from a drunken mouth, it has no lasting impression. Derek keeps him moving along, and all is back to normal in seconds – apparently he's the village asshole. I wonder what pain or anger that man is trying to drown, what his story looks like to create a character so removed from the welcoming kindness of everyone else. Who can ever know the battles we wage within ourselves?

Back on the water, an unrelenting headwind picks up early the next morning, spraying water in our faces with every stroke as we fight hard to gain ground. We hug the shoreline to maximize every inch of possible advantage against the *mwera* wind, but it seems there is always another point to conquer.

"Look where we are! We've been to a lot of cool places, eh, sweetheart?" I say to Christina. She turns and smiles back at me, and we dig our paddles in hard for the final push. We need to get back to Nkhata Bay before exhaustion claims us, and we finally arrive at Monkey Business just before dark. They're shocked to see us, especially the guy who thought we'd never make it. He looks at his watch for the date.

"Six days only?! Eish, you are too strong. Nobody is doing this trip. In my working time here, for eight years, you are the only ones to paddle back."

For a long time, my principal fear in coming back to Africa existed in knowing that our lives could be easily taken by a brainwashed 14-year-old with an AK-47 slung across his shoulder and a cigarette dangling between his lips. That worst-case-scenario had played out several times in my mind as I thought of our approaching journey into the more dangerous *Heart of Darkness* Africa that lurked to the west. Said teenager would be manning a makeshift roadblock somewhere in the jungles of the Congo, where child-soldier indoctrination runs as rampant as dengue fever. From our captor's point of view, two human dollar signs had magically appeared as a physical manifestation of his prayers, delivered on two wheels in front of the shaking barrel of his rifle. I pictured him with a stern look on his face, ordering us off the bikes in a language we didn't understand, forcing us to the ground with venom in his eyes. Then the rest of his hypnotized rebel-warrior friends, who up until six months ago were innocent kids kicking around a limp soccer ball in a field, would saunter out of the forest like zombies and surround us like a pack of hungry wolves. If we were lucky, they would beat us senseless, take every last possession we owned, including the clothes off our backs and the shoes on our feet, and leave us to rot in the jungle. At least then we'd have a chance. If we were unlucky, we'd be just two more casualties in Africa's dark and tormented story.

Yes, I did worry that I too would die in Africa, and Mom would have to live under the heavy weight of grief for as long as her heart held out. As Christina and I began this adventure, I fought to push such horrible thoughts from my mind, but they crept in from time to time, especially early on, with so many unknowns yet to come. Both of my uncles, Larry and Joe Lawson, also passed away tragically before their time, and I carried around the morose idea that I was next – that the curse of the Lawsons would continue with this expedition, a risky undertaking to keep Sean's legacy alive, on which I knew I was gambling a lot, Christina included. Anytime the thought of death began weighing heavily on my mind, I would picture Chris and me hoisting a bottle of champagne in the middle of a whitewashed hillside street in Tangier, Morocco, triumphantly celebrating the end of the African Odyssey. Sometimes I'd even imagine Sean there with us, shimmering opaque like Yoda at the end of *Return of the Jedi*, or maybe more like Obi-Wan Kenobi...

The sound of Christina groaning inside the tent pulls me out of my thoughts. Just two hours ago, she said that her throat felt a little weird and she wanted to lie down for a nap. Now she's curled up in the fetal position underneath both of our sleeping bags, teeth chattering as if she's been locked in a freezer.

"Am I going to be okay, Todd?" she asks. "I'm so cold. I've never felt like this before."

Sean said those exact last words to me while lying on the pavement in Johannesburg five days before he died. All the ifs and should-haves from years ago instantly start coursing through my brain. *We should have listened to the travel health nurse and taken the goddamn Lariam. If only fucking Zubair had shown up on time as promised, Sean would have gone to the clinic sooner.*

This is not even the first time we've had a malaria scare. In Nicaragua, on the outskirts of Managua, Christina was in the throes of a full-blown fever when she whispered, "Todd, I think I should go and see a doctor."

For a stubborn, headstrong woman, it was a rare moment of vulnerability. I was attracted to her toughness, and she didn't often show this side, so I knew something was wrong. I had never even seen her sick before: she practised yoga every day, stuck to a vegetarian diet and tackled physical challenges with strength and determination. The thought that she might have had malaria sent shivers down my spine. I stayed calm but inside was scared shitless. *Please, dear God, don't let this be malaria.* I had to help her out of bed, pleading with her to summon enough strength to walk down the street to the doctor's office, where she was diagnosed with the flu.

Now, five months into our mission, I'm beginning to realize that I'm not so afraid of a bullet from a rebel child-soldier as of the microscopic penetrating needle of a female *Anopheles* mosquito. My mind starts racing, and all I can think of is Dr. Debbie's voice: *Make sure you call me immediately if anything happens.* My brain fills itself with an instant slew of negative scenarios: What if she *does* have malaria? The closest hospital is three or four hours away, and she can barely move.

Christina won't even be able to hold on to me, she can barely sit up. *Am I going to strap her to my body and ride a rocky road in the mountains while she's wracked by a fever, for fuck's sake? What if we didn't catch it in time?*

"Todd… please tell me I'm going to be okay," she says with such worried eyes that I can't help but think of the last time I saw Sean on his own two feet.

Christina's plea for help shakes me to the core. Watching her shivering uncontrollably pulls my mind into a vivid church experience from our first days in this country, in Lilongwe, where a Zion Church pastor had whipped his followers into a shaking, sweating, hallelujah-chanting frenzy. Inside the dirt-floored church, a young man had stood with his eyes squeezed shut, his teeth clenched, praying with such fervour that spurts of spit flew from the corners of his quivering mouth. Below him sat a legless lady in a smart blue business suit, quietly praying with her hands outstretched towards the pastor. As the service reached its peak, people rushed to the front of the room, the volume as loud as a rock concert. In words we could not understand, the pastor held the heads of the devout firmly in his meaty paws, laying his hands on those who came to seek the Holy Spirit to heal themselves of sickness or sin. Shaking their heads, he delivered a "prayer from the Holy Spirit" until they collapsed backwards into the arms of others, who gently laid them to the ground. One woman lay in a trance-like state for five minutes or more, crying and shivering…

Christina can't stop shaking, and I realize I need to act fast. Rummaging through our stuff, I find a key piece of survival gear packed inside a green Tupperware container: our malaria test kit. Also inside the box is a small oral thermometer, which I place under her tongue.

"You're going to be okay, babe. I'm right here. Let's take your temperature. I'm also going to do the blood test for malaria. Everything will be okay, though, sweetheart," I try to say as reassuringly as possible.

"Do I have malaria?" she says, faintly. "My body hurts so much."

"No, sweetie. Just try and get some rest, okay?"

The thermometer reads 104.6 degrees Fahrenheit, the danger zone. With trembling fingers, I rip open the test kit and read the instructions with utmost attention.

1. Open the packet and remove.
2. Open the alcohol swab. Grasp the 4th finger on the patient's left hand. Clean the finger with the alcohol swab. Allow the finger to dry before pricking.
3. Prick patient's finger to get a drop of blood.
4. Use the capillary tube to collect the drop of blood.
5. Use the capillary tube to put the drop of blood into the square hole marked "A."
6. Add buffer into the round hole marked "B."
7. Wait 15 minutes after adding buffer. (NOTE: *do not* read the test sooner than 15 minutes after adding the buffer. You may get FALSE results.)

How to read the test results:

POSITIVE
A line near letter "C" and a line near letter "T" means the patient is POSITIVE for malaria.

NEGATIVE
A line near letter "C" and no line near letter "T" means the patient DOES NOT have malaria.

C or T. CT. Christina Tottle. Christina and Todd. A line by *C* is good, *T* is not. I start chanting in my head like a sports fan: *C is good, C is good. Gimme a line by the C.* Her shivering finally subsides, and she falls into what seems a more restful sleep. Even the prick of the needle doesn't wake her. Now I must wait 15 minutes. *Should I go to the hospital no matter what the test says? What if it doesn't work anyway?* It could be bunk after rattling around in the back of a motorcycle for 6000 kilometres. Shaking on the inside, I take a proper deep breath and rub the Nyami Nyami around my neck for protection from the gods. *Should I just go and find a doctor right now? Should I try and find a phone to call Dr. Debbie?* Hesitation cost me my brother's life, and I don't want to make the same mistake again. Christina's family would never forgive me.

I'd never forgive myself. I try not to think of my mom, her kitchen, that argument.

The flickering light of a candle lulls me into a gentle trance. Bright, hot, dancing in the wind, it reminds me of the spirit within Klara Knapek, one of Christina's best friends, who died three weeks ago in a tragic accident in the mountains near Whistler. Since we couldn't fly back for Klara's celebration of life, we decided to have our own wake and went looking for solace and beauty along the shores of Lake Malawi. As we reached the shore, a bulky orange moon rose slowly from the watery horizon like bread in an oven. We'd broken our no-night-riding rule for the first time but arrived safely at a campground, where a night watchman lit a fire for us within minutes.

"What is the name of this place?" I asked him.

"You are here in Nkhotakota," he said, accentuating the two *K*s. KK. Klara Knapek. How fitting.

I asked if he had any *chamba*; Klara liked to smoke, so why not celebrate her naturally? Without hesitation, he walked back to a small shack and returned 15 minutes later with his hat full of 23 (Klara was born on December 23) individually wrapped teardrop-shaped packets made from torn pieces of a brown paper bag. Soon after, a group of four young men approached us, looking serious but inquisitive. I happened to be filming a candlelit close-up of Christina, so I let the tape roll.

"Hello my friends from Canahdah," said the enthusiastic leader of the pack. "This is Malawi, the wahm haht of Afreeka. Here, we are good pee-pahl, kind pee-pahl."

"Yeahh," said the three others in perfect harmony, like they were singing the chorus in a choir.

"Me, I want to say, that, those people from Canahdah, they are very nice pee-pahl."

"Yeahh."

"I hope to come to Canahdah one day to visit you."

"Yeahh."

"When I get to Canahdah, you will make us famous."

"Yeahh."

"Because the Canadjian people, they are good pee-pahl. Like Mala-wi pee-pahl."

"Yeahh."

"Wow. Thank you," said Christina, laughing at their little call-and-response show. "We love your country too. Tonight we will celebrate our friend Klara, she's up there right now, dancing on that big orange moon."

"Ohhkay, laydee, thank you. We will all celebrate Miss Klara tonight."

They seemed so sincere and genuine, I secretly wished I could tell their mothers how impressed I was of their demeanour. These kind strangers were typical of most of the people we'd met in Southern Africa. We had yet to experience any form of animosity, had yet to be robbed of any possessions, and had not once seen an instance of physical abuse. I assumed that the man who sold us the *chamba* had sent the kids over to talk to us, so I gave them a couple of packets of weed, and they walked away down a moonlit path while I rolled a joint.

"This is for you, Klara," Christina said, holding up a bottle of wine to the moon. "Shine on, you crazy diamond."

I jolt out of the memory as if electrocuted and scramble to check my watch – it's been eight minutes exactly. I lean into the candle, holding the test gingerly to its glow, as if the whole world might explode if it's positive. Nothing yet. Keep waiting. I find myself thinking of those people in that church again, how loud and strange I'd found it all. But here, now, all is silent up on the hilltop. Except for me, whispering – pleading – to anyone, anything, *Please get us through this.* Suddenly restless, I leave the tent for a breath of fresh air and to seek some help while Christina is still asleep. We're staying at a place called the Mushroom Farm, an off-grid eco-lodge/campsite above Lake Malawi's northern shores, on the Nyika Plateau. From Mzuzu, it took us more than four hours to get here, up a dusty dirt road with dozens of steep switchbacks, to more than 7,000 feet above sea level – untouched, unplugged and very remote.

With Lake Malawi shimmering in the afternoon sun below, the sweeping view helps ease my mind for a brief moment. In the open-air common area, I hear three women speaking in a Canadian or

American accent. When I approach them, they see the worry on my face and ask what's wrong.

"My wife is in the tent right and she's pretty sick. I've never seen her like this before. It happened really quickly. I took her temperature just now, and it's 104 degrees. I also just gave her a test for malaria, and I'm waiting for the results."

A petite brunette with a bob haircut and kind eyes responds first. "Hi. My name is Karen, this is Elizabeth and that's Tracy. We're all registered nurses from the United States. Maybe we can help? Where is she now?"

The supreme fortune of finding not one but three registered nurses within minutes is not lost on me; it feels like three angels have arrived on our doorstep. I open the palm of my hand to show Karen the rectangular plastic stick from the test kit. It's been the longest 15 minutes of my life. A thin red line soon appears inside the window near the letter C. I look at the instructions again, then at the three nurses. Negative.

Thank fucking god.

"I had malaria last week," says a voice from the back of the room. "Hi, sorry to interrupt, but I overheard your conversation. I'm Simon, from England. I was lucky. You feel it coming along, my whole body was aching. So I went to the chemist in Mzuzu and got some drugs. I think it was Coartem? When you feel it coming on, there's a sinking feeling in your belly, 'cause you know how bad it can get. I've heard a lot of stories of kids in the villages getting malaria. But the parents can't get to a chemist on time to get treatment. Sometimes a lot of the kids die before the parent returns."

"Thanks, Simon, I'm glad you're okay," says Karen. "Todd, your wife will be fine. These tests are actually quite accurate. We'll go and take a look at her now."

Nick, the South African owner, offers me a quaint chalet at no extra charge so the nurses can undergo a proper diagnosis on a bed.

"We've all been there before," he says. "I don't want her to go through this in a tent."

With Christina's arms draped around our shoulders, Nick and I walk her, still shaking like a leaf in the wind, to our new abode.

- CHAPTER 21 -

Perched on a steep hillside, with a king-size bed and a million-dollar view, it's easily the nicest place we've stayed in Africa.

"She most likely has strep throat," says Tracy. "Ironically enough, all three of us have just been through it, and it seems she has the identical symptoms. It can be a wind-borne infection, carried with the dust in the dry season, so riding up here on your bikes is likely how she contracted the virus."

In an almost unbelievable stroke of luck, the women have an extra prescription of antibiotics left over. "Make sure she finishes the full course," Tracy says. "Make sure she gets plenty of rest, and keep her well-hydrated. She should be okay in a few days. Todd, you should also get some rest. It sounds like you guys have a long way to go."

MR. EACH AND EVERYTHING

TANZANIA, BURUNDI, RWANDA, UGANDA • July–August 2008

Tanzania receives us with a luxuriant smile, as exotic as its name, rich and green and splattered with shiny banana leaves on the road, reflecting the morning sun. Blankets of wispy fog cling to crops of tea, coffee and cocoa, and curl over tiny cylindrical mountains sprouting up from the fertile land like they've been pushed into place by the fingers of an underground giant. We've arrived in the land of Swahili tongue, where little English is spoken in these rural parts, stumbling and smiling our way through the basic greetings, asking shop owners to write the amount of our purchases on paper, like the man who scratches the price into his forearm using his fingernail, the white etching easily legible against his black skin. Rivers of women walk with a dignified elegance to and from town markets, balancing heavy loads of plantains atop their heads. Most of them turn with ease to shoot us a stoic glance as we roll on by. I'm struck by their powerful grace, how it seems that nothing could ever cause them to drop their bounty upon the earth.

Zanzibar sounds far too enticing to pass up – and we have the time – but first we look up a guy named Mike Fighton in Dar es Salaam, East Africa's largest city. Mike is the older brother of Tygo from Usisya Beach Lodge, only bigger and less boisterous. He works at an English pub called the George and Dragon, and we find him during a packed Saturday night, weaving his way through pint-swilling expats. Outside on the patio, a fellow *mzungu* spots Willy and Jessie, fully loaded and filthy on the sidewalk outside.

"You guys have ridden all the way from SA on these 200s?" he says with a look of mild astonishment.

He tells us his name is Lester, and that his trans-African motorcycle dreams were dashed after an accident put him in the hospital. He woke up not remembering a thing.

"Yeah that hospital time wasn't so *lekker*. Better than here, though," he says. "I almost died from falciparum malaria in Tanzania. I had to be flown out of the bush, and they put me on the drip and everything. I was lucky... I could have died."

"Thankfully you caught it on time," I say. "My brother wasn't so lucky. He died from the same thing in South Africa."

"Sorry to hear that, *boet* (brother). Where did he get it?"

"I'm pretty sure it was off the coast of Mozambique."

"When was this?"

"July of 1999."

"And did you know a guy named Barry Herman?"

My ears and eyes nearly pop out of my head. "What?! You know Barry Herman?"

"Yes, I was the guy who bought your bikes."

"Holy shit, what a small world," I say, shaking my head at the chain of events that led to this moment. I had to leave JoBurg before I managed to sell the bikes and left the task up to Bryan Allott.

"Lemme get this straight," Christina says, astounded. "Sean meets Barry years ago in Thailand, you and Sean stay with Barry in Johannesburg, Lester buys your bikes from Bryan, and now you meet totally randomly nine years later in Tanzania?! Your mom is going to flip when she hears this story."

It's not the first time I've experienced such small-world serendipity. A few months after Sean passed, I took a trip to Thailand and Cambodia by myself, to spread Sean's ashes in Railay Beach and to get away from life for a while. Fate had shown her hand.

Sunday, December 17th, 2000
Bangkok, Thailand

I bid farewell to Cambodia this morning, one of those places
you'd like to return to but don't know for sure if you'll ever
be back again. I can't believe when I walked into Number 9
Guesthouse in Phnom Penh, the guy at reception looked at me
and said: "Sean?"

"Excuse me?" I said, cocking my head in disbelief.

"You look like my friend Sean from Canada."

"My brother's name is Sean."

"Sean Lawson?"

"Wow, you know my brother?!"

Soon all the guys started gathering around me, saying,
"You're Sean's brother?! Thank you for coming here. How
did you know Sean is staying here many times?"

"I didn't know. The speed boat guys just offered a free ride
here so I said okay. And here I am."

They showed me LAWSON '97, carved into the pole on the
patio and took me to meet Vay, Sean's motocross coach.

"I am sorry to you about Sean," Vay said. "We became good
fren. He always ask me teach him motocross. He is crazy
guy but all Cambodians love him. He is very warm guy too,
welcome with anyone. I am now happy that I ride the rally
with him. God bless you and your family, Todd."

Crazy random Sean-connections aside, Zanzibar lives up to its mysterious tropical reputation but is much too expensive for our dirtbag
blood. So after three glorious days swimming in the Indian Ocean and
nights wandering the narrow, full-of-life streets of Stone Town, we're
back on the mainland, heading north to Arusha and good news: the
nets are here.

Mrs. Faye Cran, or "Mama Kuku," as she's affectionately known, is
a Tanzanian-born English widow in her late 60s who takes us under

her wing. She's intensely energetic and proactive, a lifelong contributor to Rotary International, and instantly becomes like a grandmother to us. Faye puts us up in her slowly decaying mansion high on a hill overlooking a forested lake, where we're treated like distinguished guests for the week it takes to wade through a mountain of meetings, emails and phone calls between Rob Mather and a few local Rotary members. Staring at more than 1500 kilometres of remote gravel roads in the coming days, we try not to take the royal treatment for granted.

"I think you can start with some of the schools outside of Arusha," Mama Kuku says. "The schools are not really remote, like you want, but at least it will get you started on your way. These nets have been donated by the Canadian Rotarians, and your fundraising, I believe. We need people like you to make sure these nets are hung properly in these dorm rooms."

The next evening, as the giant ball of African fire descends below the horizon, we arrive at Manyara Secondary School and are invited by the secretary to pitch our tent inside one of the classrooms. Early in the morning, the cement floor vibrates underneath our tired bodies from metal-legged tables being slid around the room, screeching and scraping past our heads. It's worse than nails on a chalkboard, and it's not even six a.m. The headmistress, a steely, stern-faced woman, sees fit to bring her delinquent students inside to punish them in front of us. They're told to kneel down and hold their hands out while she lashes at them with powerful strokes of a wooden switch. Cringing at the site of pain-stricken faces, Christina steps out for a breath of morning air, where a pack of boys run around the courtyard kicking a soccer ball, while some of the girls drape wet laundry over the limbs of a dead tree. The children eventually come together in the middle of the courtyard, waiting for their day to begin.

"Good morning, students," says a tall man in a grey suit, his green tie too short to stretch over a bulging belly.

"Good morning, headmaster!" they shout back in unison.

"Today is a special day. We have some friends who have come from Canada to help us. Their organization has supplied us with new mosquito nets for your beds. Show them respect, be cooperative, and please have your dorm rooms clean. They will be coming around shortly to begin the exercise."

We start with the girls, who giggle and prance around the narrow dorm room, helping to neatly tie each net to the metal skeleton of their bunks.

"I am happy for my new bed net," says Chikundi, a 15-year-old with a dignified smile. "Before, too many mosquitoes flying around my head, keeping me awake. I want to sleep so I can study well and learn, but in the day I am too tired. I think now I can sleep better. Thank you, mister and madam."

From day one, the Against Malaria Foundation has coordinated our fundraising efforts, magically turning donated money into mosquito nets and, most impressively, getting them to us on the ground in East Africa. What seemed like a noble idea for so long is suddenly happening for real, and it feels meant to be. The kids manage to hang a net over every dorm bed, and we have a surplus left over. Cramming the remaining 30 nets into our army-green saddlebags, spurred on by this early success, Christina and I feel ready to journey into remote northwestern Tanzania. Our little mission is finally beginning to sink in. We know our efforts are but a tiny drop of water in the vast river of aid flowing into Africa, but still, we ride away from that little school filled with emotion and hope, knowing every one of those 300 children will now sleep better and learn more readily, freeing up room in their lives to dream a little bigger.

With the comfort of paved roads now behind us, we enter a never-ending obstacle course of sharp rocks covered in dust so thick and fine it feels like riding through flour. At day's end, next to a slow-running stream, hordes of people fill up yellow plastic containers of brown water, hauling them onto ox-driven carts. As we're setting up camp, a man approaches with a look of concern stretched across his weathered face.

"Hello, my friends, I am the Phillip. Please excuse me, but the village leaders have decided to warn you... warning that you are not allowed at all to sleep under the valley here. The law does not allow for visitors to be here alone, to sleep here alone. So, for their securior, they have to shift you from the place you have been occupying, direct to the camp for your special secure. It's okay please? I don't have much more to express about this. That should be enough."

In spite of a couple of mispronounced words, his eloquence catches us off guard and his warbled accent makes us smile. We're puzzled, but he gives no chance for a response.

"They are very worried for your safety. There are bandits here, and they come in the night and kill you. Many people from the out-side are coming here with strange minds and thoughts… crazy men, you know."

"But we aren't worried," Christina explains, all too aware of the potential scam tactics. Somebody, somewhere might want to make money off us. "We have camped like this in many countries and never had a problem, sir. We prefer camping like this so we can meet people and enjoy the surroundings."

"Okay, thank you, I appreciate what you are telling me, and in fact I like this idea very much. But please, you must listen to me and what I am trying to tell you. It is just not permitted to stay here. It will be very bad for Tanzania if something happens and the village Chiefs will have a very big problem."

We express our dismay with a heavy sigh – nobody likes tearing down camp ten minutes after you've set it up – but his warning seems too sincere to ignore. "The Phillip" doesn't seem like he'd scam anyone.

"Thank you very much, my friends, this will be better now, and I can sleep good to know that you are now going to be safe."

Seven teenagers pick up the tent (with almost everything still in-side) and, laughing hysterically, walk it over to a wildly overpriced $15 "campsite" (they wanted US$30) a hundred yards away. The site is sur-rounded by a posts-only "fence" with no boards or barbed wire to keep us safe and "securior." Phillip returns in the morning, silver-tongued and smiling, carrying a dead fish in a plastic bag.

"Good morning, my Canadian friends, I see that you are ready to continue your journey. You have some important work to do, I think, and your travels through Africa will be tough, but I know you will be safe everywhere."

We thank him for his thoughtful words, and then he offers up a strange nugget of wisdom, laughing with his shoulders: "Go in peace, not in pieces."

Two days later, at the edge of the sprawling Maasai Steppe, it feels like we have been ripped to pieces by the world's rockiest dirt road. I want to be back with Mama Kuku and her mansion.

"How much water do we have?" Christina asks, nervously peering into the parched landscape.

"Enough for two days. Maybe three if we skip coffee."

"How much gas do we have?"

"We're about three-quarters full, but that all depends on how sandy this road is. If it's as thick as this stuff," I say, pointing at my feet, "we're probably not gonna get too far. But if it hardens up we should be okay for almost 200 klicks."

We sit in silence for a while, the uncertainty eating at us. Choices and consequences – it currently feels as though everything in Africa is whipping those two words into the wind beside us. In the eyes of many we've met, our mission is an irresponsible adventure full of unpredictable circumstances. *Where do you sleep at night? Aren't you scared of just sleeping in the bush in the middle of nowhere, with animals all around? What do you do about food? You don't travel with a cellphone, why not?*

But stacked against other adventures from legendary explorers of the past, our journey seems at times like a frivolous jaunt. We are not the first to do this, we aren't intrepid mountaineers seeking a first ascent, or whitewater kayakers scouting rivers for the first time. We are just two motorcycle travellers, nothing more. But here on the dusty roads of Maasai, I'm not thinking so humbly. If we choose to go, getting lost seems a given and the risks quite high. I'm certain a host of wild animals would be curious of the fresh meat camping in their backyard. But what is the reward? A continuation of the Journey? Another dot connected on the map? I guess we can take solace in the fact that we've got nets in our saddlebags. We're definitely heading into the "real" Africa, as we've been hearing about from other overlanders.

I hope we don't see any AKs. Moments later, a pair of Maasai women herding long-horned cattle emerge from a dust cloud. Their necks, ankles and wrists are ringed with bands of gold and swirling beads. Hoops of flesh dangle at their lobes, big enough for my wrist to fit through. The sight of these women makes me think of my mother – if she knew where we were now, she'd be worried to death. We ask for directions, but they speak neither English nor Swahili. Despite waved hands, pointed fingers and babbled words, we're still lost in the African wilderness with no GPS, no cellphone and no compass. But even in this moment of stark realization we don't find ourselves pining for technology to save our asses, nor do we regret not having it. The sole reason *why* we don't have any navigation devices is because getting lost on this vast continent was expected from the start.

"Let's just go," I say naively. "All these paths probably lead to the same place anyway."

Christina rolls her eyes but agrees; backtracking is not an option. We've only ridden 100 kilometres since yesterday, but it was a rough-and-tumble affair that took us almost eight hours from the Ngorongoro Conservation Area, where the gate guards mentioned a "secret road" around Lake Eyasi to Western Tanzania.

"Is nice road. You can see the lake, and you can reach Burundi country. Is no problem."

Is problem now. Their secret road has dissipated into dozens of crooked animal paths fingering off into the desert. Battered huts poke through the dust, but we see no other signs of life. Just as we're about to throw caution to the wind and take a wild guess where to point our tires, salvation putters up on a dust-covered Yamaha DT175 with a leopard-skin seat. The rider sports a bushy beard and a wool toque under his helmet. Just looking at him makes me thirsty. He's also carrying a helmetless passenger with googly eyes who reminds me of Mitch from Crooked Tree in Belize.

"Where are you moving to?" asks the man behind the handlebars.

Speaking in charades and broken English, we show him our scribbled list of directions written in Swahili by the park guides.

"Okay, no problem," he grins. "I am called Msekwa. We will move together. Do you have water?"

The landscape soon swallows us in a murky bowl of grey, black and brown. A gloomier place to ride I can't imagine, but it's also the most exhilarating landscape we've ridden in Africa thus far. Without the constraints of fences or roads it's a high-speed game of cat and mouse with fun little side-hits that we launch off for a little taste of controlled air time – floating on a fully loaded bike isn't something that happens every day.

Without Msekwa's lead, we'd be lost in a roadless no man's land, surely meat for the hyenas at some point. There are many cows and goats but not a blade of grass to be seen, and no lake shimmering in the distance. *How do people survive here?* We pass women carrying calabashes full of muddy water collected from shallow wells. Maasai tribesmen ride one-speed bicycles with bows and quivers of arrows strapped across their muscled backs. I stop to ask one of them if I can take a photograph, but he backs away nervously, using his bike as a shield. The encounter brings an uneasy feeling of shame – I don't want to be someone that forces another to be afraid. I'll keep my camera away from people for the rest of the day.

Freewheeling across this grim desert wasteland, we try to keep pace with Msekwa, who rides swiftly, weaving in and out of animal paths that dart between dead trees coated in dust so thick they look like mummified skeletons – thousands of them. I feel like a character in a Mad Max movie, frozen in a moment of fist-pumping adrenaline. *Finally, this is it.* Off-road adventure. Uninhibited exploration. Pure, delicious freedom. This is the Africa we've been waiting for. It feels so goddamn surreal. I can't even see the bikes or bodies riding in front of me, just the puff of dust left by their tracks. For a rider, it's a beautiful sight. Sean would be in his glory.

We stop only once, in a small Maasai village, to eat cold rice, beans and, oddly, a big boiled turkey leg. Curious tribesmen gather around the bikes and peer into the wooden food stall for a better look at our dusty white faces. A few flaunt Western clothes, but most are decked in animal skins, silver jewellery and colourful beads. One of them touches the fabric of my riding jacket and pulls his hand away quickly, as though it were being burned. The land offers no distinguishing marks and nothing on the horizon to pinpoint our bearing. Even our heaven-sent guide stops to ask for directions when we get momentarily lost amid a maze of cotton fields. The day ends with us chasing our long shadows until we come to a muddy river about 50 feet across. I think about running it because I'm too spent to push my bike through, but Msekwa talks me out of it.

"Is very deep. You walk through. We push."

In the last of the day's light, we arrive in his village, ready to drop. I look in my mirror and see a stranger in an earthen brown mask staring back at me. We've only covered 202 kilometres, but it feels like 2000. Our bodies look like tiles on a terracotta roof. At Msekwa's modest three-room home, the first thing we notice are two tattered mosquito nets hanging outside.

"We have malaria here, much malaria in the season," Msekwa tells us. "There are many suffering."

Christina explains the details of our mosquito-net mission and offers four new nets for his family – his wife, Judith, and their three children. It's a small token of appreciation for guiding us safely back to civilization.

"Please also give one to your passenger, the next time you see him in the desert."

"I thank you with my heart," he says.

In the morning, Msekwa insists on changing the dirty oil in Willy and Jessie while we eat pancakes with his family.

"You will have no problem to border. The road is rough, but the road is there. Just follow straight. Don't deviate. *Safari njema!*"

Heavily loaded with food, extra fuel and mosquito nets, our bikes are hard to keep upright in the thick gravel, but we arrive at the Burundi border at Giseru in good time – and in one piece. The sole immigration official, beer in hand, ushers us inside a cement building that looks nothing like a government office whatsoever: no presidential portraits on the walls, no plaques, no men in uniform. He seems dodgy and unsure but eventually pulls out an official stamp and hammers a three-day transit visa into our passports.

Three days! That's it? We have no local currency and barely enough food to get us through, and now we're under the gun with nets to give. Luckily, Burundi is one of Africa's smallest countries, and Christina speaks fluent French, one of the national languages.

Bedlam ensues at every stop; we're engulfed by an avalanche of white teeth and excited faces that descend upon us from both banks of the red-earth roads as if it were a survival race, kids jumping and chanting amidst a cloud of dust kicked up by a hundred hardened bare feet. Latin America prepared us well, but this is another level entirely. Throngs of people run from all directions to either greet us, meet us or try and help us with directions on the signless gravel roads. We feel like the circus that just rolled into town – an oddity, an out-of-their world sideshow that takes them away, albeit momentarily, from the tedium of chores and boredom.

"Mzungu! Mzungu!" they sing and shout, followed by the three words that seemingly every African child knows fluently: "Give me money!" So many people ask us for money, but how can we possibly help them all? You're either a philanthropist or a traveller. In Africa, you can't be both. At times, both Christina and I feel ashamed at the amount of gear we carry, worth more than some Africans earn in a lifetime, but we would rather disappoint than perpetuate the vicious cycle of point-less handouts in aid-driven Africa. Handing out a dollar here and there turns people into beggars, sometimes drunken louts. Even the most well-intentioned traveller can end up doing more harm than good by reaching in their pockets to fill outstretched hands. When we can, we help by giving some food or pencils that we've been buying for such instances. It never feels like enough, but it's something.

Within a day's ride of the Burundi-Rwanda border, cloaked in a lay-er of powdery orange sand, we find a small village high in the hills where rows of disintegrating orange-brick huts stand wearily between ripe fields of coffee and bananas. We see some people hanging out on a grassy yard in front of a family compound. They seem shy and un-certain, making us feel much the same. We don't want to bluntly ask to stay with them but do want to provide them with some mosquito nets, and now seems as good a time as any to engage. We try to communicate with an elderly lady wearing a bright orange *chitenge* wrapped around her wrinkled body, but to no avail; the elders speak only their native language. Finally a voice from behind breaks the silence. He speaks good French; Christina translates.

"His name is William, and he says his mother has invited us to sleep in her home. She wants us to feel welcome and not be afraid."

I count the heads of 64 people crowded around, but the group slowly dissipates as darkness encroaches. For dinner we cook rice and vegetables to share with the family of ten. They timidly accept and eat the meal in a separate room. I'm not sure they've ever seen rice before. Night falls fast, and cold, so we wait until morning to tell them of our project. Crowds of children, rust-coloured like the rooftops, clamber around to see the strange blue nets. We take turns pounding nails into the adobe walls with bricks, hanging nets over each of the beds in the cloister of huts – six in total. William and his family are grateful, but an argument breaks out with the neighbours, who are watching with envious eyes.

"What about me?" says a clearly pissed-off man, shouting from across the way. His clothes are in tatters, and it looks as though he hasn't washed in days. "What about my family? We also are suffering from malaria, where are these nets for us?"

"We are very sorry, my friend, but we can only carry so many nets," Christina explains in a soft voice. "We're just two people and we can't help every person in every village. We have stayed with this family, and they have generously offered their home for us. This is our way of saying thank you. Perhaps we can contact our organization, and they can put your village on the list to receive nets in the future."

"Okay, thank you," he says, calming down. "I hope one day you will come back with these things for me."

"I hope so too."

The thrill of experiencing a new country from behind the handlebars of a motorcycle really hits home as we climb high into foggy mountain passes on freshly paved blacktop and enter "The Land of a Thousand Hills." We know virtually nothing of Rwanda's geography, but it doesn't take long to notice that this country is different from any other in Africa. Glancing around at farmsteads dotted amongst the fertile hillsides, we can't see *any* litter. The ditches and streams are devoid of plastic bottles and bags, a regular blight of the African landscape. Entering Kigali later that day, we notice garbage cans on street corners and an army of workers in green coveralls picking up piles of rubbish. The city is almost spotless. A search for a computer technician to fix our broken laptop goes surprisingly well when we meet a young, English-fluent Ugandan named Martin, who gets to work immediately with a set of tiny screwdrivers. He thinks the screen may be my only problem and starts making phone calls to colleagues in Kampala in search of a new one. Martin and his business partner, Arthur, a handsome gentleman whose mouth is turned up at the corners in a constant smile, offer us free rein of the upstairs office so we can file photos and stories for the Against Malaria Foundation, *Dirt & Quad Magazine* and a new Whistler-based magazine called *Mountain Life*, founded recently by Glen Harris and Jon Burak, two friends who also knew Sean. As we pound away at our first "office day" in ages, Arthur, dressed smartly in suit and tie, invites us along for a popular Rwandan tradition, the buffet lunch. I close the laptop almost too eagerly, and away we go.

"I was young when the genocide started to happen," Arthur says at lunch. He speaks calmly and composed, like he senses us wanting to know about the horrors in his country. "We lived outside of Kigali, maybe one hour. My mother and father were both murdered, killed in the daytime in our village."

Our waitress politely interrupts, pouring water over our hands tableside into a small plastic basin, an ingrained part of the dining experience in this part of the world. We dry our hands on a fresh washcloth, and Arthur continues.

"Many people in my family also died, my uncle and three of my cousins the very next day. I had to run very fast to escape with my brother. But the next year, I lost my brother to AIDS. I was young, I think 14 years, and now everything is okay. We are a country again. This is Rwanda. Now I am not fearing for my life. I feel it is safe now, and we are all brothers."

"Oh my god, I'm so sorry for the loss of your family," says Christina, touching his hands with hers on the table. "Who did you live with when your parents died?"

"I was on my own for some time, trying hard to survive here in the city. My brother's wife took everything, all of the money. I was shining shoes, but I know computers are important, so I began to study about them. And I opened my business here."

"I admire you for your resiliency, and your courage," Christina says. "There are many people in the world who cannot imagine a nightmare like this, and you lived through it and succeeded all on your own. You should be very proud of yourself."

"Thank you, ma'am. I am blessed by God that I now have a daughter of my own."

Back at the shop after lunch, we learn Martin can't fix the laptop, and he charges us nothing for his time. "You go to Kampala," he says. "My colleague is waiting for you. He will help you when you reach there."

We still have a few nets remaining but struggle to find a remote pocket to explore and give them away. People seem to be everywhere, walking narrow pathways that bisect the mountainsides. We push on to Lake Kivu in the west, hoping to snatch a piece of lakeside paradise for a couple of days, but an ominously dark sky quashes that plan, and instead we ride higher into the mist, past the steep rocky peaks of Volcanoes National Park, shrouded in midday haze. The lushness of the forest comes as a refreshing sight – strikingly different from the spiky desert dryness of Western Tanzania and Burundi's bowl of dust. The park, its volcanoes rising sharp and steep from the thick tangle of forest below, was the base for Dian Fossey's 18-year mountain gorilla observations, and the first national park in all of Africa. Coming face to face with a massive silverback would be an experience to take to your grave, but we can't swallow the US$1,000 price tag to see the primates. Instead, we happily settle for the new friends and memories made in a country that has been to hell and seems to have risen from the ashes.

Our entry into Uganda is expensive and tiresome, and when we finally do get permission to enter the country, we find ourselves fading as quickly as the late-afternoon light. Roadside fields hold busy farmers struggling to cut furrows in the soil with ox-driven plows. Women strike the earth with handmade hoes with babies bouncing across their backs. It seems as though a quarter of all the cement buildings are painted bright pink, emblazoned with the logo of Zain, one of Uganda's cellphone carriers. The marketing is clearly working; a family that serves us rice and french fries at a restaurant has named their first child Nokia.

Christina spots a footpath that runs from the road down to a rustic homestead, where a white-haired elder is picking cotton from a pile of branches at his feet.

"*Habari zenu,*" we say politely. "Good afternoon."

He smiles but doesn't speak, his head wobbling side to side. A small crowd soon gathers, and a young man with a beaming smile walks to the front to greet us.

"You can feel at peace here. You are most welcome," he says perfectly, and intentionally loud. "My name is Dennis. Each and every thing is here for you."

"Can you please ask this man if we can stay with him and his family?" Christina says. "We are tired after a long day. We have a tent and food, all we need is some space over there on the grass if this is possible."

He turns to the old man, who continues his routine, speaking a language we cannot recognize.

"I have told these people that you would like to stay here and that you are going to help them," says Dennis. "They tell me that you are most welcome and they thank you for your visit. Don't worry, please feel free. You can have each and every thing you want."

The sun sets softly over crops of green, and we make dinner over an open fire while a crowd of 40 curious neighbours looks on. Dennis translates questions from the onlookers. "Why are you here, they are wanting to know? How did you find this village? It is too far from Kampala. They are not seeing white people."

"We are from Canada, but we have started our journey on motor-cycles from South Africa," says Christina.

He relays the message openly to the crowd, and the murmur rises in volume as they process the information.

"Ooookay. Thank you," he says slowly. "These people, they are in disbelief. They don't believe you can arrive here from South Africa with these bicycles. It is too fah."

"We are here because we want to share with this family the last of the mosquito nets we are carrying. They are for the children, to prevent malaria."

"Eeeish, there are too many mosquitoes here," says Dennis, flick-ing his index finger against his others to produce a sharp snapping sound. "Malaria is a very, very big problem, mostly in this area. By now, most of the people living here don't have nets."

A happy crowd soon forms around, and we spend the next two hours under "curiosity surveillance," as we've coined it, huddled close together next to a small cooking fire.

Pellets of moisture drip off the tent as I unzip the doors and step into thick fog to start another day. Virginia, a mother of five, is the first to wake in the house, along with her husband, Joseph, the white-haired elder. In his bedroom, he smiles as I carefully step around him and hang a net over his bed with a length of black string. Sitting up, he takes us both by the hands and asks politely, in faint English, for money to help with his illness. We explain that we don't have the funds to help him (which we don't, we barely have enough to fill our tanks in Kabale) and that our mission is solely for malaria prevention. He understands, gripping our hands firmly.

"I thank you for coming here, to our village. We have been blessed by God. We cannot forget you. We shall all pray for your journey and we hope you will return one day."

Dennis arrives and starts where he left off with his colourful speeches, helping to hang three more nets in Virginia and Joseph's mud-and-sticks home, banging nails into the walls with the head of an old hoe. Dennis accepts his mosquito net with a face-stretching smile, as if we were handing him the keys to a brand-new car.

"I shall use it to help my mother," he says proudly. "She is very sick now, so I can say this will help her. I know you must go now and continue this work, but we wish for you to return to us. Each and every thing is here for you. You can even live here how you wish."

His invitation has us thinking. How nice would it be to escape our own reality for some time and live in our own little hut in these grassy hills? But our reality is now too deeply rooted in our mission. There's more work to be done, more people to help. We'll keep pressing onwards.

– 23 –

CRAZY IN THE CAPITAL

KAMPALA, UGANDA • September 2008

Ahead in the distance, a plume of grey smoke curls up from a roadside stand of coconut trees. I wave it off as just another garbage fire, but as we approach I can see it's much more serious. The fire is billowing from the hood of a long passenger bus lying on its side, ten feet down a steep ditch. Thousands of green bananas lie strewn about the grassy forest floor. Most people seem obviously shaken by what must have been a horrific accident, crying and limping along the side of the road, looking for help. A young man, maybe 16, strides up to Christina with his hands thrust up high in the air, fingers spread wide.

"The driver of this old bus hit the side of that lorry down there," he says loudly, with impossibly wide eyes popping out of his head. "I saw everything happen, sah. I am just waiting here and BAM!" he shouts, smashing his fist in a glancing motion against an open palm. "I am not feeling good for these people. But God has been watching from above. None are dead. It could have been *all*."

Sitting in the grass near the bus, a lady presses a handkerchief to her bleeding head. An older, distinguished gentleman in a thick brown suit and shiny pointed black shoes stands doubled over, grimacing in severe pain, sucking in air through his teeth in rapid bursts.

"Do you know first aid?" he asks, rocking back and forth, working his way through the pain.

I tell him not to move his likely broken arm and fetch him two ibuprofen from my tank bag. Several ladies wearing traditional *gomesi* (colourful floor-length traditional dresses) are shrieking and praying to God as loud as a church choir, trembling and hugging each other for long periods of time. Judging by their attire, it seems like most of the accident victims are either coming from or going to a wedding. Glancing at the wreckage, we can see that the fire isn't actually coming from the vehicle, but from a brush fire ten feet beyond. Over my left shoulder, I see the skid mark – a 200-foot trail of torn-up grass and dirt that had somehow, quite miraculously, avoided colliding with a single tree amongst the thousands that dot the coconut grove. I surmise the driver either had the hand of God at the wheel, or pulled off an incredibly fast Hail Mary effort to keep the bus straight enough *while* tipping sideways into the ditch. Ten feet more to the left, and the story ends with a mass funeral.

"Him swipe dee side, driver ee pay no attenshun!" the young guy shouts.

We don't know what to do. *Do we stay and help more?* Shit happens when you're on the road, and something like this was only a matter of time; a random accident that we have no control over. Thankfully help soon arrives – an ambulance and two police cruisers that seem to calm down the ones in shock. The most seriously injured are taken away to the nearest hospital. We respectfully and quietly leave the scene, grateful that there will be no tragic death to cope with. Back on my bike, I catch myself shoulder-checking a bit more thoroughly, reminded that life can be wonderful one minute and a nightmare the next.

Later that day, our tires break the threshold of a major geographical milestone: the equator. The air feels as hot as expected, and we still have our fucking jackets on; another rule of ours to stay safe all times, for road rash is a rider's worst enemy. For posterity, we snap a few photos of the equator monument, a cement ring painted white, emblazoned with "Equator, Uganda" at the top. But a young boy, no older than eight, ruins the moment instantly.

"Give me money, *now*," he says with a demanding tone and an outstretched palm face up.

I feel like giving him a gentle smack upside the head, but instead I stare at him intently. I'm not pissed off at him for saying that, but at society in general for thrusting the notion upon him that it's okay to walk up to two complete strangers and demand money with zero hint of tact or manners.

The difficulties of everyday travel, the challenges of sticking to a shoestring budget, the daily experience of people blatantly asking for money and the struggle through all of the little interruptions of the Journey have been seeping into our travel-beaten skin lately. Pricey visas, exorbitant rates to enter national parks and game reserves, the skyrocketing cost of petrol and the high price of food put added stress on us, and even on our relationship. We can't remember ever arguing this much in Latin America. For the first time I can think of, I catch myself measuring how much longer we have on the road. *Only eight more months...* Back on the highway, with the wind in my face, I chalk such thoughts up to simply having a challenging day. *It could be a lot goddamn worse, man. Suck it up.* Time to power on.

Our arrival in Kampala comes just before dusk, and the mayhem of metropolitan Africa chokes us like storm clouds around a sunset. We still have a long, long way to reach Morocco, where we'll celebrate our successful navigation through 30,000-plus kilometres of agony and ecstasy on African soil. But first, the principal task at hand: Rob Mather and his team have worked hard on a plan that will see us joining a larger group of local volunteers in a widespread net distribution in northwest Uganda. With plates piled high with the responsibility of coordinating our own travels with the timing of the project, our unglamorous to-do list isn't getting any smaller. We tried hard, but just couldn't manage to strike anything off our list today; no place to stay, no butane for the stove, no letters in the mail. On the way to the Kenyan consulate, Christina's bike gets clipped by one of the boda-boda mototaxis that writhe through the city in a snake-like mass of intense traffic. She's uninjured, but the event brings our frustrations to a head.

"Let's go find a travel agent and fly the fuck outta here," she says, throwing her hands up in defeat. I feel much the same – city life is definitely not our forte, especially underneath this searing heat. At least we manage to make a call to Rob Mather, hoping he'll have some good news for us regarding the upcoming net distribution program in the north.

"Sorry, guys, we're at least two months away from anything still," Rob says. "I really apologize. The nets have not arrived yet, and the Malaria Consortium is finalizing all of the logistics. I realize that it might throw a wrench in your plans, but that's all I know at the moment."

Now what? Spending the next two months in Kampala is not an option, but we're committed to seeing our initiative through. After volunteering in Uganda, we had hoped to loop through Kenya and Ethiopia, then into southern Sudan and the Central African Republic en route to West Africa, but we find out the later in the day from "Aussie John," an expat who's lived in Uganda for 18 years, that entering a land border into the Central African Republic is out of the question, period.

"It's too dangerous. Can't be done," he says with utmost conviction. "South Sudan is full of bandits, mate. *Definitely* a no-go zone. You cannot travel through there. Khartoum is fine, the people are actually very nice – but in the south it's a different story. They will kill for nothing."

"What about CAR?" Christina asks, hoping for better news.

"No, it's closed, mate, you cannot get into the country. The last time any foreigners entered that country across a land border was at least six or seven years ago. There are too many militia groups operating. The only way across to Cameroon is through the Congo. You can take a boat. Should take you about three weeks, but you can take the Congo River all the way to Kinshasa, and from there you can ride to Cameroon."

We've heard of overlanders travelling north to south, and vice versa, via the normal Cape-to-Cairo route or, like the English lads we met in Windhoek, riding from Morocco to South Africa via West Africa and Angola – but we haven't heard of anybody going from east to west through the heart of the continent. *Is it even possible? Is backpacker John putting the fear factor into us about CAR? Or do we listen to him and suss out the Congo River option in two months' time?*

The next day, at a long-distance call centre in Garden City, Kampala's biggest indoor mall, we meet Hamida, a friendly 20-something with a sharp, staccato accent and a high-pitched voice that sounds like candy. We're feeling homesick, so Hamida helps us connect with our folks back in Canada before closing shop for the night. Mom seems to be in good spirits, and I can't detect much worry in her voice. It feels like she's finally embraced the fact that we're here and trusts what we're doing. All I know is that I really miss her home cooking. Worried about us driving through the city in the dark, Hamida invites us to stay in the home she shares with her siblings; music to our ears after the last couple of days we've had in this chaotic city. We follow her faded yellow Toyota Corolla across town, trying to keep up. Losing her would be a fatal blow to our tenuous sanity. Hamida's house is a humble little flat, the end unit of a long, Lego-like block of homes all made from coffee-coloured bricks and faux-terracotta tiles. The complex emanates an air of suburban African success; most people have cars in the driveway, and it's nicely landscaped, with a modest chunk of green grass separating each unit. She introduces us to her 20-something family – brother Casper, sisters Rehena and Zoe and her daughter, Betty – as well as the maid, Deborah, who shows us to our own room. The vibe is relaxed and friendly; basic, clean and safe.

Casper is quite curious about who we are, where we're from, and why we're riding through Africa on motorcycles. He's an athletic young dude, tall and lanky with a big gap-toothed grin. The idea of adventure is somewhat foreign to him; he can't grasp the fact that we're travelling for the sake of travel.

"Oh, so you are travelling to some villages, okay then. Are you not fearing? Will you give many people a net?"

Like many Africans we've met thus far, he wants to better understand life "outside" and takes advantage of the fact that he can directly interview a *mzungu* in the flesh.

"What is the food you are eating in Canada? Who is the one who is cooking when you are on the road? Will your parents be worrying about you?"

Eventually a potential two-month plan hatches: we'll head northeast through Kenya, Ethiopia and then into the Sudan (our first Muslim country), before looping back south in time to participate in the net distribution in Arua. But we're sketched out, to say the least; the brutal genocide in Darfur is still happening, and the country has been caught in the clutches of civil war between the Muslim, Arabic-speaking north and the more indigenously African south, a religious war that has raged intermittently since 1955, one of the longest-running civil conflicts in the world. *Will we be able to get a visa? Do we even want to travel here?*

We make plans to hook up with Martin from Kigali at his mother's home in the bustling Kampala suburb of Zzana. His mother, Margaret, is like a Black equivalent to my own mom – always laughing and fussing over us and "what what," as they say. "I am feeling very happy when you are eating," she says. "If I am not sitting with you, don't think I am not liking you."

With a warm smile and a hostess-at-heart personality, Margaret adopts us on the spot. Christina even takes to calling her "Momma Maggie," which brings endless laughter and delight.

"Please stay here as long as you like," she says. "It is no problem. We love having visitors. I want you to feel free here."

Another family, another place, another set of group dynamics to work out as our interconnected worldwide web continues to grow. The kitchen becomes a lively ball of energy: rinsing veggies, peeling potatoes, learning tricks of the home-cook trade. The ladies of the house are surprised when I volunteer to do the dishes. They vehemently oppose until Christina takes the mother-daughter duo and physically pulls them out of the kitchen by their arms, all three giggling like schoolgirls at recess.

"Christina, you are like my daughter," says Maggie. "So fun and happy, my child. Maybe I can kidnap you," she says jokingly. "Maybe you can stay for three months."

Three days later, I venture downtown to tackle more errands while Chris hangs back, nursing some heavy period cramps. When I call her to ask if she needs me to pick up anything on my way home, she's sobbing uncontrollably on the other end.

"Just come home as soon as you can Todd, *please*. Maggie has lost the plot."

"What do you mean, *lost the plot?*"

"She's screaming at me, telling me I'm useless and just 'cause it's that time of the month doesn't mean I can lie around and sleep all day. I just want to get out of here, Todd, please come now, babe. She's going crazy."

When I walk into the house, I can hear Maggie yelling at full volume.

"Christina, give me those trousers!"

"I need these jeans to ride my motorcycle, but I can give you something else if you like."

"You are only giving me what you don't want!" she shouts back. "Give them to me now."

"Why are you saying these things?" Christina shouts back in defence, crying. "What did we do so wrong to you? I don't understand!"

"Just get out of here and never come back," Maggie says defiantly, pointing at the front door. "You are nothing to me now!"

Out of thin air, Martin's sister Gloria magically arrives and tries to bring Maggie down from her schizophrenic rage. *Did we overstay our welcome? It's only been three days. What flipped the switch?* Maggie stomps away into the laundry room, slamming the door behind her.

"She's done this to all of us, and one by one we've all left, even my father, more than once," Gloria explains. "I don't know what happens or why she does this, but please, please know this is not what we want. We love you like family. She is not well."

We leave immediately and manage to find a cheap hotel room nearby. In the morning, still shaken, we head straight to Martin's house.

"I spoke to her," he says, shaking his head in shame. "She told me that she made a big mistake and is sorry."

"I don't know what to say, Martin, but I hope she can get help," Christina says. "Your family is amazing together. It just seemed so sudden, I still don't really know what triggered her."

"She has done this in the past, many times. I think the doctors call it an acute episode or such things like this. My father has left because of this, my brothers, everyone. It is a major problem, but I don't know what to do. She doesn't change. She thinks she is always right, and we cannot get through to her. We have tried many times. You guys, I am so sorry."

The experience leaves an obvious black mark on our first few days in Kampala, a city we would have avoided altogether had it not been necessary to obtain another pricey visa, this time for Kenya. Martin embraces his wife and child on the front steps and watches us walk away. I doubt we'll ever see him or Gloria again.

FatBoyz is pumping. The dance floor pulses with swinging booty and sweaty bodies, our table covered in drinks and beer bottles. Christina and I are the only white faces in the place. Hamida's sister Zoe, the one with a model's beauty and a tall, slender frame, introduces us to a friend of hers from Nairobi whose name we can't hear, so we just call him Mr. Kenya. He's blinged out with a massive gold chain around his neck and a black Kangol hat à la Samuel L. Jackson. He invites us to sit down and tells the waitress to bring anything we want. Judging by the amount of hugs and handshakes coming his way, he seems to be an entrenched regular. Hamida's brother, Casper, swills big bottles of Nile Special, hitting on every hot woman that passes by. Suddenly, under the flickering disco lights and blaring music, he charges across the dance floor, hops over the railing on the other side and starts delivering a flurry of violent punches into the face of a random patron. The bouncers step in immediately, hauling them both outside into the parking lot within seconds.

"You killed Walter!" Casper screams over and over again at the top of his lungs. "You fucking killed Walter, and now I'm going to kill you! You fucking killed Walter!"

The melee swells quickly, with friends from both "teams" rushing outside, as people do when a fight breaks out. We're suddenly caught in the middle of it all. I try grabbing Christina's arm to pull her away, but she takes a wayward fist to the face from one of the screaming women in the crowd.

"You better shut your mouth, boy, or i'ma git my gun and end your story right here so all these people can see," yells the recipient of Casper's violence. "Get the fuck outta here, boy, you don't know shit."

But Casper is unrepentant, spit flying in the face of what seems to be his bitter enemy. "Fuck you! You killed Walter!"

We have no idea who this guy is, or who Walter is. The bouncers take charge, flinging Casper to the pavement. Then Mr. Kenya enters the fray, shoving his face into Casper's, almost touching noses.

"I'ma pop 'im," he says calmly to everyone around, while looking directly at Casper, one inch away. "Let me go get my gun and i'ma pop 'im."

What? Aren't you guys friends? Weren't we all just all drinking together inside?

The threat's intended purpose rings hollow with Casper, though. He keeps the screaming going full tilt. Mr. Kenya is getting more agitated. This is his turf, and he seems to be the gatekeeper.

"Just get him out of here or i'ma kill him. I don't know what's gonna happen if he comes back here and cause drama again. We don't need dis around here."

Casper tries to charge but stumbles, and before I know it I'm lying on my back with Casper on top of my chest, on his back; a writhing, spitting, seething madman screaming with vengeance and fury like I've never before witnessed in my life. My small 150-pound frame struggles to keep him restrained, but spurred on by adrenalin, I summon reserves of strength I didn't know I had. Casper is either going to kill his enemy or get killed by Mr. Kenya, so I clutch him tightly to my body using an improvised mix of leg and arm holds that somehow, in the midst of these intense moments of human rage, manage to keep him subdued. I'm surprised I'm able to keep this wild animal at bay, and wonder how long I can keep it up – he's still spitting and screaming like a rabid beast.

"I'll fucking kill you," he keeps repeating into the air. "I'll fucking kill you, you killed Walter!"

Walter, we will learn later, is Zoe's ex-fiancé, poisoned to death less than a month ago by someone who resembles the random patron that Casper wants to kill. Finally a cab pulls up, and we struggle to get Casper in the back seat. At one point, with psycho eyes bulging out of his head, Casper demands that Christina get in the front seat. *Why don't we just throw Casper out and take the cab home ourselves? Why do we care so goddamn much?*

When we arrive at their house, his sisters are already there to receive him. He turns into a wild animal again, hitting a corrugated metal fence with a flurry of punches. The noise is deafening, surely waking up half the neighbourhood.

"This one is the only one who can control him," Zoe says, pointing at me.

I finally snap and, roaring like a caged lion, fling him to the ground with as much strength as my exhausted body can muster. The shit-show has got to stop. He resists again, but I hold him firmly with both hands clutching his blood-stained shirt. Two of the little daughters, no more than 5 years old, are now awake and out in the street. I feel ashamed they have to witness such violence. *How did we get in the middle of all this?*

Zoe tells us she suspects who may have poisoned Walter but that "it's too late now."

We escape the house before sunrise while everyone is passed out, our heads drowning in a pre-hangover slurry after one of the most bizarre nights of our lives. I can't shake the mental battle swirling in my head. Why is all this drama following us around in Kampala? Did we bring it on? Is there a lesson to be learned in all of this? Or is this just part of what goes on in cluttered urban Africa? The crush of population. The guns. The violence. The noise. Thank god we have our Kenyan visas in hand.

From Christina's Journal:

Saturday, September 13th
The Hairy Lemon
Nile River, Uganda

Africa: before we left I knew it would be hard. Todd had been here before, but me, never. My concept of hard was perhaps the difficulty of riding in deep sand, or the struggle to understand a child with a gun. But now that we're here, we're faced with more than that. Maybe it's just because of what we just experienced in Kampala?

   Nature is such a great healer. Decompression is what we need right now.

For most of this Journey, our ash-spreading has been spontaneous, but this time is different. Sean had always talked about this great river, another of the world's geographic features that had fascinated his wandering mind. With our feet dangling in the waters of the mighty Nile, I know a special send-off needs to take place. Christina creates a couple of neat little leaf boats that perfectly hold a sprinkle of Sean's ashes. I feel compelled to say a prayer out loud. *Hi, Sean... we've had some rough times lately, and I know it's all part of the Journey, but please stay close with us on the next leg of this adventure. We set you free in the Amazon, and now you'll flow freely in the Nile.* Pushing our little boats into the current, we watch them float north in silence.

– 24 –

HIGHWAY TO HELL

KENYA • September 2008

Keen-yah. When I hear the word spoken from the tongue of a local Maasai, it sounds like the very soul of Africa. As a child, my perception of Kenya consisted of teeming herds of wildlife roaming the savannah on a Sunday night nature show. But now the Kenya in front of us is a paved two-lane highway, a heaven-sent motorcyclist's dream full of fast, sweeping corners that slice through the sprawling scenery of the Great Rift Valley, dissected by green-and-yellow farmland like squares on a checkerboard. The perfect road washes away Kampala's negative energy as swiftly as the wind. It's amazing what a good day of riding can do to one's soul. With the city stress gone, Christina and I are feeling lighter in our connection now, free again and happy. So much of our relationship has been based in and around nature, and moments like this, riding fluidly between a waterfall-spewing cliff bank and a forested valley floor, keep strengthening our bond. Clusters of pink flamingos crowding the shores of Lake Baringo shimmer in the distance, adding to the spectacle.

Around every bend, the landscape morphs into a million shades of different; even the clouds change as fast as we can chase them. As we descend into an acacia forest, a hundred-strong caravan of soft-footed camels slowly scatters in front of us, leaving behind towering piles of fresh dung that land with thuds. We deftly avoid T-boning these beasts, for camels are king here, vital to the nomadic pastoral liveli-hoods of the local tribes. Never in my life did I imagine I'd be engulfed by a sea of camel humps. We want to film every minute of it but need to make some miles. Soon the pavement turns into crunchy gravel again as we enter Kenya's sparsely populated northern region, home to the Pokot, Maasai, Turkana, Samburu and Rendille Peoples. Here the women stop us in our tracks, unbelievably striking with their necks swallowed by saucers of beaded jewellery – layers upon layers of them, thick and dense and undoubtedly heavy, with tiny silver keys and sil-ver rings hanging from them like ornaments on a Christmas tree. *Do they ever take them off?*

Near the end of the day we come across six Turkana women bal-ancing calabashes of water upon their heads. Large hooped earrings dangle from their open earlobes. None of them smile, but they aren't unfriendly either. Christina gingerly presents the eldest one with a small copper charm. She accepts it in her frail hands and reciprocates by unclipping a miniature key from her necklace and placing it in Christina's palm; a silent, fleeting exchange between two strangers that puts a cultural exclamation mark on another brilliant day. I wish we were pulling a stack of 500 nets behind us in a trailer, but with no definitive timeline as to when we're needed for the net distribution project in Arua, we're free to roam again at our own pace. Our only job now is one we love – photographing and journalling, practices that have been at times both rewarding and laborious. Reliving our days uploading photos to the laptop every night in the tent gives us great satisfaction, and I'm thankful I made the decision to study this fas-cinating medium. I still have Sean's camera – with Roy's 40-year-old camera strap – that I use when I want to shoot black- and-white film or transparencies.

With darkness looming, a wooden sign that says *Mugie Ranch* lures us off the road. It looks promising as a place to camp. We enter slowly and helmetless, soon greeted by a friendly, middle-aged man who in-troduces himself as Claus Mortensen, a "Kenyan-born Dane," he says with a wink. "Don't ask me how."

Mugie Ranch is a private wildlife conservancy that's been Claus's home for the last 30 years. He lets us pitch camp on the grass near his house.

"Did you hear the lions last night?" he says over strong black coffee in the morning. "They were making a hell of a racket."

"Yeah, I think so," we say sheepishly. We thought the groaning was a cow in heat.

"Are you guys in a hurry?" he asks.

"No, not really, but we only have three more days to make it to Ethiopia. We only have a transit visa."

"Thomas," he says into a fuzzy CB radio. "I have two guests here from Canada. See if you can take them to find the lions."

Lions in Keen-ya? Yes, please. In Tanzania, we were turned away at the gates of the Ngorongoro Conservation Area *and* Serengeti National Park (*No motos allowed!*), so to be sitting in a roofless jeep, hunting lions with our cameras on a private safari, is a special treat. Thomas, a gentle giant of a man and one of the park's 12 local rangers, taps us on the shoulder to show us one creature after another – giraffe, impala, warthog, buffalo, springbok, jackal and five black rhinos running at a steady clip parallel to the road. No matter how many nature shows or books you watch or read about African wildlife, your mind will never be fully prepared for the real version, almost too magical to comprehend.

"Come back for lunch, but take the long way if you like," Claus instructs through the radio. Ten minutes later, Thomas spots three lions devouring the carcass of a freshly killed pregnant buffalo. Their faces are covered in blood, entrails spilling out onto the dry grass. We're so close to the beasts we can hear the sound of flesh and bones being ripped off of the dead body. It's the primal law of the land, and we've got front-row tickets to the killing game – a circle of life that's as old as the continent itself.

Progressing ever north, the once-heavenly road now has more corrugation than a shantytown, wreaking havoc on Jessie and Willy. The thick steel chain that we use to lock our bikes together is jolted loose from my front skid plate. Before I notice what's happening, the knobs of my back tire grab hold of the chain, ripping it clean off and crack-ing the hub of the rear wheel in an instant. We spend the next hour wrapping the hub in binding wire before limping onwards to find our home for the night: a makeshift camp full of 130 workers laying fibre optic cable from Nairobi to the Kenya-Ethiopia border at Moyale, an 800-kilometre project. Miraculously the wire job has held, but my rim is bent from hitting hundreds of unavoidable sharp rocks embedded in the road like shark fins jutting out of the water. In the morning, some eager and friendly camp mechanics spend nearly three hours straight-ening out my back rim and reinforcing the wire job on the rear hub. The camp cook, David, feeds us delicious *mandazi* (African doughnuts) and chai tea.

"Kenya is becoming advance," he says, spitting out a big green wad of khat, a plant only found in the Horn of Africa, known to enhance concentration and stimulate body and mind. David gives me a handful to try. It's intensely bitter, what I imagine the taste of a dry forest might be. Laughing, he continues. "These men they are laying this wire from Nairobi. The connection is coming. The world is getting smaller, like this," he says, squeezing his thumb and forefinger together.

Twenty kilometres from Marsabit, I can smell something burning; the hub is now entirely cracked through, rubbing against the brake drum and scorching it. To add to the misery, Christina points out a puncture in my back tire – a large rusty nail protruding from the rub-ber. It's too late in the day to fix, so I ride slowly into town to seek out another bike doctor. This time, Willy will need an operation. Even though Marsabit is bigger than we thought and has plenty of motor-cycles cruising around, there isn't a spare hub to be found, and we don't have time to wait for one to be shipped from Nairobi.

"You cannot fix this tire," says a tall man, quite arrogantly. He's dressed in a white kaftan, smoking a cigarette, looking like he wants to be conceived of as important amongst a small crowd of onlookers. His face is as black as night. "You first take truck to Moyale. There you can fix it. Not here."

"We *can* fix it here, and we will," I respond sharply.

The incessant heat has sapped my penchant for politeness or diplomacy. Luckily, one of the mechanics is keen to try my idea: to create a makeshift metal "bracelet" that can hold the cracked hub from shattering into pieces. After seven hours of tinkering and hammering, we leave with bloody knuckles, a repaired puncture and two pieces of curved iron fastened together with four strong bolts that fit snugly around the hub. It's a crafty piece of African ingenuity built right before our eyes – not perfect, but it should get us to Moyale. Less than 30 minutes later, I feel my back tire swerving like a snake's tail.

Not again. No fucking way.

I generally believe I can summon enough even-keel energy when the going gets tough, but that talent went out the window many sweating, scorching miles ago. Now everything is pissing me off, including Christina, who's barking something about not fixing the tire properly.

"For fuck's sake, Chris, these goddamn tire levers keep pinching the tube, and it's so shredded it won't keep air. We're basically fucked."

We've been getting along so well lately, but I don't think either of us wants to be around the other right now. I can't remember the last time we've had any alone time, a solid block of hours to just do anything we desire by ourselves. The constant grind of 24/7 togetherness is starting to show, and there's no escaping each other, not in this scorching heat. *Have we reached our boiling point?* But in these desolate lands, everyone helps one other; it's the only way to survive. Before we know it, a big white angel of a truck arrives, rambling towards us on four massive tires. Yes, the crew of the giant cargo truck *can* take me and my bike to the next town! I chain Willy into the truck bed and sit down on 50-kilogram sacks of maize, beans and Pakistani rice while Christina rides on ahead, joyously free from the weight of her pack and saddlebags (and me). We arrive at the police outpost in Turbi just after 11 p.m., dirty, tired and almost ready to throw in the towel.

"Here, we are always travelling like caravan, with other cars," says a shirtless officer, handing us two small cups of tea. "Never alone."

Chalk up another lesson born from naivety. The officers let us set our tent up on a patch of dirt adjacent to their building. Just before bed,

Sean makes a visit to my mind, and I think about what he'd be doing if he was still alive. I imagine he'd be some kind of adrenaline guide to famous rock stars looking for an out-of-box adventure in a far-flung corner of the world, showing his guests the Third World ropes by riding on the roofs of buses and eating bugs for breakfast. He'd be the guy who'd show his clients no-holds-barred experiences where having no rules was the only rule. He'd probably be stoked at the predicament we're in right now. I can hear him saying, "It's not a real adventure unless something goes sideways."

Or upside down and backwards.

In the morning, one of the cops, a shirtless, pot-bellied man named Djembe, helps me patch my other spare tube, getting Christina and me back on the road to crash and bang our way towards Ethiopia with only five hours to make it to the border before our visa expires. Unfortunately the Chinese-made tube is as thick as rice paper, and the rocks are simply too sharp. For the umpteenth time in the last five days, I suffer *another* flat tire. With no more patches left and no spare tube, the only option is to ride it flat.

Is that a car coming towards us in the distance? Could it be yet another angel?

This time it's a pimped-out Land Cruiser driven by Danilo – a stereotypical Euro overlander on safari – decked out in head-to-toe khaki, Tilley hat and all. He tells us he's made it all the way from Germany to Kenya in *one month*. He also happens to have two spare cans of instant-fix tire goop in his tool kit. With no time to waste, we fill the back tire with the strange white foam, and I try as hard as humanly possible to avoid the minefield of rocks on the final 80 kilometres – a fool's errand on this stretch of road.

Before long, the insta-fix comes oozing out of the spoke holes like foam from a rabid dog's mouth. With no other option, I'm forced to ride the remaining 50 kilometres on a flat tire with a bent rim and a broken hub, bumping along and laughing at the absurdity of it all. The peaceful zen of utter defeat. Finally the road turns to tarmac and leads us to the Kenyan immigration office, 30 minutes before closing.

"Don't worry, you're only human," says the gentle officer, taking stock of our situation. "We call that road the highway to hell. I would not have fined you anyway, even if you were late. You can stay here if you like, no one is bothering at night."

We're too tired not to accept, and fall asleep in his little border outpost on two wooden benches before we even eat dinner.

VERONICA'S GREAT ESCAPE

ETHIOPIA • October 2008

Of course we want to see the tribes of the Lower Omo Valley, with their incredulous lip plates and distinctive tribal make-up. This is the Africa we came for, not a goddamn strip mall in Kampala or a cockroach-infested hotel room on the outskirts of another capital city stuck waiting for an expensive stamp in our passports. Our serendipitous yet fleeting encounters with Turkana and Rendille People in Kenya left us completely spellbound, and as we cross into Ethiopia – what some refer to as "the cradle of civilization" – we can't help but hope for more of the same. As a photographer, I have fanciful daydreams of encountering more tribal cultures so I can selfishly capture some "award-winning" images of these fascinating people on the soil they've called home for thousands of years, but the reality is, in Africa it's another day, another moral dilemma.

"It's like visiting people inside of a zoo," says Willem, a Dutch backpacker who recently encountered the Mursi People near Jinka.

"Yeah it was a real shame," adds his wife, Rahel. "They only paint themselves and dress up for tourists, and they just ask for money for *every single photograph*, for everything, really."

Ah yes, travel in the age of the almighty dollar sign, where tradition takes a back seat to the modern tourist. Willem and Rahel go on to explain how it's impossible even to visit the area without a paid guide, or, as they put it, "a conduit for the degradation of these cultures. We could see the guide almost bargaining for his commission with the people before we were allowed to see them. It was basically just business."

Thankfully, exploring the world by motorcycle has allowed for a lot of random cultural immersion without buying a packaged tour, and Christina and I would much rather organically stumble across Indigenous Peoples as we forge our own path. *A human zoo?* No, thanks. I can live without the photographs.

So out of the dusty desert and into the highlands of the Great Rift Valley we go, where our Westerner preconceptions of disease-ridden, poverty-plagued, famine-and-drought Ethiopia are quickly replaced by a patchwork of fertile green-and-yellow lands, people playing ping pong and billiards on outdoor tables, and roadside stalls stocked with colourful collections of bananas, oranges and avocados. The distractions are plenty, but none more so than the people themselves. In Ethiopia, we must be more cautious of hitting pedestrians than of the thousands of donkeys, goats, sheep, horses, chickens and cows. People here rarely look both ways before they cross the road and seem unable to properly judge the distance and speed of an oncoming motorcycle very well. We always ride with our headlights on for safety, but every second pedestrian seems to take personal pleasure in letting us know that yes, indeed, our lights are on and we should turn them off. Using our horns freely becomes the daily norm.

On the outskirts of the hillside community of Wondo Genet, our young new friends – 15-year-old Mulugeta and his slightly older buddy Tamirat – show up at six a.m. sharp, keen to show us their spectacular forested hills and waterfalls. Stepping out onto the dewy grass, I take in the beauty during a morning pee, then dive into packing up our daypacks while the boys wait outside, lifting weights the African way – with a metal bar attached to old coffee tins filled with concrete. The rising sunlight brushes the tops of the trees alongside the road and makes for a perfectly peaceful scene, until colobus monkeys, swinging low from branch to branch, suddenly snatch our breakfast samosas straight from our hands. Hiking the steep single-track trail away from camp, we're soon gifted with stunning vistas of green peaks shrouded in light, misty fog and littered with forest banana trees and small huts clinging to the hillsides. With sweat already beading on our foreheads, I begin to appreciate our guides' insistence on an early start. It feels good to get into the mountains again, even in the African heat. Suddenly, Mulugeta turns around and says sharply: "Do not look!"

Of course I do, instinctively glancing past him to see a pool of the most electric, crimson-red blood running down the trail, still wet and slimy and almost too bright to be real.

"Oh my god," Christina gasps, holding her hand to her open mouth. "Is he dead? Oh no. We have to tell someone immediately."

The man is lying on his back, eyes and mouth still open. I feel his wrist for a pulse and his chest for a heartbeat. Nothing. It's unsettling to be the ones to first come across him, and, personally, even weirder to be touching a dead man. The last time that happened to me was when Sean died. I hate the thought of it, but know I need to shoot a few frames of the dead man to show the police. Could it have been an accident? Did he fall and hit his head on a rock?

"This is the first time for me to see this," says Tamirat. "This town is not troubled."

I believe him. Wondo Genet seems like a beautiful and healthy place – green, lush and peaceful. Christina starts sobbing uncontrollably while Mulugeta holds the side of the man's head, a pained expression on his face as he murmurs something in his native language. We descend back to town at once, struggling to process what we've just witnessed, and arrive at the police station to find a team of six officers suiting up in blue camouflage uniforms, rifles slung over their shoulders. They've obviously been notified, but we don't know how or by whom.

"You must come back up the mountain," one of them says to me in an urgent tone. "You will need to describe everything exactly as you saw it. We go, now."

Back on the trail, it's immediately evident that word has spread, and fast. It seems as if the whole town is coming up. Weaving our way up amongst a constant flow of men and women, easily a hundred people holding their distressed faces in the palms of their hands, chanting and crying, all moaning rhythmically on their way to witness their neighbour, brother, husband, uncle, son or friend now long gone from this world. *What if that was us? What if we'd hit the trail an hour early?* When we reach the scene of the crime, someone has covered the dead man with a pale-blue bedsheet, but that doesn't stop people from lifting it up – they need to physically see his face to believe it. It's no sight for a small child, but my attempts at keeping scores of them away proves futile. There are simply too many.

"He was hacked by a machete, murdered with a single blow," says one of the officers. "We are asking for more information from the people here."

"He was carrying a large sum of money," Mulugeta translates for us. "But I cannot understand how anyone knew he was going to be on the path so early in the morning. It is a mystery."

"This is unbearable, Todd," Christina says, tears pouring down her cheeks as the crowd keeps closing in. "I feel so helpless."

Another wave of screaming women reaches the murder scene, huddled together on the path, jabbering away in Amharic, a language we cannot understand. That barrier protects us, in a way, not knowing every little detail – but as complete strangers, we're also besieged with sideways glances from people who think we may have had something to do with the crime. I inform the officers that we're going to head down; we still have one more thing to do – clear our friends' names. Nobody knows yet what really happened, and we have not been questioned at all. I give the chief of police a burned CD of the photographs of the entire morning, proving Mulugeta and Tamirat were with us when we left town together and when we discovered the body. The boys apologize profusely, not wanting this rare, isolated incident to taint our memory of their hometown.

"This is a good place. We hope one day you will come back. Until then, you will be with us here," Tamirat says, knocking his heart with his fist.

We load the bikes and head east, once again reminded that life is fleeting and every moment counts.

A lone knock on our one-star hotel room door reveals Veronica, a South African who wants to leave a message for her American friend Amelia, who happens to be shopping at Addis Ababa's central market with Christina.

"Please tell Amelia I have found another hotel not far from here. I need to move, because I am afraid," she says timidly. She's short and stout, with a pretty, round face that's framed with a balloonish jet-black afro.

"Why are you scared? Who are you scared of?"

"I need to hide from my husband. His name is Carlos."

She tells me he's beaten her several times before, once even sending her to the hospital after a miscarriage six months into her pregnancy.

"The girls will be back soon. Let's have dinner tonight, all of us, and we can talk about everything, okay? We will all move to your hotel as well."

"Okay thank you, Mr. Todd. I will see you this evening. Thank you."

Christina, Amelia and I arrive at the Tsaday Hotel at 8:45 p.m. to bad news from the hotel manager, who speaks barely-there English. "This is business," he says to me. "You are again pay now!"

Is he asking us to pay? We haven't even checked in yet.

Through a staff member translating, he explains that Carlos showed up when Veronica was washing her hands underneath the tap outside of her room. He hit her on the face and demanded that she come with him. She tried to defend herself, but he overpowered her and pulled her out of the compound and down the rock-strewn alleyway. Hastily, we throw our bags in a small room and lock the bikes together with our thick metal chain. A concerned Muslim lady in a long purple dress, who swings her arms purposefully as she walks, guides us from hotel to hotel in search of our new friend.

"This area no good," she says with worried, squinting eyes. "Bad time. This time many teeves in this area. We go back your hotel. When we get your hotel, we are safe, then I am going my home. This is Ethiopian tradition."

Instead of going back to the hotel, we find a nearby café and discuss our three options over a serving of sour, spongy injera flatbread and a thick, hearty soup called *wat*. One, keep looking all night; two, report it to the police; or three, go get some sleep and continue looking for Veronica when the sun rises. We decide to go to bed, and return to the Tsaday well past midnight. Veronica and Carlos creep in soon after – he probably thought everyone would be asleep. Veronica's worried face spells *help me*, and Christina grabs her by the hand, swinging her into Amelia's room, locking the door. An angry hotel security guard arrives carrying a big wooden stick that he taps repetitively against the ground while locking eyes firmly on Carlos, who's sobbing like a child, saying sorry a thousand times. Eventually, a military guard and two cops take him away without a struggle.

"I don't know what to do," says Veronica. "He won't let me be, even though I want to leave him. I've tried to divorce him many times."

Early the next morning, we act fast to get Veronica to the South African Embassy for protection. She's been in this abusive marriage for two years; Carlos beats her and cheats on her and takes all her money, but is an ultra-smooth talker who can always turn the situation to his favour by creating an aura of innocence that wins cops over. He's skilled at making it look like the abuse is *her* fault, but she has no money, no family nearby, and no way of escaping either the relationship or the country. Her only hope lies within the walls of that embassy on the other side of the city.

"We met in South Africa, but he changed completely when we got to Ethiopia," she says, packing her only bag as fast as possible. "I didn't know who he was anymore. I became so very scared of him, but I thought I still loved him."

I start my bike and Veronica hops on, clutching me tightly. Just as I'm about to ride away, Carlos storms onto the property, shouting: "Don't take my wife! Please give me my wife!"

"Go, go, go!" she screams hysterically. I hit the throttle, but Carlos, shockingly, throws his body in front of my tire in desperation. I knock him over, but he clutches the spokes of my tires like a crab, screaming: "Don't take my wife!"

I want to run him over. Incredibly, although there are several people now witnessing the melee, nobody else tries to help. I'm yelling and cursing through my helmet at the security guards to get Carlos the fuck out of my way as he lies sprawled and crying at my front tire. The girls pry his fingers loose one by one as the manager pulls the keys from my ignition without me noticing. *What the fuck?!* I smack the top of his hand with a closed fist and the keys fall to the ground. He's pissed off, but I only care about getting Veronica to safety, now. Christina flicks me the keys, and I start Willy again as the small crowd swarms around Carlos.

"Grab him from behind so he can't jump in front of my bike!" I yell to Amelia. Some hotel staff and a few guests now come running in, even the ladies from the kitchen, adding to the intensity and chaos.

"Hold on!" I shout to Veronica, who's gripping me so firmly I can hardly breathe. I spot a window of opportunity amongst all the human bodies and bolt out the gate. I can see Carlos in my rearview mirror, chasing us down wildly. Veronica screams in horror, "He's coming... GO!... please GO!!"

Before we hit the first corner, I'm already in third gear, swerving between cars and pedestrians to gain some distance. Carlos has no chance, and I speed off towards the South African embassy with Veronica holding my sides so tightly I have to grab her arm and tell her to relax.

"Sorry, Todd, it's the first time I've ever been on a motorcycle," she says, looking over her shoulder in fear.

"It's okay now. We'll be there soon, and you will be safe."

We arrive at the embassy, and the girls aren't far behind. Stepping off Christina's bike, Amelia looks as angry as a hornet, belying her mousy, spectacled face framed by long, straight red hair.

"She needs protection right now, please," I say to Miss Karachi, the name-tagged Indian woman sitting behind a glass window. "She cannot go back out there. Is there any way the embassy can get her home today? This is an emergency, we're worried for her life."

Veronica is still too shaken up to converse, but Miss Karachi gets on the phone immediately.

"Unfortunately the policies state that her family must arrange for the money to be sent to Foreign Affairs in South Africa. Once the fax of a receipt is sent to us, then we will arrange the flight."

"Can we just pay for her right now to get home?"

"No, sir, I'm sorry, but we must follow procedure in these matters. There is nothing I can do."

Fuck policy and procedure.

The woman also tells Veronica that she must first go to the police station.

Fuck the police, they already had him and let him go.

Then, unbelievably, Carlos arrives with three other cops and his older brother. As we suspected, the cops aren't on our side. They don't believe a word Veronica says and they're asking *us* to forgive *him*.

Forgive him? I want to punch his fucking head in.

"I have no respect for you as a man," I say to Carlos's face, which causes him to cast his eyes to the floor.

Apparently Carlos *did* get arrested shortly after the incident at the Tsaday Hotel, but his uncle paid 10,000 birr (US$100) on the spot to set him free. Now Carlos is trying to negotiate with the crooked Addis Ababa cops to get his wife back, but Amelia is not backing down.

"You so-called police officers," she says vehemently, staring them down one by one. "No matter how sorry he is, he will just keep doing this. He should be in jail, and you know it."

She's adamant that someone in the embassy call one of Veronica's family members in South Africa to arrange for the flight home. After two more tense hours inside the embassy, Veronica is taken to another area of the building with barely a chance to hug us goodbye. As she's being escorted towards an official embassy sedan (and hopefully back home to South Africa), Carlos drops to his knees, screaming, "Please don't take my wife!"

"She's not your wife anymore!" screams Amelia, shooting him a venomous look.

Carlos reminds me so much of Casper, and I only hope, for humanity's sake, that they both become better people. The next day,

Amelia informs us that Veronica will be on a plane bound for home in 48 hours. I'm happy. We helped give her a chance at a better life, and I pray things work out for her.

It takes us a couple of days to reach the shores of the stunning Lake Tana, the largest lake in Ethiopia (and the source of the Blue Nile), where, past the coffee shops and pizza joints of Bahir Dar, we find a place to make camp along a shallow stream. In the morning, peeking my groggy head out of the tent, I see our polite new friend Marta sitting a respectful distance away, humming a tune, the last to leave of the large crowd that formed a horseshoe around us as we set up camp last night. Marta speaks the best English and helped translate the standard "Who are we? Where do we come from? How did we get here?" queries. Today she knows we want to visit Blue Nile Falls and is there to watch over our things while we go for a wander.

Hiking always makes me introspective. Maybe it's the rhythmic monotony of putting one foot in front of the other, thoughts drifting as my increased heart rate feeds the clean wild air into my brain. Regardless, it happens almost every time. On the trek up to Blue Nile Falls, I find myself replaying flashbacks of the previous days, experiences like Msekwa and the jealous neighbour in Burundi who wanted nets for his family. I think of Martin and Maggie, hoping that she'll get some help for the sake of her family. And Casper and his tortured soul; will justice ever arrive for him and his sisters? Will they ever find Walter's killer? Is Veronica now finally free from the shackles of domestic violence? We came here to hang nets in rural villages; were we naive to be surprised by these violent urban experiences? At some point, the scenery pulls me away from the flashbacks, and I shift to thinking just how lucky we are to be able to witness such staggering beauty in a place so far from home. We're surprised to see Blue Nile Falls refreshingly uncrowded and pristine, given the fact it's one of the top tourist draws in the country.

Much like in Rwanda, there's not a speck of litter nor a plastic bag or bottle to be seen, no hotels or resorts poaching the natural atmosphere and no lines of people to ruin the experience. Instead, we're treated to green fields and forests, rainbows and mist, the perfect place to rejuvenate mind and body by lathering ourselves in cold mud and letting the power of the Nile wash us clean. It's a far cry from the hordes of backpackers and overland buses in Victoria Falls, and nothing like the Ethiopia of fallow fields and endless famine portrayed by mass media.

"It feels like we're in some sort of fairytale land," Christina says to me as we watch an old lady spin yarn with a hand-spindle from a pile of sheep's wool at her bare feet. "Maybe this exact spot was the birthplace of humanity?"

The child hawkers that greet us outside the park gates are as impressive as the falls themselves, laying down their tried-and-tested tourist pitch with completely polished perfection.

"Hello, ma'am, how are you? What is your name? Oh, that is a very nice name. My name is Hana. You buy scarf and calabash from me, okay. Did you have a nice visit inside the falls? Is very nice, yes? You buy from me, okay, Ma'am Christina! I am Hana. You don't forget me, okay."

Heading back to our camp, we come across a small clear-water creek. Three male teenagers posted at the water's edge offer to carry us across, using scare tactics to make a quick buck in the process.

"There is malaria here in this water, from the algae, you know. You cannot walk across," says the eldest of the trio.

"Okay, thank you," Christina says, rolling up her pants before casually piggybacking me ten feet across the algae-less water.

Arriving back at our river camp, Marta graciously accepts one of Hana's beautiful scarves but refuses to take any of the money we offer for her six hours guarding our belongings.

"Everything is fine with your things. Nobody is disturbing. I just want you to be my pen pal. Is that okay?"

Much like a family of five sisters we met at Lake Awassa a few days ago, she's really taken a liking to Christina. Unabashedly affectionate in a sisterly way, holding her hand, brushing hair, painting her nails.

It's nice to watch such authentic connections unfold. Africa's been such a blessing for these moments of real, pure reciprocity.

In the morning, much to the delight of coffee-addict Christina, Marta's mother, Blessing, invites us to their home for *jebena buna*, a coffee ceremony tied closely to womanhood. In homes across all of Ethiopia, *buna* is part of daily life, an essential element of culture and society. Blessing starts by roasting green coffee beans in a pan over a three-legged charcoal stove, waving the hot pan around us as smoke releases the intoxicating aroma, meant to heighten our anticipation of the coffee to come. Once the beans are fully roasted, she pours them into a mortar and begins grinding them with a pestle before putting the ground beans into a beautiful clay *jebena*, the coffee pot. Then she starts burning something else over the hot coals.

"This is frankincense," she says in quite fine English. "We use it to add more aroma for the experience. Do you know it? It smells like all of Ethiopia."

She dumps a tablespoon of sugar into each of four small cups and elegantly pours the steaming black nectar from almost two feet above, not spilling a drop, before stirring each coffee with her spoon held upside down.

"Ethiopian coffee, traditional style *jebena buna*. Please enjoy."

They want us to visit longer, but we need to stay on pace. Rob Mather has notified us that the net-distribution program is set to start happening in less than six weeks, in northern Uganda, and we still have a lot of ground to cover. We head north towards the Sudanese border (with costly visas in hand), riding at 6,000 feet above sea level on a red road that splits the green earth like a runway, zipping past old rusted tanks and artillery machines from Ethiopia's warring past. Ahead of me, Christina stops abruptly to warm her cold fingers at a fire burning on the side of the road, then quickly turns away when, amid the smoking pile of tires and wood, the putrid stench hits her – 31 burning camel carcasses wafting into the air.

"They die in accident," says a bystander. "Only one is survive."

I ask how much one camel is worth.

"Three thousand birr," he says, raising his eyebrows for accentuation. I quickly do the math in my head.

"Some poor family just watched three grand go up in smoke," I say to Christina.

"Much money Ethiopia," he finishes, walking away with his T-shirt covering his mouth and nose. "Camel too much money."

SLOW BOAT THROUGH THE SUDAN

KOSTI TO JUBA, SUDAN • November 2008

I never thought we'd ever set foot in the Sudan, and now I'm not so sure how I feel about riding through this baked desert. Compared with the freedom of Latin America, where our only responsibility was to each other and to stay safe, I now feel stifled. For some reason, I'm pissed off for just being in this country. *Why are we even here?* It seems like an expensive detour; our visas alone cost more than US$250. We could have easily holed up somewhere rustic in Tanzania for two months while we waited for more nets, or enjoyed the beauty of Ethiopia for longer, but no, we gotta keep on charging north like a pair of stubborn mules – for what? Just to say we went to the Sudan? It all seems a bit ridiculous.

"Todd, maybe you don't realize this now, but there are literally thousands of kids that are going to get a net because of your idea," Rob Mather wrote in a recent email. I felt like he was placing me too high on some kind of humanitarian pedestal. Did I deserve it? I'm no angel. I drink and smoke and like to cause trouble, sometimes just for fun. What business do I have helping innocent children? I have to remind myself that it's not about just me, though; it goes so far beyond. Deep down, I know I'm a good person and truly want to help. Helping people is like a drug, a powerful sensation that we've experienced many times already. We don't have nets now, but we will soon. *Just enjoy where you're at, man. Enjoy the ride. Be patient.*

North of the border at Metema, thousands of shredded plastic bags cling to dry shrubs and trees – an unsightly scar on a featureless, dust-cloaked landscape. We frequently pass donkeys, goats, dogs and several other unrecognizable carcasses, hit by speeding cars and left to rot in this outdoor furnace. The freshly killed ones display grotesque bellies distended like balloons. Others, left for months in the brutal desert climate, are now nothing but skin stretched over skeletons. The one saving grace is that Christina and I have each other; riding through this landscape alone would be hell on wheels. As the brown desert blur passes by endlessly, I can't remember a more boring stretch of countryside in any country we've ever ridden. Brief stops at little roadside shacks to drink well-water and eat tasty *ta'amia* (falafels in pita bread) help break the monotony, as do strangers who invite us to join them for afternoon tea and *shisha* (flavoured tobacco smoked from beautiful glass water pipes), or the kind couple at a gas station who give us a full tub of strawberry yoghurt, miraculously cold and delicious. At the end of the day – out of the scorching heat like a real desert mirage – appears the Rahad, a tea-coloured river that snakes through the barren, cracked earth. Before the mirage vanishes, we jump in to refresh our sun-battered bodies and scope out the shoreline; it seems like a fine enough place to set our hammocks between two thorn trees to swing all night long, but our senses are tingling; this is just our first day in the country, and we don't yet know the lay of the land. Any concerns for our safety are answered by a pair of smiling armed guards, who greet us in Arabic.

"As-salamu alaykum." Peace be upon you.

A friendly wink and a pat on the butt of the rifle tells us they'll be protecting us tonight. In the morning, they bring us tea and donuts – a consideration towards foreigners that seems to permeate Sudanese culture. At a small internet café on the outskirts of Khartoum, we meet an inquisitive, worldly man named Mr. Namjaddin, who pays our bill, escorts us to the far end of town to inquire about our impending voyage down the Nile River and invites us to a lavish dinner at his home. He even has his driver pick us up at our hotel.

"Some women are allowed to drive cars in the Sudan, but motor-cycles, no," he says, passing a plate of dates and cheese to Christina. "You can expect many people staring at you. Some will not know how to accept a woman on a motorcycle. Be prepared for this."

Khartoum marks the farthest point north in our African Odyssey, 22,000 kilometres from our first tracks in Pretoria many months ago. At this stage in the game, it doesn't feel like we're travelling *through* Africa anymore, but more as if we're rooted into the continent, clenched in a warm hug of humanity. Had we not been bound by our obligations, we could have easily soared past Khartoum, north to Egypt, and wrapped ourselves around the northern coast of Africa to our celebratory champagne in Morocco; adventure done and dusted. But the anti-malaria mission *is* the destination. We owe it to our donors, and ourselves, to see it through. At the Kosti New Port, we manage to find passage on the only barge heading south on the Nile River to Bor, some 2000 kilometres away. I was expecting a more grandiose version of the Nile than the one presented in front of us: river banks littered with everything one can imagine, from old tires to aerosol cans to floating plastic bags crammed with garbage. Only papyrus reeds and water lilies impart nature's presence. Although we're heading south, our forthcoming voyage *up* the Nile (one of the world's few rivers that flow south to north) is the only way we can get back to Uganda while avoiding the "ethnic cleansing" genocide to the west, in Darfur. They tell us it will take three to five days to reach Malakal, so we hit the market early, stocking up on sugar, eggs, bread, little foil-wrapped tri-angles of processed cheese, onions, potatoes, bananas, oranges, grape-fruit, coffee, garlic, chocolate, rice and as much fresh water as we can fit into our bottles and bladders. Twenty-five dollars later, our pack is full and it's time for breakfast, seven a.m. and already sweltering hot.

At a tiny outdoor food stall with three tables and those ubiquitous white plastic chairs found in every country in the world, the cook opens the lids of a few pots to reveal a variety of greyish boiled stews. *For breakfast? No bloody way.* We've taken a few gastronomical risks in Africa so far, and some have paid off, but there looks to be no ap-pealing reward for us in those big black pots. Christina notices some eggs and points at them enthusiastically. The cook takes notice and, flashing a cartoonish smile full of massive shiny white teeth, perfectly mimes the cracking open of an egg, repeatedly. The sunglass-wearing businessman sitting next to us starts laughing hysterically in a high-pitched wheeze, laughing so hard he succumbs to a coughing fit. Once he regains control the eggs show up, four greasy blobs and a few square slices of white bread on a single plastic plate, which the cook/owner/waiter spins onto the table with a flick of his wrist. He ducks back into the kitchen and returns with a huge wooden salad spoon obviously too big to stir the coffee in our tiny cups. What a comedian. I love his style.

Eager to get on the river, we wind our way through dusty streets jammed with swerving moto-rickshaws and bicycles until we find our ship. Her name is *Jimeiza*, and she stinks like shit, piss and dried fish – but at least she's headed in the right direction. She's long and wide, a massive cabled-together hulk of a barge carrying a few fuel and cargo trucks, hundreds of sacks of onions and about 50 passengers, for now. Tourists normally head north, towards Egypt, but we are a double anomaly: heading the wrong direction, with our white skin blaring in contrast next to the pitch-black tones of the Sudanese gathered at the government dock to check us out. Carefully we walk the bikes up a wooden plank onto *Jimeiza*'s dock and lock them together. Next we hump all our gear into our meshed-in, open-air room on the top floor, near the captain's quarters, and start setting up our tent on the rusted-steel floor, naively thinking we'll have the place to ourselves for at least one night. We're barely settled, and in walks a guy I spotted at the security office in town. He's wearing faded jeans, a green polo shirt, and white Adidas running shoes fresh out of the box. He scans the room briefly then lays out a section of cardboard to begin his afternoon prayer.

"*Allahu akbar! Ashadu an la ilaha illallah!*" he chants, standing up, his arms folded at his stomach. "God is great! I bear witness that there is only one God!"

He prostrates on the mat, rubbing his forehead softly on his piece of cardboard, repeating the sequence in succession for a few minutes like a yoga sun salutation. After he's finished, he stands up and says, "My name is Khalid. Blessed be Allah. Do you have any questions about religion or about the word of Allah?"

"No, thank you."

"What is *your* name?" he asks, his voice now much louder, like he wants others to hear.

"My name is Todd."

"Mister Tony, I have some questions for you. I have three, in fact. You first wait," he says bluntly, ducking out to grab a small suitcase. "What do you think about what I have heard in the news about the marriages of these homosexual people in Canada and Europe and these states like this? I want to know what you think about the issue? What is your opinion?"

The question, and the accusing manner in which it's been delivered, catches me off guard. *Is this guy for real? I just met you one minute ago, man.*

"For me, it is about the choice of the individual," I say after taking a moment to think about my response. "There are many different types of people in this world, and love takes many forms. Love doesn't discriminate one way or the other. These people have the choice to marry who they want to."

"Ahh, but the word of Allah does not permit such things, my friend. Why can't you embrace Islam? God has told us, from the early days of Adam, that this is not the way – this cannot be the way. I don't understand how a man can marry another man."

"You may not understand, because this is against your religion and not part of your culture, but there are billions of people in the world, and many different cultures. You may not believe in it, but these people do, and it is their choice."

Rolling his head towards the sky laughs condescendingly, immediately firing another question at me.

"And what about this legalizing of the prostitutes? You know, here in Sudan there is no news. I cannot get the news. But I am from Kenya, and I have heard some news that in some countries they are legalizing prostitution and the government is taking from it."

"I don't know anything about it," I say, hoping he'll stop talking and go away.

He laughs the same ignorant, patronizing laugh and rolls his head again. "I think you will embrace Islam, my friend, I can see it. They are there in Canada, Muslim brothers. They can help you follow the word of Allah. Even me, my family is Christian, and I was Christian for more than 20 years."

"Why did you turn to Islam?"

"Because the word of Allah is true. There is only one God, and Allah is he. It says in the scriptures, it is there in the Holy Quran. The Bible has been changed. The Holy Bible has been changed more than 30 times, but the Quran has never changed. For more than 1,230 years, it has not changed. And tomorrow it will not change. It will never change."

A microcosm of Sudan's *jalabiya*-wrapped splendour, the *Jimeiza* hums with people peeling potatoes, chopping onions, women gathered around boiling pots of stews and sauces stirred with a stick rubbed between their palms, similar to the method of trying to light a fire without a match. Some people smoke or just watch the river go by; others play card games and dominos. Thankfully, most everyone is friendly, but there are always a few bad apples...

"You give me money for cigarette! You buy me one cake. I want now!"

The polite ones, and there are a great many, are constantly inviting us to join them for tea or food or to smoke *shisha*. One afternoon, a group of men beckon us over to share their afternoon meal, which at first glance appears anything but inviting. My eyes fall upon a greenish-brown disc of mush that looks like it was smacked upon the plate from a spade held waist-high. Not wanting to be rude, I dig my fingers into the mucilaginous mystery, then dip the handful into a stainless-steel bowl of brown gravy before sliding it down my gullet. It's actually quite tasty. After lunch, water is scooped straight from the river with old metal tins and poured into the locals' thirsty mouths. Then, while we're docked along the riverbank, I watch a guy take a shit (a "long call," as they say here) off the back of the barge, but he's positioned too high above the water's surface, unable to dip his hand in the river to wipe his ass. Seemingly unconcerned, he simply pulls up his baggy white cotton pants and casually strolls away. Not more than 30 feet behind him, a cluster of men fish beside another group bathing, coating themselves in a thick, foamy layer of white soap.

There are enough bewildering moments onboard the *Jimeiza* to keep us thoroughly entertained, but we realize rather quickly that *we're* the circus sideshow, and understandably so. This stretch of the Nile is so remote, so far removed from any kind of tourist interaction, that many of these people have never before seen white skin and long hair, even on television, let alone in the flesh. We're a fascinating spectacle to them, especially amongst some of the younger children, who touch our skin and hair as if we are magic itself. One afternoon, our Nuer tribesmen friend Azim, with six characteristic tribal scars wrapped across his forehead, says, "Look, Master Toddy" and points to the sky at a huge African fish eagle soaring above. The eagle swiftly banks to the left and cocks its head in our direction before dive-bombing into the river, emerging with a large silver fish clutched in its talons. Christina reaches for the locket around her neck, pulls open the faded-silver cap and flings Sean's ashes into the river, a spontaneous gesture that fills me with a renewed sense of love for her. Christina never met Sean, but the attention and affection she shows when I talk about him has helped me heal – I know they would have been great friends.

Azim tells me that he's going to name his next son Toddy. I guess I'm flattered. I've been called many variations of Todd in many different countries: Ton, Tops, Tol, Tommy, Tomas, Mr. Don, Mr. Tony, Tim, Tone, John, Tor, Tok and other weird names. What's consistent is that hardly anyone ever remembers my actual name. Christina, on the other hand, with her three-syllable name that flows beautifully off the tongue, is just the opposite. The Latinos loved her and had no problem remembering her name, and it's much the same here in Africa, but the one-syllable Todd doesn't hold the same weight. I'll have to remind my mom that she didn't give me a very international-sounding name. At least Azim likes it, or something close enough.

Aside from narrow pathways created by livestock (the lifeblood of the Sudanese), the only signs of civilization in this endless sea of papyrus reeds are thatched-roof huts constructed mere feet from the river's edge. From an outsider's perspective, it's a puzzling scenario – what happens in the rainy season, when the water rises? How do they cook their food with no trees for firewood or charcoal? Many dugout canoes ply the river, but we barely see any trees anywhere. But it all seems to work out. Families still earn a living by paddling these primitive canoes full of fresh-caught fish alongside boats and barges, selling various catches-of-the-day to hungry passengers and crew. Long, perilous voyages are often undertaken on do-it-yourself reed "barges" that float downstream with nothing more than a long pole as propulsion.

"On this type of reed boat, it will sometimes take two months to travel the distance that we will in one week," says our captain, Abdurahim. "Many are dying. They cannot swim, and they drown, or the crocodiles can eat them. It is too far."

We've now been two weeks aboard this "boat," and she's growing every day as more monstrous barges are lashed to us with thick rusted wire cable, winched snugly together so everything moves as one mammoth unit. It's a floating village at least 400 feet long and 100 feet wide, with no fewer than 500 people packed into every available space on board. Checking out different corners of the ship's dynamic pulse requires deft footwork around milky puddles of greasy water, prayer mats and cardboard mattresses. Two sheep that have to stand in their own feces chomp on clumps of grass and reeds. Splashes of spit from chewing tobacco mix with bits of paper, but nobody takes the effort to sweep or clean the space around them. Plastic bottles and cigarette butts are strewn about the deck, and the incessant reek of sweat, piss, shit and squalor forces us to breathe through our mouths. Aside from our tent, there is only one other area of respite, at the bow, where the slight breeze of motion helps make the stench less putrid, even under the searing Sudanese heat. Here, the quiet beauty of the mighty Nile passes slowly and silently beneath the rusted hulls. Chris and I venture here daily to watch sunsets of poetic beauty punctuated by the flight of hawks and graceful white egrets overhead. Idyllic villages appear and disappear along the riverbank as we ride the gentle sweep and sway of the river's course.

One evening as dusk rolls in, we join in a *shisha* circle, taking seats amidst the swirling sweet smoke. The peaceful energy is abruptly disturbed by an arrogant youth who's clearly quite proud of his grasp on the English language, much like Khalid.

"Hey, my friend. What are doing here?" he asks me, reaching for the wooden end of the tube to inhale. "Where are you going?"

"We're going to Bor, and then to Juba by motorbike," Christina explains. "Then, from Juba, we go to Uganda."

"My friend, I want to beg you for something," he says. "You have a lot of money, you help me now. You buy me just one cake?"

I do my best to ignore him and reach for the hookah hose. His friends seem to catch on to his scheme and laugh at him.

"My friend," he repeats, louder now. "I am talking to you because we are speaking the same language, so we are friends. When you meet people with the same language, are you not friends with them?"

He doesn't allow me time to respond and continues with his monologue.

"These people, they don't know what I am saying to you, they do not speak English, so don't worry about anything. You can buy me something or give me money – it is no problem. I don't eat today. I am hungry, my friend."

He's part of a large military contingent onboard who prepare meals and eat together, so I'm not falling for his bait. He's looking for a handout but won't get it from us. I don't blame him for asking; I'd probably do the same if I were in his shoes. But give him money, and the whole boat would come asking. We try to connect and chat with the others in the smoking circle, but he chimes in again after seeing us swatting mosquitoes off our ankles.

"Brother," he says. "You don't like mosquitoes to bite you?"

"No. Do *you?*"

"Yes, I like mosquitoes biting me."

"Why?" Christina asks, astounded by the hubris of his tone and comment.

"I like them to bite me because they are feeding on my blood," he says, laughing at her.

"Do you know about malaria?" Christina asks him calmly.

"Yes, I know about it. More than the book. More even than you."

"And what do you know about malaria? Do you know you can die from malaria?" I say.

"No, you cannot die. There are medicines you take. No problem, my friend."

I hang my head in disbelief. "It kills many, many people in Africa every day, including right here in Sudan."

"That was some years ago. Now it is HIV/AIDS that is the one killing. Can't you people do something about this? What is being done?"

"Do you know there are thousands of scientists working on a cure every single day? They are trying very hard to cure this disease."

He *tsks* loudly and shakes his head as if to say, "No, they're not."

Heading back to the top deck, we realize just how good we have it compared to many of the people onboard who've endured a lifetime of poverty, famine, drought, conflict and a rash of humanitarian crises. While we enjoy the luxury of showering and cooking in the comfort of the captain's quarters and lying on soft, cushy air mattresses inside of a mosquito-proof tent, men next to us sleep squished together like sardines on nothing more than flattened cardboard boxes. But they don't complain. They simply say, *"mafi mushkila"* before crawling under: "No problem." Our respect for all Africans continues to grow. Their resilience in the face of daily adversity is astonishing.

But our best friend on the barge, a kind soul named Sadiq, the ship's mechanic, seems especially distant lately. On the top deck before sunrise one day he asks Christina, "How you sleep? Good?"

"Yes, *tamam*," she says, proud to show him that we're learning some basic Arabic. "Did you sleep well also?"

"Aah, yes, but I sleep alone. I am alone," he says, bowing his head. "I have almost one month now away, no family. They are living in the south, in Bor. Too many years I am doing this. Always boat, always river."

Always river, indeed. After 22 long days, we finally arrive in Bor, with sweat and sunscreen stinging our eyes as we lug our gear onto a hard-packed beach. Hoping good news awaits and the net distribution project in Arua is on track, we bid a long farewell to Sadiq and the Captain, who gifts me a pair of baggy white cotton pants. After so many days the water, clicking in my helmet strap and revving Willy's engine energizes my soul. The anticipation of mobility – the road, the wind, the speed – and the exciting idea of finally getting to place some nets has me feeling like a superhero ready to save the world. We pass the disembarkation inspection and ride on, dodging potholes and deep rainy-season ruts as we inch closer to Ugandan soil.

Just two hours in, a roadside soldier suddenly draws a rifle from his shoulder and points it at my chest. Terror strikes my heart for a split second, but he lowers the weapon almost immediately and beckons us to approach.

"Is three months go prison for this violation," he says in loud, broken English after we roll to a stop. "Why you no go around the sign?! You pay $100 dollars each person. You have violated Sudanese law, you know. Maybe we hold you overnight, you have taste of Sudanese prison!"

"I'm sorry to cause any offence to you, sir," I say calmly. Suddenly I don't feel like a superhero anymore. "We did not see the sign, sir, we're sorry. We did not do this on purpose."

"Her," says another official with a deep crease between his bulging eyes, pointing at Christina. "Why is she doing this with her eyes?"

"The road is very dusty," I say. "She's just trying to clean the dust from her eyes."

"Don't lie," he barks back, waving an accusatory finger in my face. "You spend a night in prison, and then Monday you have court for your case."

What the fuck? Does he think that her eye-blinking is some kind of secret code?

He tries to instill fear with his mean face, but we're now well aware of the scare-for-money tactic, which has happened to us a few times so far in Sudan. I deftly ignore him and start digging into my tank bag for our passports and papers. He demands that we open *all* our bags; he wants to see if we're hiding any guns.

"Sir, we are only passing through your country," I say in my nicest possible voice, deliberately slow and steady. "We are sorry if we have done anything wrong."

"You go inside!" he says sharply, pointing at a small stick-and-mud hut.

Following us, he sits down on a wooden chair, not once taking his eyes off ours.

"From where are you?" he says in an incriminatory tone.

"We are Canadian."

"Where are you going?"

"To Uganda."

Trying to butter him up with innocence and gratitude, Christina continues: "How far is the border? Sir, we are sad to be leaving Sudan, the people have been very kind to us. We love your country too much."

Someone outside calls for him, and in a moment of impatience he slides his chair back violently. "I am tired of talking! You pay $200!"

We glance at each other hopelessly, then at the desk. Our passports are still there. Part of me wants to slip them into my pocket and leave. Then an older man named Charlie enters the room.

"There is no problem," he says, scooping up our passports off the desk. "But please not remember Sudan for this guy. We are just together, you and us. But next time, you go around the roundabout the proper way."

"What roundabout?"

"Over there. You see the tire in the road. You must go around the tire."

Christina shoots me an incredulous eye-roll, but we're in no mood to argue. *THAT is a fucking traffic circle?! That's his sign?*

Finally he waves us on our way. "You go now!"

We go, fast. Juba, the ramshackle capital of South Sudan, lies waiting just a few kilometres away, and we've had a long day. The only place to stay is in a campground run by an industrious Ugandan expat named Esther. We strike up a conversation with her over dinner in the basic restaurant, mentioning our run-in with the police and how unnerved we were at the prospect of a fine, seeing as we have almost no money left. Just before we retire for the night, she unexpectedly presses a tightly rolled US$100 bill into Christina's hand, and doesn't charge us for our meal. *Did that just happen?* We're not complaining, just stunned.

"Oh it's nothing," she says of the money. "It can happen to anyone, even me if I'm in another country."

"Thank you so very much," Christina says, grasping her hand. "This means a lot to us. We are actually out of money, and we didn't know how we were going to pay the camping fee."

"Please don't worry, you are my guest and I want you to feel at home here."

If we had a dollar for every time we've heard that in Africa, we could buy the whole bloody campground. But in spite of Esther's generosity, my heart feels heavy for this place. The massive NGO population has run roughshod over the local economy, inflating the price of oranges and apples to almost two US dollars *each*. The city is swimming in litter and filth, grating on our nerves. Near the market, one woman sets up her little onion-and-tomato table in front of a puddle of stench, and she'll be there all day long. It puzzles me to think how, and why, any of this rancid squalor can be acceptable to anyone. In less than two generations, the culture has gone from carrying woven baskets to the market, to carrying produce in a manufactured-by-the-billions plastic bag discarded as easily as a random thought. A hundred NGOs that have come to help the fallout of a decades-long civil war have ironically turned the country into a new kind of war zone. For miles on end, we pass nothing but piles and piles of broken glass, plastic bottles and steady streams of trash flowing into creeks and streams. At one point, Chris pulls over to look at a pile of broken bones, horns and teeth, the rotting remains of dead cattle. She wants me to take a picture.

"Fuck that," I yell through my helmet, fighting back the bile that's creeping up my throat.

We're not happy with Africa today. Not only are big trucks churning up huge clouds of dust, but the constant jarring of a million ruts and rocks causes painful headaches under our helmets. Then a puncture in my front tire piles even more shit onto today's heap. Luckily, I find a roadside vulcanizing shop within two minutes, but while focusing on my own problems, I lose Christina, who has difficulties of her own. She drops her bike in the thick sand and can't lift it uphill, and I'm too far up the road to hear her shouting for help. While I'm haggling with the tire guys, she's forced to take her pack and saddlebags off her bike, lift Jessie up, and repack everything all over again. When she finally arrives at the show she approaches with a look on her face that could kill a dinosaur.

"Two things," she says to me calmly. "One, check your goddamn mirror. And two, open your fucking ears."

The grubby men surrounding us break out into laughter, but it's all too much for Christina. She hits her breaking point. "I just want to go home," she says, sobbing. "I'm sick of people laughing at us. Can we just get the fuck out of this country, finally?"

I knew this day would eventually come. We both did. The majority of the Journey has been agreeable to us – the freewheeling euphoria that exists on most days holds us together and gives us something to look forward to, even after the long days and harsh trials. But we're now facing a different order of magnitude. Africa has not only crept into our skin; it's slithering underneath it like a hungry worm, gnawing away at the fabric of our own sanity. If it weren't for our steadfast commitment to Motos Against Malaria, we'd likely have booked a flight home after Kampala's soul-crushing ordeal. At one point, it was me who wanted to quit. After pinning Casper to the ground in the FatBoyz parking lot, lying on my back to restrain a spitting, snarling beast, I remember thinking, *How in the hell is this even happening right now? Is this for fucking real?* If we had spent one more day in that state of chaos, I'd surely have gone off the deep end and done something I would have regretted until the end of my days. The pressure to keep going has driven me very close to the end of my frayed rope.

But here in the Sudan, I have it easier than Christina. I don't have to suffer through the non-stop cat-calling and unwanted advances that she's had to deal with almost daily, including from the sleazy cook who made a pass at her one night in *Jimeiza's* kitchen. I don't have to cover my whole body from head to toe with clothing so as to not appear disrespectful in the eyes of Muslim men, under heat so powerful it never goes away. Christina was raised by a feminist mother, and at times her headstrong demeanour has gone against the grain in this male-dominated culture – Sudanese are not used to hearing a woman speak her mind. I hold Christina in a warm embrace and don't give a shit what the laughing men think of her or us or anything else. She is *my* partner, and to have come all this way, more than 22,000 emotional African kilometres, makes her queen of the world in my mind – a beautiful warrior goddess with superpowers that make me proud to be her man.

TUSKS TO THE SKY

ARUA, UGANDA • December 2008

"They say that somewhere in Africa the elephants have a secret grave where they go to lie down, unburden their wrinkled gray bodies, and soar away light spirits at the end."

ROBERT MCCAMMON, *BOY'S LIFE*

Bumping along the remote outskirts of Arua, we're soon engulfed by a long plume of dust billowing out from behind a flatbed four-by-four loaded with big bundles of nets. Protected by armed guards, the nets in this shipment will find their way into the homes of thousands of humble beneficiaries in the coming days. A welcoming celebration engulfs us upon arrival in Ojapi, a small village in the Maracha-Terego district. Gleeful groups of mothers dance and sing and jump high in the air, piercing the atmosphere with loud wails of "aye, aye, aye aye!" and clapping in gratitude for the two foreigners who have come to help protect their children from the dangers of malaria. It's enough to bring happy tears streaming down our dusty cheeks. Christina starts bumping bums with one of the ladies, and the scene erupts in boisterous, thundering laughter that almost shakes the mangoes from the trees. With 200 clapping hands encircling the dirt dance floor, I join in.

It's a spectacle, and almost too much to handle for the men, who laugh hysterically in the background, laying their bodies over one another in excited jubilation.

"Welcome to our home," says one of the men, beaming as he grabs my hand with both of his. "You are most welcome here. This is our tradition. This is how we welcome visitors. We want you to stay here."

We can't stay, though, we have nets to give out, so the celebrations are short-lived, and we're soon on the road again with another jubilant memory deposited in the bank.

Johnathan Kimbu and his Malaria Consortium colleague Paul Sewankambo tag along behind in a fancy silver Toyota Land Cruiser. Forty-five minutes down the road, we arrive at the Tara Subcounty headquarters together, dusty and excited. A large crowd of people, including many who have walked for an entire day, sit on plastic chairs and wooden benches under the shade of two large, leafy trees, listening intently to a broad-nosed man in a suit and tie explaining the details of the net distribution program on a white paper flip-chart nailed to a tree. The man, sporting a perfect basketball-sized pot belly, introduces Loy and Melinda, two of Paul's colleagues, who have just arrived from Kampala. The ladies quickly introduce Christina and me to the crowd of friendly faces.

"*Mi ifu ngoni!* (Good morning!)" says Christina in their native tongue, Lugbara, which produces a round of applause and respectful laughter.

"Please make sure only under-fives are registered," Melinda says, "and be sure to tell everyone that the nets are *only* for the children. There are *no* nets to be allocated for adults. Sir Todd and Ma'am Christina will be arriving on motorcycle in each village to conduct a follow-up exercise in the coming days. It's important that each net is hung properly over the *child's* bed."

To our Western sensibilities, it seems outrageous that parents wouldn't automatically use the nets to protect their own offspring from dying – but life is different in Africa. Here it's all too often an adult male's world, and men have been known to use mosquito nets to catch fish, or to resell them at exorbitant prices in city markets. Others take the nets to cover their own beds, sleeping separately from their wives and children. I can't help but wonder if this may be why Africans grow up to be so resilient and quietly courageous – once they've survived early childhood, they've already overcome a number of great hurdles in life. In the West, we coddle our children and constantly protect them from harm's way, whereas in many parts of Africa it seems like it's every child for themself.

"The nets are more effective than drugs, more effective than anything else you can think about," says Paul, turning in a semicircle to address the crowd. "As long as the net is within the household, all will be protected. Sometimes, as you know, we get resistance with such kinds of interventions, like spraying for mosquitoes, but the nets are very popular."

November 30, 2008. It's Sean's 39th birthday. Thinking back to our adventurous days together in Southern Africa, I picture him smiling down on us from the great beyond. It sounds silly, but it does seem like he's been riding with us the whole time, and I can only hope he knows what he's inspired us to do. Everyone present knows why Christina and I will be in their village; the word has spread. Most of the crowd has arrived by "footing," having walked for miles around to shout and sing their appreciation. They will all receive a long-lasting insecticidal net (LLIN), the single biggest means of preventing malaria's deadly toll. Even with all of Africa's logistical hurdles facing such endeavours, the Uganda Malaria Communities Project, with help from the Malaria Consortium, pulls off the sensitization, registration, mobilization, allocation and distribution with flying colours, all a part of the training program that we've taken part of in Arua prior to the fieldwork encompassing us now. It's a massive, highly organized group effort involving an army of volunteers throughout two subcounties (small territorial divisions within Arua's five counties). Together, we'll help distribute more than 10,200 nets, 1,400 of which have been directly donated by Motos Against Malaria supporters. This peaceful countryside, devoid of noisy generators and power lines, where people make do with candles and kerosene lanterns at night, will be our home for the next few days as we undergo the vital project follow-up.

"You see, here in Africa, we don't have nets," says a man named David, who singles us out at the end of the day to talk in person. He's wearing a ripped green T-shirt with a dirt stain from shoulder to shoulder and a wide-brimmed hat ingeniously made from tape and cardboard. "We don't cover our bodies at night, and they are not cleaning the areas around their huts. Then you will find, during the raining time, these mosquitoes, they breed around your home area if there is stagnant water."

As he's talking, I smack a mosquito off of his exposed forearm, leaving a splash of blood on his skin. Undeterred, he continues. "We are putting our water in pots, but if there is no covering the pots, this is when the mosquito is breeding. These are the *Anopheles*, the ones that are killing. So, what we need here is *sensitization*. We need *ed-u-ca-tion*. When these people are sensitized, they will know exactly what is happening."

He pauses to adjust his seating position, pensively staring into the sky.

"I am happy that people like you came to see for your own self. Otherwise, we Africans are not good."

"Why? What do you mean? Africans *are* good," Chris responds.

"Because they will hide these things, these nets and such, and not give properly you see," he says, gesturing with a hand sweeping behind his body to signify theft. "They will sneak them away for their own selfish reasons."

"That's why this organization wants us here," I say. "The people who donate money, it's important for them to know that the nets are going to the right places and people."

He listens intently and with great respect, never taking his eyes off of us even as a group of curious kids form around us.

"Do you still get malaria?" I ask.

"Me? Why not," he says, laughing. "Yes… why not."

"How many times have you had malaria?"

"Eish! Many times! But you see, we adults are a little bit stronger now. We Africans, we can take *a lot*. We don't go to these hospitals, is too fah from here, you can see. When we get malaria, we are still paining with fever and these things, but we are resistant now, you know."

At the end of the day, much to Paul Sewankambo and the Malaria Consortium's delight, all registration forms are filled out with absolute precision; the numbers are totalled correctly, everyone has kept time, with not one single argument or misunderstanding. What stands out most is the impeccable penmanship; every letter, every word, every name exquisitely written to record how many households and children under five have been properly registered. Those who cannot sign their names (or don't know what a signature means) roll their thumb onto an inkpad, leaving their thumbprint to verify they have in fact received a net.

"In this area where you are moving, it is one of the biggest breeding grounds for the malaria parasite in all of Africa," explains Paul. "Here in this region, we have some of the highest numbers of incidences of malaria-related deaths. The disease is endemic here. It is very dangerous for these people. Many children are dying, and pregnant mothers are also at risk. You will see in the next few days on your follow-up when you are on the motorbikes. I hope you are not fearing this exercise."

What he means by "fearing" is unclear, but it's obvious he's warning us to be ready. For what, we're not quite sure. Early the next morning, we first meet with Helen, a mother of five and Community Medicine Distributor (CMD) in Pajama Parish. Typical of many of the ladies we've met in the area, Helen displays a set of prominent, piano-key teeth jutting out from big round lips and short hair cropped close to her scalp. She smiles constantly, until she sits down for an interview inside her grass-roofed home.

"I am working in the health unit, and we are getting malaria in great number," she says with grave concern. "It is rather hard for us here to find medicines. Sometimes you cannot get the drugs, so malaria will continue with you. Today, we get the mosquito nets, so I think it will help us. The children deserve a life too, you know."

"And have your children all had malaria?" Christina asks.

"Yes," she says, looking out the doorway. "Every week, they will be caught by malaria. Not every day, but after every week."

"And what do you do to treat or prevent malaria in the children?"

"They told us they will bring this (anti-malarial) Coartem, but up until now they have not given it to us in the villages. Even my son has died from malaria. He was one year and six months."

Christina places a gentle hand upon her thigh, and Helen's bright smile with the big teeth returns. She invites us to share some green oranges that she plucks from a tree in her garden. Helen's friend Henry, a young university-educated health volunteer, has agreed to escort us throughout the day, running behind our bikes as we visit each hut in a cluster of nearby villages, all connected by a series of narrow footpaths hidden between tall stalks of maize that brush our handlebars as we ride past. In amongst these farms, we reunite with the pure and simple freedom of rural Africa. Packs of ragged children follow a respectable distance behind our bikes, running along in the grassy fields, chasing rolling bicycle rims guided by sticks – a time-honoured tradition known as "hoop rolling" that we've witnessed all throughout the developing world.

"The only time they see white people is on the prime time, so the kids want to come and touch your skin to see how it feels," Henry says, his head beading with sweat.

Outside one of the huts, a group of women sort through baskets full of maize kernels, picking out the rotten black ones and separating the white kernels ready to be painstakingly pounded into flour to make *ugali* (maize-meal porridge), Uganda's staple food. Christina, concerned at the solemn look of a mother with a naked child balanced on her hip, asks Henry what is wrong.

"That is due to malaria," he says, chewing a stick between his lips. "The mother is saying that he does not see properly. The vision is not there."

"Does he have malaria now?"

"Yes, he has malaria."

He seems like a healthy child, with chubby cheeks and smooth skin, but his glazed eyes tell a different story. Crawling around on the ground, grabbing his feet and ankles, his knees and legs covered in orange dust, he seems lost in his own thoughts.

"They are too poor," says Henry. "She is saying she cannot do anything."

Inside the house, a few cobs of corn are piled in the corner next to a box of dried greens. Two prized eggs balance alone on a small table. A worn mosquito net, riddled with holes, hangs over a lone sleeping mat on the dirt floor, while the new blue PermaNet LLIN is still in its plastic package on a chair. The lady's husband enters the house, curious as to our presence.

"Can you ask him why the new net isn't hung over the bed?" Christina asks Henry.

"He has not hung the new one because there is one here already, he is telling me."

"Okay, please tell him that the new net is for his children to sleep under. We can help him hang it now. In the meantime, we will ask our colleagues if there is any medication for the child."

We've inspected about 35 huts in four different villages, and the long day's emotional undercurrent has taken a mental and physical toll; poverty is hard to stomach sometimes, and educating about the prevention of malaria feels heavy on the brain. We find a private spot under a sprawling mango tree in an open field that will make a good campsite for the night. As we're pitching the tent, an elderly gentleman comes by, walking slowly with a wooden cane after dismounting from an old motorcycle.

"I am Mr. Andrew, a former commanding officer in the Ugandan Air Force, and many years of service in the military also. This is our village, and I am seen as the chairman of the village. You can feel at peace here, and there is no problem."

"Thank you, Mr. Andrew," Christina says with a warm smile.

"But I do have one question," he says. "Why do you sleep outside like this? Maybe we can move you inside, then everything will be okay."

"It's all right," I respond. "As you can see, we have now set up our bed between the motorcycles and have a mosquito net to sleep under. We like to sleep outside, and we feel very safe here."

"Okay, thank you. Then it shall be fine. I am very security-conscious, and all of our people are very friendly. We have some hardships and poverty, but we are a happy people. You will just rest here and feel at peace. Nothing can happen to you."

And nothing does, save for another magical night's sleep under the African sky. At sunrise, time stands still as we're serenaded by a chorus of chirping birds, cows, goats and roosters. Young schoolkids with their blue-and-white uniforms stare at us from behind a derelict barbed-wire fence while we make breakfast and get ready for another day in the field. Henry has left, so it's just us on our own. As it turns out, Aussie John from Kampala was right. Mr. Andrew's crackling AM radio announces that Congolese rebel groups operating in western Uganda are still waging a war against the government, and renewed guerrilla warfare in northern DRC has put an unwanted asterisk on the African Odyssey. All westbound overland borders are *still* closed to foreigners in Uganda, Rwanda, Burundi, DR Congo and the Central African Republic.

Our plan to travel along the Congo River and on to Kinshasa is dead.

There will be no jungled traverse across the continent. No celebratory champagne in Morocco. No "end of the road." After examining and exhausting all available options, there is simply no safe way to journey by road through to the West. Sadly, this will be our final day in rural Africa. To be unable to complete what we set out to do is a hard pill to swallow but, as Sean used to say quite often, "Sometimes shit just happens, and you gotta roll with it."

We'd rather go home alive than not at all.

"You two better be home before Christmas, or I'm disowning both of you," Mom joked in a telephone conversation two weeks ago. I guess she'll get a surprise Christmas present after all: two weary travellers sliding down the chimney, covered in African dust.

But for the time being, we stay focused on absorbing every detail of life this idyllic landscape can offer. With many villages and homes still to visit, we strike camp in haste, manoeuvring the bikes over another rock-strewn road into the hills of Nyadri Parish. Men meander around on black bicycles, holding the bars with one hand, their machetes clutched in the other. Strong, silent women, each burdened by 20 litres of water balanced atop her head and a baby slung around her back, walk gracefully back to their homes, where they'll spend the rest of the day washing clothes, gathering firewood and cooking. Barefoot children run with us as we weave our way along paths packed hard from years of use. They're eager to show us their new nets, and we're pleased to see most families have hung them correctly, but there are a few who sleep on woven mats on earthen floors and have hung their nets two inches too high. We take turns lowering the nets one by one, pounding long, rusted nails with rocks into the dirt walls. For those who don't have nails, we improvise using small sticks instead.

The laminated picture of Sean that's taped onto the gas tanks of our bikes catches my eye as we head to another hut. On the bottom of the photo, in white letters, it reads: *We take these risks not to escape life, but to prevent life from escaping us.* Every day, without fail, Chris and I have rubbed that picture for good luck – a sunset silhouette from South Africa, shot by our friend Garrreth Bird. The photograph perfectly encapsulates Sean's life: his face pointed up at the sky as the last of the sun's rays grace his cheeks, ropes and carabiners dangling from his harness and a camera in his hand. It looks like all the world, his world, has stood completely still for one pure slice of time. And it reminds me I still have some ashes, the last of them, hidden in an envelope in a secret pocket of my backpack. I spill the remains into Christina's cupped hands, and together we rub the ashes into the knobs of our tires and front fenders of Willy and Jessie. Just as a smile leaves an imprint on a face, I want to make sure we leave Sean's mark upon the earth of this great continent. I only wish I had the wooden elephant with us, a totem not only to Sean's life and remains but to the kindness of Africa. I'd mount it on my handlebars, tusks to the sky, and take him along for one final ride.

We've managed to visit about 120 homes over five days, but with darkness about to fall, our mission is sadly over. There are millions more kids in Africa who need a net to sleep under, but we'll have to be content with what we did with the time we had. If we save even one life, it will have been worth every gravel-crunching, livestock-dodging, heat-searing kilometre. After our final follow-up in the Pajama district, we mount our bikes and peel away, riding side by side towards our last African sunset, searching for a place to rest our tired brains and bodies. Another sprawling mango tree next to an abandoned shack reels us in – the most serene setting possible to spend our last night in the African countryside. Surprisingly, we are absolutely alone. Christina strings our mosquito net between Willy and Jessie and gets our bed ready, while I make a fire to cook on. We ran out of cooking fuel ages ago and have resorted to stick fires ever since.

A month ago, while Christina practised evening yoga on the roof of the *Jimeiza*, I spent my time sneakily putting together a surprise slide show from every single country we've visited in the last four years. I'm happy we're all alone tonight – just us and the crickets and the sense of peaceful lightness that accompanies a completed task. Christina senses I'm up to something, so I blindfold her with a T-shirt, letting the suspense build for a few more minutes while I lay out the Mexi-blanket and pour a shot of cheap rum into our coffee mugs. With two flickering candles lighting up the net for romantic ambience, I pull off the blindfold and hit play on the laptop. The Journey pops off the screen in vivid liquid crystal, a full-colour flashback of the last 50 months of our lives, set to a soundtrack of music we collected along the way.

"Aww, this reminds me of when we met, babe," Christina says, squeezing my arm with tears glazing over her eyes. "And the electricity is still there. I definitely *DO NOT* want to go home."

A vivid kaleidoscope of Latino characters lights up our faces; the memorable people who turned this grand moto adventure into an even grander humanitarian adventure: Sveen and his disco bus, Mitch and Claudette and the kids, Morris and his mom, Serena and Pascacio from Nabusimake, Eve the TV lady from Guyana, Marcel and Steven from Suriname, Grace and Paolo in Macapá, Betty from Iquitos and

Dario and the polka guys from the Chaco in Paraguay. I include a few feel-good snapshots of friends and family from home before the slides move along to Africa: wow-factor landscapes and camp shots and adventurous riding shots, our clothes soaked to the bone in Rwanda, riding the roof of the world in Lesotho, above the clouds through the Great Rift Valley. Dr. Debbie and her parents, the grasshoppers in Swaziland, Sam and our friends in Cape Town, and pictures of a hundred more faces and places we'll likely never see again.

"How can we ever thank all of these people?" Christina asks, not needing or wanting an answer.

All these people... Will they glance back in time and remember us as we did them? Will knowing we've made it safely home be all the thanks they'll need? Will we manage to keep in touch with the strangers who became true friends?

More pictures keep rolling past: potato farmers in the Peruvian Andes, tea pickers in Rwanda's green hills, the firewood gatherers in the highlands of Guatemala. They all remind me of my grandparents, who I'm glad have stayed in my thoughts so often on the road. They're my real heroes. They passed along the spirit and quest for true freedom. Mom and Brad occupied a lot of time in my head as well, but most of it was reserved for Sean, of course. Without him, we wouldn't be sitting under this tree, a mosquito net draped between the handlebars of our Yamahas, our hearts full of pride and love. When it's distilled into a 45-minute slide show, the Journey seems almost unbelievable, like wandering through a lucid dream. As the images flicker past, it becomes clear that people, not destinations or adventures, have become the driving narrative of our days.

Like Africa itself, the people have left their own marks under our skin. Christina and I have managed to keep it all together on two wheels, through all of our arguments and fights and getting lost and worried and sick and scared, through 38 countries and 79,933 kilometres, every single one of them unique, like fingerprints of the world passing underneath our tires. After the final photograph appears, we stoke the fire and sit down on Sean's blanket in the grass, raising our rum to toast the Journey – the magical life-changing adventure that will keep us young in our hearts for the rest of our days.

We're safe and at ease, and it feels like being back on the farm, sitting next to my brothers, roasting marshmallows by the fire in the birch forest; but instead it's just Christina and me under the mango tree, a billion stars in the sky, and a slice of the moon lying on its side watching over us.

ABOUT THE AUTHOR

Todd Lawson believes in passion, diversity, and the search for freedom outside. He's an avid world traveller, husband, brother, father, son, writer, photographer, creator, storyteller, mountain athlete, humanitarian, adventure-seeker, and lover of life and all its wonderful ways. Todd is the publisher, producer, and photo editor at Mountain Life Media, and co-founder of the Rise and Sean Foundation. *Inside the Belly of an Elephant* is his first book. He lives in Whistler, British Columbia.